TWILIGHT OF THE GODS

ALSO BY STEVEN HYDEN

Your Favorite Band Is Killing Me

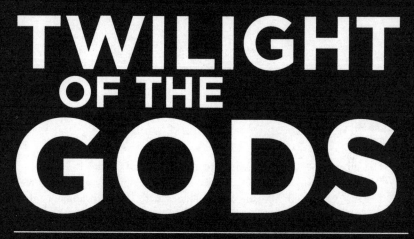

TWILIGHT
OF THE
GODS

A Journey to the End of Classic Rock

STEVEN HYDEN

DEY ST.
An Imprint of WILLIAM MORROW

DEY ST.

The chapters "I Know There's an Answer," "Draw the Line," and "Keep on Loving You" includes material that originally appeared on The A.V. Club, and "Pressing On" includes material that originally appeared on Uproxx.

TWILIGHT OF THE GODS. Copyright © 2018 by Steven Hyden. All rights reserved. Printed in the United States of America. No part of this book may be used or reproduced in any manner whatsoever without written permission except in the case of brief quotations embodied in critical articles and reviews. For information address HarperCollins Publishers, 195 Broadway, New York, NY 10007.

HarperCollins books may be purchased for educational, business, or sales promotional use. For information please e-mail the Special Markets Department at SPsales@harpercollins.com.

FIRST EDITION

Designed by Paula Russell Szafranski

Half title art © JD Photograph/Shutterstock

Part opener art © Artem Twin/Shutterstock

Library of Congress Cataloging-in-Publication Data has been applied for.

ISBN 978-0-06-265712-1

18 19 20 21 22   LSC   10 9 8 7 6 5 4 3 2 1

For Stan at New Frontier Record Exchange,

and all the other legendary rockers who died too soon;

and Rosemary, who was born right on time

CONTENTS

RAY: Everything's going to flame, man, the planet is screaming for change! We've got to make the myths.

JIM: There ought to be orgies.

—from J. Randal Johnson and Oliver Stone's screenplay for *The Doors*

I've always had this skepticism about rock, because I worshipped it and believed in it for so long, the mythology of rock 'n' roll, and I got to a certain point in my life where there are people making up stuff about me and what I supposedly did as a singer in some band.

—Jeff Tweedy

I don't want to live in a world without lions, and without people who are lions.

—Werner Herzog

"The Hero Is Born and Learns About the World . . ."

"The Song Is Over"

NOTES ON TRACK 1: The tone setter. We wanted the opening track to sum up our aesthetic and overall ethos. So we stated our core themes plainly in the lyrics—the power of rock, the inevitability of death, and the struggle to reconcile those two things. Oh, and Don Henley sucks.

For as long as I can remember, classic rock has been there for me.

Led Zeppelin, Pink Floyd, the Beatles, the Stones, Dylan, Springsteen, Neil Young, the Who, Black Sabbath, AC/DC, David Bowie—the fixtures of my classic-rock youth. But like all precious minerals, classic rock is a finite resource. One day, it will disappear. Bands break up. Albums go unplayed and are eventually forgotten. Legends die. But it still seems . . . unfathomable. For much of my life, I thought that classic rock would be around forever.

I remember when the reality of classic rock's mortality first dawned on me. It was 2012, and I was sitting inside of an arena on the outskirts of Chicago waiting for the Who to come onstage. When I say "the Who," I'm referring to half of the Who—Pete Townshend and Roger Daltrey. The other two guys, Keith Moon and John Entwistle, were long dead. Moon died exactly one year after I was born—September 7, 1978—from overdosing on pills prescribed to help him stave off his craving for alcohol. (This is the most ironic death in rock history.) Entwistle passed away in 2002, one month before I saw the Who in concert for the first time. Entwistle's death was more typical for a rock star—he was found in a Las Vegas hotel room, where he had been partying with a stripper named Alycen. In life, Entwistle's nickname was "the Quiet One," which I guess is ironic given his final moments.

Before my first Who concert in '02, I was bummed that I would never get to see the Who with Entwistle. I briefly considered not going—the purist in me wondered whether I was seeing the "real" Who. But what did I know about the "real" Who anyway? I started listening to classic rock as a teenager in the nineties, when many of my favorite bands had long since broken up, died, or devolved into tribute acts. But in my mind, the greatest rock bands the world has ever known were eternally frozen in their primes. To me, the Who was still the band on the cover of *Who's Next*.

Sure enough, my reservations about seeing the Who without its original bassist and drummer disappeared approximately 1.2 seconds into the opening number, "I Can't Explain." I was in awe of my heroes.

Loving classic rock has always been an act of faith: albums as sacred texts, live concerts as quasireligious rituals, and rock mythology as a means of self-discovery. After discovering classic rock at the dawn of middle school, I committed myself to studying rock scripture—I read all of the books, subscribed to all of the magazines, and watched all of the documentaries. I sought out the most crucial LPs of the rock canon and played them over and over until the lyrics became my personal ethos. I loved the guitar riffs, the bombastic drums, the preening vocals. But what made classic rock an obsession for me was the belief that I was plugging into something profound and larger than life. I'm not a religious person, but if there is a God, I was sure I had found Him on side two of *Abbey Road*.

The mythology is what hooked me. Some kids read comic books; others glamorize athletes. My superheroes were rock stars who either had been deceased for decades or were well ensconced in the throes of middle age by the time I discovered them. But I didn't care—that just made my classic-rock heroes all the more mythic. I worshipped Pete Townshend, Bob Dylan, Keith Richards, Jimmy Page, Jim Morrison, and Paul McCartney *because* they were distant, untouchable figures. They were like gods who I secretly believed could elevate my own humdrum existence if I had enough faith in the classic-rock mythos.

Of course, those people weren't gods at all, but rather mortals who would grow old, make comeback records with Don Was and/or Jeff Lynne, and take money from beer companies for their overpriced, nostalgia-driven concert tours. For a while I was able to overlook these realities and fixate on the myth. But that night in 2012, inside of the hockey arena outside of Chicago, my faith in classic rock couldn't completely blot out the truth.

I'll say this first: I thought the Who was incredible. How could the Who not be incredible? For this tour, they performed one of my favorite albums, 1973's *Quadrophenia,* in its entirety. Playing iconic albums in their entirety has become standard practice for classic-rock bands. The days of forcing the audience to listen to three or four songs from a well-intentioned but mostly lousy late-career album nobody cares about are basically over; time is precious, and classic-rock tours now are all about the hits.

On the way to the show, I passed the outlet mall where I'd bought *Quadrophenia* on cassette more than twenty years earlier, when I was in the eighth grade. A double-album rock opera about an alienated teenager who suffers from multiple personality disorder, *Quadrophenia* should be issued free of charge to every fourteen-year-old misfit. I used to slap the tape in my Walkman and listen to "Cut My Hair" over and over—Pete Townshend sings in the chorus about working yourself to death just to fit in, *just like I was doing,* as Keith Moon's frantic drums replicate the erratic pounding of a broken teenage heart.

Onstage in Chicago, the Who labored to re-create an essential listening experience from my youth. During "The Real Me," Daltrey twirled his microphone in precisely the manner I had always imagined him twirling his microphone. Then Townshend attacked his guitar during the suicidal rocker "Drowned," bashing out his solo with about a dozen violent windmills. These guys were still extremely good at being the Who. I loved it.

However, I was keenly aware that my enjoyment hinged on the ability to project an image onto the Who that no longer seemed wholly accurate. Despite their best efforts, Townshend and Daltrey seemed old. Like . . . *really fucking old*. That's because they *were* really fucking old—they tallied 135 years between them. Townshend's pallor was alarming; he looked like a guy who had just read the reviews for *All the Best Cowboys Have Chinese Eyes* for the first time. And then there was Daltrey, who I estimated had lost at least 75 percent of his once-mighty singing voice. When he tried to scream his iconic yelp at the climax of "Won't Get Fooled Again," he sounded like granddad hacking the gunk out of his throat.

Throughout the concert, video footage of the Who from the sixties and seventies flashed on the screens behind Townshend and Daltrey. Even the dead guys made cameos—Entwistle appeared on-screen to play a bass solo during "5:15," and Moon contributed vocals culled from a midseventies festival gig for his loony showcase, "Bell Boy." Seeing the Who in person was not unlike watching my DVD copy of *The Kids Are Alright* at home. Jeff Stein's classic 1979 documentary had built up the legend of the Who in my mind around the time I bought that *Quadrophenia* tape—this was a wild, combative band that annihilated hotel rooms and arena stages but always seemed to emerge from the chaos unscathed. Now the Who itself was encouraging the audience to gaze upon the iconic images broadcast on giant screens looming over the frail figures onstage.

It was a metaphor for what I'd been doing to my favorite classic-rock bands for years. I had let my imagination trick me into believing that classic rock would be forever vital and strong. But when you look away from the myth, what you find are wizened senior citizens who don't have a lot of time left.

How does a true believer react when he realizes that his faith in the immortality of classic-rock gods is diminished? There are several stages of grief. First, denial. ("I will pretend that any Rolling Stones album released after *Tattoo You* doesn't exist.") Then, anger. ("Why did I waste my money on *Bridges to Babylon*? In what universe was Mick Jagger singing over Biz Markie samples a good idea?") And then bargaining. ("If I sell *Steel Wheels* and *Dirty Work*, I can use the money to buy the latest Dylan box set, because owning eighteen versions of 'Leopard-Skin Pill-Box Hat' will prevent me from hyperventilating.")

What's left is acceptance. Acceptance is hard.

I'm not the only one struggling with this. Maybe you've noticed the outpouring of grief in your Facebook feed whenever a beloved classic-rocker dies. This is about more than simply missing our favorite entertainers. The loss is deeper and more personal. It's as if our own pasts are being erased. We're mourning not only fallen icons, but also a part of ourselves.

To try to make sense of classic rock's demise, I spent a year going to as many classic-rock concerts as possible. I saw Springsteen, McCartney, Black Sabbath, and AC/DC. I also revisited all of my favorite classic-rock albums and reread all my most essential classic-rock books. I marinated in the minutiae of classic-rock mythology. I tried to figure out why this stuff means so much to me. Because, since I'm an utterly average person, if it means a lot to me it must mean lot to other people as well.

And then I mourned. I mourned *a lot*. Because you can't talk about classic rock now without also thinking about death.

I started writing this book around the time that David Bowie died, and I finished it around the time that Tom Petty passed. You know what happened in between? A lot of other rock stars went.

Some were truly iconic, like Prince, Gregg Allman, Chuck Berry, Leonard Cohen, Walter Becker of Steely Dan, Malcolm Young of AC/DC, and Glenn Frey. Others were less than legendary. (You'll always live in my heart, former Megadeth drummer Nick Menza.) But they all point to a downward trend for the music I love.

As for the bands that are still around, some have gone to great (and often weird) lengths to stay on the road. AC/DC hired Axl Rose to replace ailing singer Brian Johnson. The Grateful Dead hired John Mayer to sub in for the long-deceased Jerry Garcia. Alice Cooper and Joe Perry of Aerosmith formed a band with Johnny Depp in order to perform songs originated by dead seventies rockers like T. Rex's Marc Bolan and Harry Nilsson.

But despite the undeniable signs of decay, people keep flocking to classic-rock shows. A concert staged in the fall of 2016 in the California desert featuring the Rolling Stones, the Who, Neil Young, Bob Dylan, Roger Waters, and Paul McCartney—it was officially known as Desert Trip, though the media dubbed it "Oldchella," as it was staged at the same location as the popular annual festival Coachella—grossed a record-setting $160 million over two weekends.

Some classic-rockers, perhaps spooked by seeing so many of their contemporaries fall, are trying to get out while the getting's good. In early 2018, Paul Simon, Elton John, and Lynyrd Skynyrd announced retirements to be preceded by extended farewell tours—one last cash-in before riding off into the sunset. Whether by choice or natural causes, more rock legends will be lost in the years ahead, until there are finally none of them left. When that happens, will there be a new generation of disciples who take up the cause for classic rock and carry it forward? Or is classic rock itself now a problematic relic from a time when white male musicians commanded a disproportionate amount of attention? Does it *deserve* to fade away?

A lot of the things that we as rock fans take as inalienable truths had to be invented, disseminated, and affirmed. Why is classic rock a lifestyle as much as a form of music? Where did these traditions come from, and how did they become so ingrained? And when did all that mythology come undone, sending classic rock from the cultural penthouse to the funeral parlor?

As I was asking myself these questions, I noticed that my personal odyssey through classic-rock history resembled the story lines of some of my favorite classic-rock concept albums. Many of the greatest concept albums have the same plot—you start with a protagonist who is damaged by some profound trauma, like Jimmy in *Quadrophenia* or Pink in Pink Floyd's *The Wall*. This trauma provokes a spiritual reckoning that sends our hero on an epic quest. If you're like Ziggy Stardust or the unnamed naked dude in Rush's *2112*, this quest will require reviving rock 'n' roll amid the dire, desperate environs of a futuristic, dystopian world. If you're like Rael, the lead character in Genesis's brilliantly bonkers *The Lamb Lies Down on Broadway*, it will necessitate the removal of your penis. Thankfully, my classic-rock quest is closer to Ziggy Stardust and *2112* than *The Lamb Lies Down on Broadway*.

My journey to the end of classic rock starts in my boyhood bedroom, where everything exciting in my life entered through the same portal: the radio.

"Welcome to the Machine"

NOTES ON TRACK 2: On this one we went back to our roots—school, teenage rebellion, the radio, Tesla (the band, not the car), and learnin' about sex, drugs, and prog rock. All the stuff that made us who we are today. It's important to remember where you come from, man.

I t was just so . . . evocative.

Radio was how I learned about classic rock—DJs told you which bands mattered the most and assembled those bands into playlists that related an overarching narrative signifying an era. Over time, I learned about all of the stuff that was left out of classic rock, and how it disproportionately excluded certain kinds of artists—pretty much anyone who wasn't a bushy-haired white guy signed to a major label. But I didn't know about any of that back then. These were my "young and innocent days," to quote the great rock philosopher Ray Davies, when the magical world I found on the radio seemed like "soft, white dreams with sugar coated outside." Anything that wasn't on the radio when I was in seventh grade might as well have not existed.

Looking back, I sometimes envy the kids who get to discover new bands on the Internet. When I became a music fanatic, I fantasized about having access to more music than I could ever hear in a lifetime. My very own warehouse full of CDs and vinyl. But now that my boyhood fantasy has become reality in the digital realm, it's nowhere near as mind-blowing as I imagined it would be. Even for someone my age, streaming music became as normal as listening to the radio with shocking quickness. As for the people who were born into the streaming age, they don't know what they have. The miraculous is now mundane. "Everything" has always been possible, so it sort of feels like nothing.

The Internet isn't nearly as good at telling stories as the radio was. It's an endless conversation with a billion segues, whereas the radio kept it simple, stupid. For all of its many flaws—wall-to-wall commercials, obnoxious DJs, payola, cultural segregation, a bizarre affinity for the music of Rick Astley—the radio had a certain dramatic flair. Songs could really make an entrance. The DJ would do a short introduction, yapping about the local county fair coming up this weekend until the vocal kicked in. Then . . . you heard "Baba O'Riley" for the first time. Or "Iron Man." Or "Born to Run." It was like a lightning bolt crashing into your life. The general lack of information back then was crucial, because it made the possibility for genuine surprise real and magical. There was a time when the Who, Black Sabbath, and Bruce Springsteen were completely unknown to me, and then the radio ushered in a world where those people were suddenly visible. I'm just saying: ignorance isn't bliss, but it does have its advantages.

After that, you started noticing this music everywhere. I never thought I'd feel nostalgia for hating songs I used to love because I don't have control over how many times I hear them. But what can I say? I miss the storm-chasing aspect of radio, where you keep on listening through commercials and bum tracks and annoying patter by crummy jocks because you're hoping to catch another bolt of lightning.

This never-ending pursuit for musical thrills started for me around age eleven or twelve. I commandeered the family boom box, set it up in my bedroom, and proceeded to listen to music all the time. This is going to sound pretentious but it's the God's honest truth: I was now tuning in with a conscious desire to *know* about the artists, as opposed to just passively listening as a captive audience member. Up until my tween years, the radio was just a machine in the car that occasionally played songs that I liked, such as "What a Fool Believes" by the Doobie Brothers (my first-ever "favorite" song) or one-hit wonders by groups with names like Nu Shooz and MARRS. I gave music about as much thought as the cheap, partially torn faux leather haphazardly lining the seats of the burnt-orange family Nissan. What came out of the radio was like upholstery to me—I acknowledged its presence, but just barely. But now, I decided that "being a music fan" would form the core of my burgeoning teenage identity. It was time to learn, so I studied the stories that radio had to tell.

By the late eighties, radio had transitioned from a medium directed by forward-thinking disc jockeys to a new system defined by corrupt relationships between corporate radio chains and palm-greasing record-industry conglomerates. The result was a radio landscape where the opposite of musical revolution reigned. Mainstream radio offered a severely mediated perspective on contemporary music—in order to be heard, you were pretty much required to have the backing of a corporation that rigged the market to keep out less powerful competitors.

It wasn't until Nirvana released *Nevermind* a few weeks after I turned fourteen in the fall of 1991 that I was made aware that there was such a thing as "underground" music. Seeing the video for "Smells Like Teen Spirit" on MTV for the first time remains my greatest lightning-bolt moment of all time, though it only happened because Nirvana had left Sub Pop for DGC—they weren't *really* underground by then. But exposure to tightly regimented radio formats had already programmed my brain to think about music in a certain way, starting with the belief that there really was such a thing as "classic rock."

Classic rock didn't exist as a genre until the early 1980s, when stations in middle-American cities like Cleveland and Houston that had once aspired to a progressive mix of new music and obscure album cuts began relying on the same old familiar songs by the most famous and successful bands of the sixties and seventies. In 1982, a radio consultant famous for being a pioneer in market research, Lee Abrams, invented a format called "timeless rock," which parceled out a conservative selection of cuts by up-and-coming bands into an otherwise rigidly constructed playlist designed to appeal to aging listeners who only wanted to hear what they already knew they liked. This was the seed that sprouted classic rock, which rapidly became a dominant radio format by the end of the eighties.

For listeners like me, who didn't know what radio was like before this change occurred, classic rock seemed like an entrenched concept that had been passed down organically from up on high. But that wasn't really the case: radio had codified a generation of bands—the Beatles, the Rolling Stones, Led Zeppelin, Pink Floyd, the Eagles, the Doors, Fleetwood Mac—as "classic" because it was convenient marketing. At fourteen, I had no way of knowing that. Teenagers like me just believed whatever the radio told us. Of course, it helped that the best classic-rock bands *really were great*. Two things can be true—classic rock can be a marketing scheme, and it can also be transcendent. What I know is this: hearing "Hey Jude," "Wild Horses," and "The Chain" went a long way toward convincing me that the radio was the best friend I had in the world.

The most popular radio station in my town was WIXX, which played Top 40 music. I particularly liked the Top 9 at 9 nightly countdown, which was supposedly based on listener requests, though I don't recall WIXX ever playing all that many requests. If you called up and asked for WIXX to play Madonna's "Vogue," it might end up on the air in an hour or two, but only coincidentally.

The Top 9 at 9 consisted of a reliable mix of dance pop (like Paula Abdul and Milli Vanilli), kiddie-friendly hip-hop (Young MC and DJ Jazzy Jeff and the Fresh Prince), and the latest power ballad by whichever hair-metal band was favored by MTV at the moment. The biggest power ballads on WIXX included "Heaven" by Warrant, "Every Rose Has Its Thorn" by Poison, and "Love Song" by Tesla, which was so popular that WIXX had to eventually retire it after the song topped the countdown so many times. Tesla *ruled* northeastern Wisconsin.

WIXX turned me into a music consumer, convincing me to buy tapes with my own money. My earliest purchases were prompted by WIXX's most overplayed songs—"She Drives Me Crazy" inspired me to buy Fine Young Cannibals' *The Raw and the Cooked*, "Miss You Much" was my entry into Janet Jackson's *Rhythm Nation 1814*, and "Opposites Attract" attracted me to Paula Abdul's *Forever Your Girl*, which was otherwise fatally skimpy with the MC Skat Kat cameos.

WIXX made me care about artists, an important first step. But when all of that bubblegum goodness on WIXX started to lose its flavor, I became curious about what else was available a little further up the dial. So I flipped a few notches to the right of WIXX—yes, I literally had to turn a radio dial on my bedroom boom box—and found the local classic-rock station, WAPL.

The artists on WAPL were clearly of a different vintage than Janet Jackson and Paula Abdul, though not quite as different as it might seem now. In 1990, classic rock wasn't that old yet— many of those artists still had a place in pop music. Billy Joel, the Rolling Stones, and AC/DC were still producing successful radio singles (from *Storm Front, Steel Wheels,* and *The Razors Edge,* respectively) and MTV played their latest videos, which in retrospect was a bad idea for MTV as well as the artists. Looking back, Billy Joel setting fire to photos of Lee Harvey Oswald and Oliver North in the "We Didn't Start the Fire" video didn't help him or the music channel seem any cooler. New albums by Bruce Springsteen, Don Henley, Phil Collins, and Sting were similarly relevant, if not exactly hip. Van Halen's first record of the nineties, *For Unlawful Carnal Knowledge,* debuted at No. 1, and the LP's signature single, "Right Now," spawned a clip that won Video of the Year at the 1992 MTV Video Music Awards, the same year that Krist Novoselic smashed himself in the face with his own bass guitar during Nirvana's instant-classic performance of "Lithium."

Even old classic-rock songs could become hits in the early nineties—thanks to exposure in the smash *Saturday Night Live* spin-off film *Wayne's World,* Queen's "Bohemian Rhapsody" reentered the pop charts and peaked at No. 2 in '92, nearly seventeen years after it was originally released. Today, "Bohemian Rhapsody" is still a great rock anthem, while "Schwing!" is a joke that precisely zero people have found funny in the twenty-first century.

When grunge became the defining musical movement of early nineties youth culture, classic rock's prominence was affirmed once again. While you'd be hard-pressed to find any discernible classic-rock influence on today's pop acts—unless you count Justin Bieber's habit of occasionally wearing Metallica T-shirts, but let's please not do that—the bands of my youth were proud products of the classic-rock continuum. If you liked the biggest rock groups in the world at the time, an appreciation of classic rock was inevitably baked in.

Many grunge bands made this connection explicit: Nirvana covered David Bowie on *MTV Unplugged in New York.* Pearl Jam made a whole album with Neil Young. Alice in Chains hired Ozzy Osbourne's ex–bass player. With grunge bands, there was always a sense of perpetuation—they didn't seek to kill classic rock, as the punks supposedly set out to do. (Though in the end, bands like the Clash, the Ramones, and Talking Heads wound up absorbed into classic-rock history anyway.) Grunge bands wanted to carry the torch, and in the process integrate themselves into a larger, ongoing story.

Then there were bands that had no contemporary presence whatsoever and yet *seemed* contemporary to me because I happened to live in a small, sheltered Midwestern community. In my town, REO Speedwagon and Journey never went away like they did in more urban parts of the country. I'd been to enough car washes and county fairs in my life to know their hyperemotive hits by heart, along with the most spun tunes by the likes of Boston, Styx, Kansas, and Supertramp. I was aware that this music wasn't new, but it was still just as ubiquitous in my world as any current Top 40 hit, thanks to stations like WAPL.

All of this developed into an obsession that went much deeper than my dalliance with the pop stars on WIXX. It wasn't just the music—WAPL presented a self-contained culture that was deeper, stranger, and riper for exploration.

In my room, I set about closely studying the ins and outs of classic-rock radio, just as I had once pored over pop radio. On WIXX, figuring out why the station played the songs it did was easy—they were simply the most popular tunes in the country at the moment. Every Sunday, I had dutifully listened to Casey Kasem's *American Top 40,* so I knew what time it was. Casey was like the president of pop music—he even looked like a Lebanese Ronald Reagan—so whatever he said was the law in those parts.

On WAPL, however, the airplay standards were more nebulous, if not downright ambiguous. Apparently, some songs were so "classic" that they aged into "oldies" territory, as represented locally by WOGB, which played rock 'n' roll from the fifties and early sixties. Elvis Presley, Chuck Berry, and Buddy Holly are as classic as "classic rock" gets, but WAPL never played those artists, as they were considered oldies and thus segregated from the likes of Rush and Lynyrd Skynyrd.

Some artists straddled the oldies and classic-rock worlds. For the Beatles, *Sgt. Pepper's Lonely Hearts Club Band* was the dividing line—WOGB played early Beatles hits like "She Loves You" and "Eight Days a Week," and WAPL played staples from the post-acid years such as "Hey Jude" and "Come Together." For the Rolling Stones, the dividing line was "Sympathy for the Devil"—WOGB stuck with "Satisfaction" and "Get Off of My Cloud," whereas WAPL spun "Brown Sugar" and "Tumbling Dice." For the Kinks, the line was between "You Really Got Me" and "Lola"—those were the only two songs by that band that I ever heard on the radio, so WOGB was granted custody of "You Really Got Me" and WAPL was handed "Lola."

Weirdly, classic-rock radio also seemed to favor bands that people no longer cared about over bands from the same era that still had some cachet decades later. I had already read enough rock criticism to be aware of the Velvet Underground, but it was difficult to actually hear any of Lou Reed's seminal gutter poetry on local radio, because WAPL preferred to play Grand Funk Railroad. Ditto for the leading lights of punk and new wave—I couldn't hear the Ramones, Elvis Costello, or Talking Heads because local radio stuck to the Cars, Kansas, and Chicago.

Looking back, it's hard for me to fathom how innocent I was. I did not yet know how to get the Led out. I had not yet traversed the murkiest, proggiest depths of human consciousness. I was not yet baptized in the church of classic rock. Once I was, nothing would ever be the same.

Was my childhood love of classic rock really *just* an outgrowth of having limited listening options on the radio? Does this fully explain my *continued* interest in this topic over the course of more than two-thirds of my life?

Not really. And I know this because of Joseph Campbell.

When I was a kid, I had no idea who Joseph Campbell was, even though at the time he was a minor celebrity thanks to a popular PBS series, *The Power of Myth*, which originally aired in 1988. (Campbell died eight months before the show premiered.) Today, Campbell is remembered as probably the most famous mythologist ever. The author of classic books such as *The Hero with a Thousand Faces* and the four-volume *The Masks of God*, Campbell also coined the phrase "Follow your bliss," which I assume seemed profound in the eighties before it became annoying forever after.

In *The Power of Myth*, Campbell is interviewed by honey-voiced broadcast journalist Bill Moyers over the course of six episodes, during which they discuss how myths developed over many centuries, as well as the ways that myths from different cultures tend to resemble one another. Campbell believed myths serve a universal purpose, acting as a through-line in the history of humankind from the earliest societies right up to the present day. He viewed myths as "themes of the imagination," borne in the collective unconscious and "moved by its own inward experiences . . . that are asking for fulfillment."

Often, this need for fulfillment is served by hero worship, whether it's for Jesus, Muhammad, Abraham Lincoln, or some other seminal figure. "A hero properly is someone who has given his life to something bigger than himself or other than himself," Campbell said. This process of giving yourself to something bigger usually involves a physical quest, like a war or an act of heroism. But it can also be a spiritual journey, in which a person "has learned or found a mode of experiencing the supernormal range of human spiritual life, and then come back and communicated it."

"It's a cycle, it's a going and a return, that the hero cycle represents," Campbell tells Moyers. For Campbell, this "going and return" exercise was a metaphor for growing up, a process in which each of us has "to get out of that posture of dependency, psychological dependency, into one of psychological self-responsibility."

I think what drew me into classic rock was the mythology of it, which satisfied the part of my psyche that demanded connection to a vast, awe-inspiring entity.

We're conditioned to believe that young people don't know or care about anything that happened before they were born. That's sort of the whole point of being a teenager. But what I loved about classic rock as a kid is that it seemed to have been around forever. Classic rock was there before I was born, and I was sure that it would still be there long after I was gone. Plugging into that made me feel part of classic rock's permanence.

Classic rock represented a continuum that had started long before me and reached all the way to the grunge bands that I

loved in the present moment. It felt like the opposite of pop music, which was proudly disposable and all about the here and now.
Pop was inherently nihilistic, whereas classic rock had roots that
you could trace as far back as you cared to go.

If I can play armchair psychologist for a moment: another
reason I think I was drawn to classic-rock mythology as I entered puberty is that I didn't have a reliable male role model in
the house. My parents divorced when I was two, and aside from
an occasional weekend visit to my dad's place two hours away
from home, I didn't have a strong connection to my father. As we
all know from *Tommy*, the Who's classic 1969 rock opera, losing a father early on can make a kid unnaturally obsessive about
his hobbies. Instead of becoming a pinball wizard, I gravitated
to rock music. Guys like Pete Townshend would be my father
figures from now on.

In *The Power of Myth*, Campbell reminisces about worshipping as a child this "great big old tree" that grew in the backyard
of his family's summer home. For Campbell, the tree represented
"forces and powers and magical possibilities of life that are not
yours, and yet are all part of life." Classic rock was my great big
old tree.

After studying the ins and outs of classic-rock radio in my
bedroom, I deduced that two albums were greater than the rest—
Led Zeppelin's *IV* and Pink Floyd's *The Dark Side of the Moon*.
So those were the tapes that I asked my brother, Paul, to buy me
for my fourteenth birthday.

Led Zeppelin IV was so cool that it wasn't technically called
Led Zeppelin IV—it didn't even have a proper title. Jimmy Page
insisted on going forward sans title when the band released the
album in the fall of 1971. He didn't even want the band's name on
the cover. Instead, there's simply a nineteenth-century oil painting
of a man with a pile of sticks on his back hanging on a battered, pa-
pered wall. This was Page's protest over the critical establishment's

constant slagging of Zeppelin's previous albums. He wanted the band's newest work to exist without the baggage of Zeppelin's image and to create its own context.

Fans called it *Led Zeppelin IV*, as opposed to *Led Zeppelin 4*, because Zeppelin albums had the weight of Super Bowls. But Zeppelin's fourth was also known as *Untitled, Runes, ZoSo,* or *Symbols,* as each member of Zeppelin was signified by an enigmatic emblem on the album sleeve. No matter what you called it, *this shit was mysterious.* I felt I could listen to *Led Zeppelin IV* a thousand times and never fully plumb its depths.

When I put the Zeppelin tape in my boom box for the first time, I knew the actual songs wouldn't surprise me, as every single track on it was played on WAPL. Most albums—even other recognized Greatest LPs of All Time—typically don't get that kind of exposure. There are usually at least one or two tracks that are considered filler. Fleetwood Mac's *Rumours* sold more copies than *Led Zeppelin IV,* but you never hear "Oh Daddy" on the radio. But that's the thing about *Led Zeppelin IV*—every song is important. And when you hear those songs in sequence, the whole thing has a special alchemy.

Side one is "Black Dog," "Rock and Roll," "The Battle of Evermore," and "Stairway to Heaven"—this is the "overplayed" half of *Led Zeppelin IV.* Turn on any classic-rock station right now and there's a decent chance that one of these songs is currently hey hey mama–ing all over the airwaves. The reason why those songs are still being played all the time is because they're *amazing.* Side one of *Led Zeppelin IV* is so great that it's actually a little dull to talk about. Nobody needs another treatise on how the visceral punch of "Black Dog" and "Rock and Roll" is perfectly matched by the spectral folk of "The Battle of Evermore" and then synthesized into the acoustic and electric duality of "Stairway to Heaven." It's like explaining why oral sex is an enjoyable pastime—*don't blowjobsplain, dude.*

There are two unwritten laws about *Led Zeppelin IV,* and the first is that your favorite track must come from side two. The other law is that *Led Zeppelin IV* is too popular to be your favorite Zeppelin album; this is why rock critics who try too hard always make a case for *In Through the Out Door* being Zeppelin's best.

The second half of *Led Zeppelin IV* is the "deep cuts with credibility" side. I came to understand that anyone professing love for "Rock and Roll" seemed like a philistine, whereas an endorsement of "Misty Mountain Hop" distinguished a true Zeppelin connoisseur. The side-two law even extends to the members of Led Zeppelin—when Robert Plant and Jimmy Page reunited in the nineties for *Unledded* and *Walking into Clarksdale,* Plant was reluctant to play "Stairway to Heaven" on tour but was fine with revisiting the seventh track on *IV,* the overpowering Bo Diddley-style shuffle "Four Sticks." He's the truest Zeppelin connoisseur of all.

The inherent elitism of the pro-side-two argument vis-à-vis *Led Zeppelin IV* would be toxic if it weren't sort of true—the closing track, "When the Levee Breaks" is just flat-out better than "Stairway to Heaven," and not *only* because it doesn't have any of the high school prom associations. "Stairway to Heaven" is what happens when the lights are on; "When the Levee Breaks" is strictly lights-out material, conjuring the feral sound of pure sexual and spiritual foreboding. Never in recorded history has the loaded phrase "going down," which Plant moans over and over in the song's final moments, seemed so seductive *and* terrifying.

But that's just the music. What really sold me on Zeppelin was the band's mythology, which I discovered in Stephen Davis's scandalous 1985 biography, *Hammer of the Gods.*

Davis's book came out when Zeppelin was at a relatively low ebb—the band had broken up five years earlier, in the wake of drummer John Bonham's death, and Zeppelin didn't seem all that significant in the middle of a new decade defined by synthesizers and emerging hip-hop culture. But for young fans like me, *Hammer of the Gods* was absolutely crucial in establishing the Zeppelin mystique. The prologue alone is incredible. Take this opening passage:

The maledicta, infamous libels, and annoying rumors concerning Led Zeppelin began to circulate like poisoned blood during the British rock quartet's third tour of America in 1969. Awful tales were whispered from one groupie clique to another, as Led Zeppelin raided their cities and moved quietly on.

Later in the same paragraph, Davis references some of these "awful tales," which involve "drinking vaginal secretions direct from the source" and "eating women and throwing the bones out the window" and "tumescent girls immersed in tubs of warmed baked beans before coitus." There are subsequent references to "invocations and gyromancy in candle-lit hotel rooms," "maidens publicly banged on tabletops in raunchy rock scene nightclubs," and "sex magic and endless orgies." The prose here is so purple that it should've hung in Prince's closet. But it nevertheless succeeds in making you want to snort the rest of *Hammer of the Gods* directly up your nostrils.

All three surviving members of Led Zeppelin swiftly (and unsurprisingly) denounced *Hammer of the Gods* upon publication. Jimmy Page claimed that he literally threw the book out the window of his house, which I assume was a castle perched on some distant mountaintop. Robert Plant blamed the multitude of bad vibes on Davis's primary source, Zeppelin's former road manager Richard Cole, arguing that the depravity credited to the band was actually perpetrated by Cole. Even the normally reticent bassist John Paul Jones had a pithy put-down for *Hammer of the Gods*. "It's a sad little book," Jones declared.

I must respectfully disagree with the men of Zeppelin. *Hammer of the Gods* is the opposite of sad—it remains the most enjoyably ridiculous work of rock 'n' roll pulp semifiction that I've ever read. I wouldn't call Davis a *good* writer, but when it comes to glamorizing scumbag behavior and making rock stars seem like larger-than-life demigods, he's an unparalleled master. (This will not be the last time that I cite Stephen Davis in this book.)

If *Hammer of the Gods* is exaggerated, I prefer to chalk it up to artistic license. Davis had to lie a little (or maybe a lot) to get at the larger truths of what made Zeppelin (and classic rock) so alluring to subsequent generations.

Along with millions of other impressionable readers, I learned about the hoariest tall tales of the Zeppelin saga from *Hammer of the Gods,* including the so-called Mud Shark Incident (in which a groupie was penetrated with the tip of a shark's nose in a Seattle hotel room in 1969) and the legend about three-fourths of the band allegedly selling their souls to the devil in exchange for Zeppelin's tremendous success. (Only Jones supposedly refused to do business with Mephistopheles.)

I also learned about other important tidbits of rock mythology from Davis: Robert Johnson's fateful deal with the devil for his own musical immortality at "the crossroads" back in the 1930s; the evil magnetism of early-twentieth-century writer Aleister Crowley, the self-proclaimed "wickedest man in the world," who inspired Jimmy Page as well as Mick Jagger, David Bowie, and the members of Black Sabbath; and the mind-warping powers of "backward-masking" evil subliminal messages into rock songs.

According to legend, if you played a vinyl version of *Led Zeppelin IV* backward on a turntable, you would hear "Hail to my sweet Satan" buried inside the otherwise beatific mix of "Stairway to Heaven." I didn't own a record player, so I couldn't verify whether this was true. However, one year after I read *Hammer of the Gods,* a youth pastor visited my church to preach against the dangers of backward masking in general and *Led Zeppelin IV* in particular. If his intention was to scare the congregation, it had the opposite effect on me—everything I loved about the salacious *Hammer of the Gods* was now confirmed as fact.

Let's go back to Joseph Campbell's definition of a mythological hero and the motif of a quest. The members of Led Zeppelin went on a *physical* quest. I understand that some readers might be offended by equating the guys in Led Zeppelin banging nubile members of the infamous L.A. groupie cabal the GTOs at the Continental Hyatt House with acts of heroism. It's undoubtedly true that the drugging and whoring lifestyle that Zeppelin epitomized is emblematic of the questionable white-male fantasies that have long animated interest in classic rock while also stultifying its ability to evolve with the rest of the culture. But, again, when I was in middle school, I wasn't smart enough to see that. What made Led Zeppelin attractive to me was that this band had traveled to the extreme outer edge of depraved and downright *dastardly* behavior, and returned to civilization to share what they had witnessed. That's what I heard whenever I listened to *Led Zeppelin IV*.

Pink Floyd's vision quest on *The Dark Side of the Moon*, meanwhile, was much different. Zeppelin's music went outward, whereas *Dark Side* was directed inward. Preoccupied with alienation, clinical depression, man's inhumanity to man, and the possibility of losing your damn mind at any moment, Pink Floyd deployed outer space as a metaphor for the vastness of inner space. And inner space is where teenagers spend the majority of their time.

Unlike Zeppelin, which defined how a band was supposed to fucking *rock*, Floyd moved at a lethargic pace. *The Dark Side of the Moon* operated on the body clock of a teenager with mononucleosis. The guitars dragged, the organ fills sagged, and the swelling chorus of female backing singers swooped in like a dreamy hallucination. It fit my inner chemistry perfectly. (Later, when I started smoking pot every day in my twenties, *Dark Side* also suited my *altered* chemistry.)

The deliberate dearth of kinetic glamour carried over to the band members. Whereas the guys in Led Zeppelin dressed like sex-hungry geishas, the members of Pink Floyd favored sweaters, blue jeans, and sneakers; they looked like their mothers had dressed them. In Pink Floyd's *Live at Pompeii* DVD, which includes footage from the making of *The Dark Side of the Moon*, the cameras ponderously linger on Pink Floyd eating lunch in the studio canteen during a break from the recording sessions. It's entirely possible that *this* was the most interesting part of making one of the most popular classic-rock albums of all time. It's like Pink Floyd was trying to be as boring as possible while also being insanely popular.

When I heard *Led Zeppelin IV*, I had no connection to the worlds that Zeppelin described—I hadn't read enough Tolkien or *Hustler*, much less been exposed to the menagerie of carnal delights that Page and Plant and Bonham (though not so much Jones) had at their disposal throughout the seventies. But Pink Floyd's misanthropic soundscapes were in tune with what was happening in my own angst-ridden headspace. Led Zeppelin represented an ideal of what I wished I could be, but Pink Floyd depicted what I actually was—gloomy.

Led Zeppelin IV has the breadth of an epic journey, veering from austere folk foreplay to metallic hump-funk to demonic postcoital blues. *The Dark Side of the Moon*, meanwhile, feels like one long song. The music's lack of dynamism suits the one-note solipsism of the lyrics, which express a desire for human connection without ever truly embracing a reality situated beyond the contours of Pink Floyd's perfectly constructed sonic architecture.

The gestures of empathy are strikingly adolescent—"Don't be afraid to care"; "Look around, choose your own ground"; "Money, so they say, is the root of all evil today." The instrumental "Great Gig in the Sky" is an attempt to musically convey what death feels like, but it's also the record's sexiest moment, which is the perfect way to contextualize death for teenagers. (This has been true going back at least as far as *Romeo and Juliet*.) In the end, the most moving parts of *The Dark Side of the Moon* explore the (frankly terrifying) likelihood that the inside of your own skull both is inescapable and might in fact be the worst place to be—this never seems truer than when you're just starting puberty.

Both albums encompass the twin poles of teenage desire: *Led*

Zeppelin IV is about conquering the world, and *The Dark Side of the Moon* is about trying to overcome your own hang-ups. But Pink Floyd had its own outsized mythology that lent the interior monologues of *The Dark Side of the Moon* a magnetic, shadowy mysticism.

First, there was the album cover—like Zeppelin, Pink Floyd made it a point to never put pictures of themselves on their records. Instead, both bands favored inscrutable iconography without any tangible meaning (which always seemed to give the music packaged inside *more* meaning). *Dark Side*'s famous cover depicts a prism against a stark black backdrop refracting a ray of white light into a rainbow. Is this a statement about how each of us is part of a larger, collective consciousness? Or does the cover of *Dark Side* seem profound simply because it resembles the black monoliths in *2001: A Space Odyssey,* drawing in naïve teenagers like they're alien-bred chimps? The answer is: the former *and* the latter.

At the core of Pink Floyd's mythology is the band's original front man, Syd Barrett, a handsome, charismatic singer-songwriter whose mental health rapidly deteriorated right as the Floyd released its 1967 debut, *The Piper at the Gates of Dawn.* While Barrett reportedly suffered from schizophrenia, it was his experimentation with psychedelics that made him a mythological figure among Floyd fans. Even listeners who hadn't actually heard *The Piper at the Gates of Dawn* (or preferred the band's post–*Dark Side,* stadium-rock period, which I did as a budding classic-rock head) gravitated to Barrett as a kind of sentimental cautionary tale. As far as Led Zeppelin had ventured into the wilderness of the outside world, Barrett had seemingly traveled just as deeply into himself, and returned a scarred, broken man. In 1968, when his increasingly erratic behavior threatened to derail Pink Floyd's burgeoning career, Barrett was kicked out of the band.

Pink Floyd's most popular work subsequently drew on the power of what Barrett signified; even after he was no longer in the band, his spirit haunted its records. *Dark Side*'s most pivotal track, "Brain Damage," is a song about reconciling insanity. ("There's someone in my head / But it's not me.") Pink Floyd's next album, *Wish You Were Here,* is a more overt tribute to Pink Floyd's "crazy diamond." (A disheveled Barrett actually paid the Floyd a visit during the *Wish You Were Here* sessions. He looked so bonkers, his former bandmates didn't recognize him.) The last of Pink Floyd's "Syd" trilogy, *The Wall,* is a concept album about a fragile rock star who is driven to hide behind a mental barrier that he must ultimately transcend. Again, Pink Floyd forwarded the idea that the rock 'n' roll lifestyle was responsible for turning Barrett insane.

For Barrett, there would be no transcendence, at least not in his personal life. As an archetype, however, Barrett will probably live forever. (He shed this mortal coil in 2006.) He is the defining example of one of the more enduring rock myths, the Romantically Damaged Loner Genius Recluse. This is an artist who is supposedly so brilliant that he is rendered tragically fragile, forcing him to retreat from the outside world.

This myth has been revived time and again, for either musicians afflicted with severe mental illness (like Brian Wilson, Roky Erickson, and Daniel Johnston) or those overwhelmed by an intense flash of early stardom (which describes shooting stars like Lauryn Hill and Jeff Mangum of Neutral Milk Hotel). Barrett's story is informed by a bit of both scenarios. Like all myths, the Loner Genius Recluse narrative requires the audience to do most of the work via their imaginations. It's what the genius *didn't* do that will forever seem most enticing. While Barrett reemerged in the early seventies to release two solo albums adored by cultists, for the most part his legacy derives from his unrealized potential.

For all of the ambiguous mystique that made *The Dark Side of the Moon* and *Led Zeppelin IV* ideal reservoirs for (to quote Campbell) "inward experiences looking for fulfillment," there was also the comfort of their established narratives. It was one thing to follow pop music as it unfolded in real time—that just felt empty in comparison, as ephemeral as yesterday's papers. But classic rock told ancient fables about the highs and lows of success, the excitement and danger of sex, the intoxication and degradation of drugs, and the myriad paths to enlightenment and eternal damnation. It was an awe-inspiring universe loaded with stories that had a beginning, middle, and end, just waiting to be explored.

I knew as a Led Zeppelin neophyte that the band's career ended in tragedy (i.e., the drummer drinking his weight in vodka and asphyxiating on his own vomit). Before I put on *The Dark Side of the Moon* for the first time, I was aware that the album's primary architect, Roger Waters, was later exiled from the band in the eighties by guitarist David Gilmour and drummer Nick Mason, an echo of Syd Barrett's departure from Pink Floyd in the sixties. Knowing this stuff didn't "spoil" the bands for me—it made their music seem richer and steeped in significance. Their stories were like shadow plays that explained the adult world and all of the wondrous, terrifying possibilities it had to offer.

"Rock and Roll"

NOTES ON TRACK 3: What it's all about, baby. Also: Don Henley still sucks.

Before we proceed any further, let's get one thing straight: this book discusses *classic rock,* not *classic* rock. *Raw Power* by the Stooges is a *classic* rock record, but it's not a *classic rock* record. Meanwhile, *Hi Infidelity* by REO Speedwagon is not a *classic* rock record, but it is a *classic rock* record. *Classic* is a value judgment, whereas *classic rock* denotes a particular era of music signified by bands who may or may not be shitty. I am delving into the latter.

Clearly, my definition of "classic rock" is shaped by classic-rock radio. I've already talked about the arbitrary lines that radio put between artists derived from the sixties and seventies. The overriding factor in determining who was classified as classic rock — and who was classified as folk, punk, new wave, or metal — was mainstream popularity. If you sold millions of albums, played arenas, and benefited from a major record label plying disc jockeys with cocaine and microwaves in order to get your music on the radio, you were classic rock. If you were beloved by critics, played clubs and theaters, and earned way more street cred than dollars, then you were slotted in one of the "cult artist" genres.

Qualifying for classic-rock status is a double-edged sword. On the negative side, it's never been hip or respectable to be called a classic-rocker. Let me give you an example: Billy Joel and Randy Newman are both piano players whose music was informed by Brill Building pop, jazz, and classical music. Neither of them has ever "rocked," exactly, but in their day, they scanned as rockers due to their irreverent attitudes and their proximity to unassailably rock peers.

In the late seventies, Joel and Newman both had hits about an overbearing person who asserts his superiority over another, relatively small person. But at the time, Billy Joel's "Big Shot" was scorned by critics even though the public loved it, and Randy Newman's "Short People" was defended by critics even though many listeners found it offensive. Why? Because Billy Joel is a classic-rocker and Randy Newman is a cult artist. Consider this: you are classic rock because you're successful, and you're successful because radio considers you to be classic rock. Today, Billy Joel performs "Big Shot" in stadiums and Randy Newman plays "Short People" in theaters because constant exposure has implanted Billy Joel into exponentially more lives, even though the typical music critic will still argue that Randy Newman's songs are exponentially smarter.

You could also see this disparity in the reactions to the deaths of Lou Reed and David Bowie. From a critical perspective, Reed and Bowie pretty much are on equal footing. Reed's band the Velvet Underground was an essential influence on Bowie early on, though Bowie arguably took Reed's "kinky sexuality plus canny pop hooks" songwriting formula further than Reed did. Bowie is respected as an iconoclast, but even he would've probably conceded that he was not as independently minded as Reed, who capped his career with an uncompromising (and largely unlistenable) double album of tuneless jams recorded with Metallica. Bowie was a taboo-smashing provocateur, whereas Reed was an all-time gadfly. In terms of credibility, they're both gods.

In terms of mainstream popularity, however, it's a different story—David Bowie is way more famous than Lou Reed. When Reed died in 2013, his passing garnered all of the necessary tributes. His legacy was thoroughly vetted and saluted, and his compatriots and collaborators reemerged to pay their respects. Diehards were allowed to defend *Metal Machine Music* publicly without being challenged. Bowie himself put out a simple four-word statement: "He was a master." The story was big for twenty-four hours, somewhat big for another forty-eight hours, and then it gently faded.

When Bowie died, however, the outpouring of grief went on for weeks—and not just from the press, but from fans on social media all over the world. Seemingly anyone who had ever heard a David Bowie song took to Twitter and Facebook to proclaim, "Bowie's music was the soundtrack of my life!" Even though Bowie hadn't scored a lasting pop hit since the mideighties, those people weren't exaggerating.

When I was growing up listening to WAPL, I heard one Lou Reed song—1972's "Walk on the Wild Side," which was produced by Reed's good buddy David Bowie and later sampled by Marky Mark and the Funky Bunch on "Wildside," the moody follow-up single to the early nineties middle-school-dance staple "Good Vibrations." For a while, "Walk on the Wild Side" and Marky Mark represented the totality of my Lou Reed knowledge. Wisconsin radio might have been limited, sure, but I heard many David Bowie songs, and from several different eras, on WAPL. There was his first, borderline-novelty hit that cashed in on the moon landing and the popularity of *2001: A Space Odyssey* ("Space Oddity"). There was the cream of his glam-rock period ("Changes," "Suffragette City," "Starman," "Rebel Rebel"). His Plastic Soul ("Young Americans") and Thin White Duke ("Golden Years") incarnations were represented, as were his dalliances with Brian Eno in Berlin ("'Heroes'") and his reemergence as the savvy godfather of the MTV-feted, early eighties New Romantics ("Let's Dance," "Modern Love"). Classic-rock radio provided subsequent generations with a survey of Bowie's most important work of the seventies and eighties while glossing over Reed. This, undoubtedly, informed how both men were grieved, and, right or wrong, it has determined their relative importance for contemporary listeners. David Bowie is classic rock, and Lou Reed is a cult artist.

Now, if I were to simply say that classic rock is whatever is in regular rotation at 101.7 the Bear or whatever the classic-rock station is in your town, it would barely function as a workable definition. So let's set some historical benchmarks. The story of why classic rock mattered needs a definitive beginning, middle, and end.

Classic Rock Begins with *Sgt. Pepper's Lonely Hearts Club Band*

To find the beginning of classic rock it's helpful to consult 1970's *The Sound of the City,* by British DJ and writer Charlie Gillett, an invaluable eyewitness account of how "rock 'n' roll," a term used synonymously with "youth-oriented pop music" in the fifties and early sixties, matured into "rock," a self-conscious art form that was set apart from supposedly craven music for adolescents and tweens.

According to Gillett, the separation of rock from pop was driven by record companies that wanted to establish legacy artists who could sell albums, as opposed to trendy pop combos who came and went based on their ability to churn out singles for pop radio. Legacy artists rewarded the investment of promotional resources by sticking around longer than pop stars, and pricey albums generated higher profits than relatively inexpensive singles. The music press aided the record industry in this process, Gillett argues, by glorifying the people who made the music, sowing a cult of personality around rock stars that subsumed the music. "Real" fans were encouraged to buy every album by their favorite artists, because each new release was the latest episode in an ongoing narrative. These were the seeds of classic-rock mythology.

Also vital were live performances—while pop groups proved their mettle on AM pop radio, rock bands made their reputations (and moved units of their latest studio work) by what they did on the concert stage, where improvisation was encouraged. Over time, the audiences for rock shows identified themselves as a countercultural tribe—as Gillett writes, "they adopted any number of visual ornaments and personal habits to make sure its associations were clear for all to see: not only to establish a togetherness with others of similar tastes, but to declare a distinction from the rest of the world." In other words, hippies grew crazy facial hair and wore fringe jackets and clunky necklaces to differentiate themselves from the Man, *man*.

Gillett didn't consider the transition from rock 'n' roll to rock as progress. He preferred the innocence of early rock 'n' roll to the druggy self-indulgence of rock. This is also true for Nik Cohn, who was openly disdainful of the emerging "rock" culture in his 1969 book, *Awopbopaloobop Alopbamboom*, another early survey of rock history. In Cohn's view, rock was defined by "its new solemnity and piety, its instant acceptance of pisspot bards as messiahs," and above all, "its loss of energy and humor, all the things that made [rock 'n' roll] so compelling in the first place."

If there's one event that crystallized the changes Gillett and Cohn espouse, marking our launch date for classic rock, it would have to be the release in the summer of 1967 of *Sgt. Pepper's Lonely Hearts Club Band,* the album where the Beatles officially stopped being lovable mop-topped pop stars and became serious rock intellectuals. This is slightly reductive—the previous two Beatles LPs, 1965's *Rubber Soul* and 1966's *Revolver,* are also examples of the Beatles' increased sophistication when it comes to songwriting, record making, and cultural politics. But the symbolism of *Sgt. Pepper*—the psychedelic cover, the drug references, the mustaches—is ultimately what matters most here. It *looks* like a serious work of art, or at least it did in 1967. *Sgt. Pepper* wasn't a collection of singles, it was presented as a cohesive forty-minute block of music. It was, many felt, "more" than rock 'n' roll.

Sgt. Pepper separated classic rock from oldies radio and created a line of demarcation that never really went away. There are many great and important rock records that came out before *Sgt. Pepper,* including Bob Dylan's *Highway 61 Revisited* and *Blonde on Blonde,* which arguably advanced rock as a serious artistic form much further than *Sgt. Pepper* ever did. But, again, it's the perception of *Sgt. Pepper* as a bellwether that has proven crucial. Before *Sgt. Pepper,* rock 'n' roll had virtually no artistic pretensions. It was unapologetically ephemeral. Rock, however, aspired to be as lasting as the dustiest folk ballad or lionized classical music symphony. And, for better or worse, that idea was crystallized by *Sgt. Pepper.*

Classic Rock Ends with Nine Inch Nails' *The Fragile*

Two things happened at the end of the nineties that changed rock music forever. Number one, Napster demystified albums, by breaking them down into individual tracks and making those tracks extremely easy to steal. In the process, all of the stuff that made albums seem special—cover art, liner notes, the money you had to save in order to buy them—was rendered obsolete for the average listener. Like that, the most sacred component of classic-rock mythology, the album, was reduced to data clogging up your hard drive.

Number two, the space that music created for young people to gather and pool their energy was no longer required, because now people could assemble in the Internet's virtual sphere. Now, instead of going to a rock show to find like-minded people, you could commiserate on message boards, where you also had the luxury of anonymity, liberating the inner asshole in us all. Over time, as streaming video rapidly improved, you didn't even have to leave your house to hear live music. Instead, you could stay at home and create your own music festival out of videos shot on smartphones. It was free, and you didn't have to wait in line to use a filthy Port-a-John or buy overpriced beer.

The result of Napster and YouTube is that classic rock as we know it no longer exists. There are still great rock bands, and there are still rock bands that are part of the classic-rock continuum, in that they are influenced by classic-rock bands and they are carrying those traditions forward. However, these post-classic-rock bands—the White Stripes, the Killers, Arcade Fire, the National, and the War on Drugs are notable examples—don't have the cultural impact of classic-rock bands, and they never will. That's not the fault of the bands—they exist in a world where the infrastructure that supported classic rock has been obliterated. Today, the best new bands have virtually no shot at exposure via radio, which is still vitally important for breaking new artists. Meanwhile, the record industry has reverted to a pop-centric focus—as it always does—as a reaction to a prolonged economic downturn.

When I became a serious rock fan in the early nineties, the music was readily available on radio and MTV. The record business was so strong that major corporate labels were willing to take risks on bands from the extreme margins of pop music. Even the Butthole Surfers, one of the weirdest and most abrasive bands of the eighties American indie underground, had a radio hit in the nineties. But those avenues have long since been closed to modern rock bands.

Classic-rock bands sell millions of records, play huge concerts, and have four to six songs that everybody knows. The last decade to produce bands like that is the nineties, which is why Pearl Jam, Nirvana, and Smashing Pumpkins tracks now get played on classic-rock stations along with Zeppelin and Pink Floyd. The biggest bands of the nineties reached the same critical mass that bands in the sixties, seventies, and eighties did. Ubiquity is the common thread that connects classic-rock bands. But technology broke that thread at the start of the twenty-first century.

The best way to illustrate this is to talk about the third Nine Inch Nails album.

In 1994, Nine Inch Nails became one of alt-rock's biggest bands in a conventional classic-rock manner—they released a popular single, "Closer," from the tortured opus *The Downward Spiral,* and performed a showstopping set at Woodstock '94, in which the group's mastermind and singer, Trent Reznor, slathered himself in mud and writhed around like a shit-stained shaman. Unlike Kurt Cobain and Eddie Vedder, who famously shunned the trappings of rock stardom, Reznor slipped some of that old Jim Morrison Lizard King mumbo-jumbo into his goth-guy persona. While his sensitive, feminist-minded peers seemed uncomfortable with expressions of sexuality, Reznor wore tight leather pants and panted that he wanted to fuck you like an animal.

But Reznor was also a proponent of old-school studio wizardry. For his follow-up to *The Downward Spiral,* called *The Fragile,* Reznor spent years crafting songs out of dense soundscapes littered with brilliantly executed sonic flourishes that only the most obsessive listeners would ever notice. This was to be Reznor's version of *The Wall,* Pink Floyd's landmark double album about how arena rock is an expression of cultural alienation. Whatever *The Wall* signified for big-time rock 'n' roll in the late seventies, Reznor's album would represent for the late nineties.

Everything on *The Fragile* was in its right place—Reznor even employed Bob Ezrin, coproducer of *The Wall,* to help him sequence the songs properly. The artwork was meticulously rendered so that the listener could stare at it for hours without ever fully discerning its "real" meaning. Great pains were taken so that *The Fragile* would sound amazing on an expensive stereo. Reznor made music in pricey, professional studios—he wasn't some amateur working on a laptop, which would soon become the preferred recording method for the next generation of rock tunesmiths. Ultimately, Reznor made *The Fragile* an immersive 105-minute experience that demanded the full attention of anyone who hoped to understand it. It was classic rock through and through.

Here's what *The Fragile* wasn't: an album that was well served by being chopped into stray tracks that are sampled for ten seconds on Napster before being discarded forever. If *The Fragile* wasn't received on Reznor's own uncompromising terms, it would seem boring and formless.

Unfortunately for Reznor, "boring and formless" was precisely how *The Fragile* was perceived when it came out in the fall of 1999. Nine Inch Nails' brand name ensured that *The Fragile* would debut at No. 1 on the albums chart, but by the following week, it had tumbled all way to No. 16, the biggest one-week drop in chart history at that point. The record that replaced *The Fragile* at the top of the charts was Creed's *Human Clay*. The other big sellers in 1999 were Britney Spears's . . . *Baby One More Time,* Backstreet Boys' *Millennium,* the Dixie Chicks' *Fly,* and Santana's *Supernatural.* Nineteen ninety-nine was also the year that Napster became a cultural phenomenon and the disastrous Woodstock '99—that misbegotten nu-metal showcase blighted by multiple sexual assaults and Fred Durst–inspired riots—temporarily sullied the reputation of music festivals. Reznor's classic-rock orthodoxy just didn't fit with the public's idea of what pop music was anymore. He had taken so long making an album that conformed to a faded era's idea of art that he aged himself out of his window as a commercial pop act.

After *The Fragile,* there would be plenty of *classic* rock records. But *classic rock* records were now extinct.

Let's attack the "What is classic rock?" question from a differ-ent angle. Which band best defines what classic rock is in terms of sound, attitude, impact, and narrative arc? Put another way: if an alien landed in your backyard, and for some reason you decided that exposing this extraterrestrial to classic rock was of the utmost importance, which band would you choose?

Since I'm the one posing this ridiculous hypothetical, I suppose I'm also on the hook for an answer. But it's not easy. My first instinct is to pick a band I love, because music fans always want to believe that whatever it is they like is the center of the universe.

I initially wanted to pick the Who, because the Who epitomizes what a real rock band should look like: muscular blond lead singer, angry-genius guitarist, stoic playboy bassist, and lunatic alcoholic drummer. Plus, *Who's Next* is the ultimate stadium album of the classic-rock era, which explains why deep cuts from that album keep showing up as jingles in truck commercials and theme songs for network TV crime procedurals. But the Who don't quite fit the bill as a *defining* classic rock band, as Pete Townshend's preoccupation with rock operas makes the Who too iconoclastic to be truly emblematic of anything other than themselves.

All of my other favorite classic-rock bands are disqualified on similar grounds. Led Zeppelin set the template for how rock bands are supposed to sound onstage and screw around backstage, but how many bands have pulled off that wholly unique Zeppelin mystique? Pink Floyd is the ultimate "head" band, but Roger Waters used arena rock to critique arena rock, so it seems odd to make his band the figurehead of a genre that he sort of hates. Queen is the gold standard for rock showmanship, but who in the hell is comparable to Freddie Mercury? A hard-rock band fronted by a flamboyant, barely closeted gay man that plays disco, rockabilly, and show tunes steadfastly resists codification.

Bruce Springsteen? He's a little too pure to signify the dark, seedy side of classic rock. Black Sabbath? They're a little too evil to represent classic rock's earnestness. The Beatles or Rolling Stones? Possibly, though again, those bands have their own vast, rich mythologies. Can you compare the most distinguished rock bands in human history to the Moody Blueses and Bachman-Turner Overdrives of the world?

No, there's only one band that fits the bill as classic rock's defining band. My heart doesn't want it to be this band, but my head confirms that there's no other choice. The evidence, I'm afraid, points solidly down a dark desert highway, where cool winds blow back your hair.

Of course I'm referring to the (fucking) Eagles.

You have no doubt heard of the Eagles, but in case you're reading a book about classic rock with no prior knowledge of the seventies, hotels, or California, here's a quick primer: The Eagles were the most popular American rock band on the planet between 1972 and 1980. Early on, they were known for easygoing country-rock tunes about loose women from Winslow, Arizona, and loose women who are also liars from Los Angeles, California. These songs are collected on the 1976 compilation *Their Greatest Hits (1971–75)*, the bestselling album of the twentieth century, and the second-biggest seller overall, trailing only Michael Jackson's *Thriller*. Later, the Eagles added excellent rock guitarist and problematic presidential candidate Joe Walsh for a stadium-rock reboot in the back half of the seventies. At that point, the Eagles' music became implicitly concerned with the effects of cocaine on L.A.'s music culture, which coincided with the Eagles' members becoming explicitly concerned with procuring cocaine whenever they weren't onstage.

Then they broke up, swearing to reunite only when hell froze over. What occurred next is perhaps the most un–classic-rock aspect of the Eagles' story: The drummer, Don Henley, became the most successful solo artist of the group. (Classic-rock drummers typically die, race stock cars, or marry Barbara Bach.) The second-most successful Eagle, Glenn Frey, called his solo debut *No Fun Allowed*, so I don't need to tell you that "second-most successful" is a relative term here.

Inevitably, hell eventually froze over. The Eagles reunited in the nineties, and subsequently played their most popular songs from that '72-to-'80 epoch in arenas and stadiums around the world for the next two decades.

The numbers suggest that the average person is more likely to love the Eagles than hate them. And yet everyone I know who cares about classic rock *despises* the Eagles. There are many reasons for this, starting with the Eagles' dubious credentials as a rock band. "Take It Easy," "Witchy Woman," "Desperado,"

"Peaceful Easy Feeling"—this is not the résumé of a band that knows how to rock. Even people who worked on Eagles records doubted their rocking prowess. Glyn Johns, the legendary rock producer who worked with Zeppelin, the Stones, and the Who before producing the first two Eagles albums, openly disdained any attempt that the Eagles made to go outside of their soft-rock niche. "They were a harmony band. The sound they made vocally was extraordinary," Johns said in 2016. "But Frey, because he came from fucking Detroit, thought they were a rock 'n' roll band. But they wouldn't know rock 'n' roll if they fell over it."

Then there's the arrogant mentality of the band members. Eagles songs are often decried for taking a bullying, judgmental stance in the lyrics toward anyone deemed morally or intellectually deficient—and most of the time, those people happen to be women. In Eagles songs, ladies are either after your money (like the gold digger in "Lyin' Eyes") or they're straight-up wenches (like the strumpet in "Witchy Woman"). Henley and Frey were never cool in the way that Jimmy Page was cool. They were cool like the captain of the high school baseball team is cool. They were clean-cut, hardworking jocks, the kind of guys who will tape your ass cheeks together if you dare pass out early at the party.

(The influence of *The Big Lebowski* also can't be discounted in spreading the epidemic of Eagles hate. It's sort of impossible to talk about the Eagles now without acknowledging how the Dude *hates the fucking Eagles, man.* In terms of classic-rock theory, Jeffrey Lebowski ranks among the most influential music critics of the past twenty years.)

Above all, the Eagles are stymied by the old truism about familiarity breeding contempt. As recently as 2014, Nielsen SoundScan reported that American radio stations were still playing "Hotel California" once every eleven minutes. This statistic is even more incredible when you consider that "Hotel California" is only the second-best white reggae song in the classic-rock radio canon, behind Zeppelin's "D'Yer Mak'er." Any song that's been played as often and for as long as "Hotel California" is bound to gin up hatred. I don't know how many love/hate cycles I've gone through with that damn song. For a while, I hated "Hotel California" so much that I talked myself into believing my own cockamamie theory about how the song's decadent SoCal patois was indirectly responsible for the nineties ska-punk abominations of Sublime. After all, isn't pink champagne on ice just a gateway drug for *40oz. to Freedom*?

But whether you love the fucking Eagles or you blame the fucking Eagles for fucking Sublime, the fact remains that no other band better encapsulates the arc of classic rock's cultural prominence. And you can plainly see this if you watch the 2013 documentary *History of the Eagles*.

The 2010s have been a banner decade for music documentaries—in terms of not only quality, but also quantity. There's a good chance that if your favorite rock band, no matter how obscure, doesn't have its own documentary yet, it will only be a matter of time before that's rectified. This is probably due to the so-called long tail theory, which dictates that servicing a million niches is now preferable to attempting to reach an increasingly fractured mass market. But I think it's mostly because watching old footage of rock stars doing drugs and carousing with groupies in the seventies will never cease to be awesome, even if you can't stand *those particular* rock stars.

Of all the classic-rock documentaries that have been produced in the past decade, *History of the Eagles* is rivaled only by *Rush: Beyond the Lighted Stage* as the best of the bunch. But whereas *Beyond the Lighted Stage* is a heartwarming story about lifelong friends who happen to be in the world's biggest prog band, *History of the Eagles* is a much darker story about craven capitalists who labored for years over spotless, perfectly constructed pop-rock songs, and then played them forever on the road, even after they openly expressed their intense dislike for one another.

"There's a philosopher who says, as you live your life, it appears to be anarchy and chaos and random events smashing into each other," Joe Walsh sagely intones at the start of *History of the Eagles.* "Later, when you look back at it, it looks like a finely crafted novel." Like all things Joe Walsh has ever uttered, this statement might sound insane but it's actually true, at least when it comes to the Eagles. If you're looking for a three-hour summation of how classic rock went from the pre-corporate folkie idealism of the late sixties to nostalgic late capitalism by the end of the nineties, *History of the Eagles* is the best lesson you're going to find.

The documentary is split into two parts, with part one covering the seventies and part two dealing with the reunion years. It goes without saying that part one is the more entertaining installment—this is where we see the Eagles hosting after-show parties (dubbed "the third encore") with bathtubs full of Budweiser and TV sets that have been hurled out of fourteenth-floor windows. Stories are related about smuggling baggies loaded with joints and Valium through customs in the Bahamas, and riding shotgun down the L.A. freeway in a Corvette driven by a drug dealer at ninety miles per hour, and trashing a hotel room in some Podunk town to the tune of $28,000 in damages. We learn that original bassist Randy Meisner was drummed out of the band because (according to Walsh) he "wasn't alpha." We witness the band members' evolution from bushy-mustachioed innocence to well-heeled, *American Gigolo*–style chicness. Everything that happened to classic rock in a macro sense happened to the Eagles in a micro sense.

Part two is anticlimactic in comparison, though in some ways it seems more honest, diluting the initial romance of *History of the Eagles* with endless lawsuits, long-festering resentments, and hugely profitable but otherwise uneventful stadium tours in which the set list scarcely changed. The only passion displayed comes whenever a professional adversary gets their comeuppance, whether it's the Eagles' erstwhile producer Johns, prodigal guitarists Bernie Leadon and Don Felder, or former benefactor David Geffen.

"I'd rather die than let you fuck me," Geffen seethes in one of my favorite scenes from late in *History of the Eagles*. It's said in reference to Henley and the Eagles' angry-dwarf manager, Irving Azoff, but the quote could've also worked as a title for the documentary: *I'd Rather Die Than Let You Fuck Me: The Eagles Story.*

In 2016, three years after the release of *History of the Eagles*, Glenn Frey died, from complications caused by medications he was taking for rheumatoid arthritis. In the film, Frey looks as healthy, handsome, and jocky as ever. About six months before he died, Frey concluded with the Eagles a two-year, hundred-and-forty-show tour that was launched in conjunction with the documentary. Now, when you watch *History of the Eagles*, knowing that Frey is dead, the documentary's resonance as archetypical classic-rock mythology only deepens. Frey checked out, but he can never leave the Eagles' story.

Let's go back to the song "Hotel California." When I hear it now, I don't notice the *pret-tay pret-tay bois* white-reggae affectations. Instead, I fixate on two things: the harmonized guitar solos by Walsh and Felder, which sound like Iron Maiden on quaaludes, and the lyrics, which are a hero's journey straight out of Joseph Campbell. "Hotel California" scans as a warning about the hedonism of seventies Hollywood, but it's really a glorification of the passage from innocence to experience that classic rock has always promised. There are sex and drugs and (moderately heavy) rock 'n' roll in "Hotel California." There is also death in that song, which is more meaningful now than when I first heard it on WAPL as a teenager.

Classic rock once seemed to contain secrets about how to live if you were the type of person inclined to search for truth inside liner notes and rock biographies. But now it has become a way for the classic-rock audience to process mortality. Because the members of the Eagles aren't the only ones trapped forever inside "Hotel California." We all are.

"I Know There's an Answer"

NOTES ON TRACK 4: What you're holding isn't just a collection of tracks. It's a unified statement. A musical novel. We're operating on a deeper-than-normal level. If you don't get it all at first, that's okay. We don't fully understand what we're doing either.

As a music journalist, I get used to having the same conversations over and over. For instance, whenever I interview an artist about a new album, it usually goes like this: She will talk about how much time was spent figuring out the order of the track list, and how the interaction of the songs informs the cover art. She will wax rhapsodic about how this new opus isn't *really* a concept album, though the songs are linked in subtle, imperceptible ways that she doesn't feel like divulging because *it's up to the listener to figure out the meaning for herself.* And then she will sigh heavily and admit that this is all for naught, because people don't care anymore, and they'll just pick out the songs they like and plug them into a Spotify playlist.

Albums still exist, but their existence feels precarious. Given the variety of different formats for music consumption, the album has been reduced to just another item on the menu. It is an artistic and economic construct that many listeners have outgrown. Sometimes I think that the only reason albums are still around is because artists still insist on making them. If the survival of the album format depended solely on the market, it would have been discarded long ago.

In Paul Thomas Anderson's *Boogie Nights*, there's a famously excruciating scene in which a wigged-out drug dealer played by Alfred Molina waves a gun at a gang of wigged-out porn stars— Mark Wahlberg, John C. Reilly, and Thomas Jane—who plan to rip him off. Before they can make their move, however, the gang is forced to listen to Molina's rant about how he hates being told how and in which order to play his favorite songs. This maniac would rather take "Jessie's Girl" from Rick Springfield's *Working Class Dog* and "99 Luftballons" from Nena's *99 Luftballons* and plug them into a "totally awesome" mix tape.

This is how most people regard albums today. Listeners prefer the interactive musical experience of making a playlist versus the more passive construction of a ready-to-serve album. What passed for cokehead logic in the early eighties is now conventional wisdom.

You can't miss the album's steady downward arc. People have been purchasing fewer albums every year since the early aughts, to the point where buying a CD or downloading an album seems either quaint or like a total rip-off. In an average week, an album can now move around fifty thousand units and wind up among the bestselling LPs in the country. To put that in perspective, consider that in 1983, Def Leppard sold one hundred thousand units *per day* at the height of *Pyromania* mania. And the British pop-metal band was still kept out of the top spot on the albums chart by the even more popular *Flashdance* soundtrack. Michael Jackson's *Thriller*, of course, was also doing blockbuster business at the time, though by modern standards every album in the Top 10 during an average week in 1983 was a monster.

In the 2010s, the record industry rejiggered sales statistics to account for the collapse of the album business. Track equivalent albums (TEA) and streaming equivalent albums (SEA) bundle downloads and streams into ad-hoc LPs, essentially for the sake of juicing the numbers. Imagine if Major League Baseball tried to stave off a sharp decrease in home runs by counting four singles as a round-tripper, and you get the idea.

People stopped buying albums for many reasons, but the most important is that they don't *need* albums anymore. Music consumers were once conditioned to buy music that was implanted onto tangible objects that they would display in places of honor in their homes. But now consumers simply pay a monthly subscription fee for access to a centralized database of music files that everybody uses. Listening to music now is like going to the beach—you build a playlist out of songs stored in the celestial jukebox, like a child making a castle out of sand. But once you leave, the sand stays at the beach. You don't own the sand, you borrow it.

The fudging of album statistics is standard record-industry cheesiness (and undermines the idea of albums as a unified work, rather than just a collection of songs), but I understand the reasoning. The industry needs to prop up the album as a relevant concept because nothing as significant has come along to replace it. Music fans love their playlists, but there is no specific playlist on Spotify that has the cultural cachet of *Thriller*, Guns N' Roses' *Appetite for Destruction*, or Taylor Swift's *1989*. Just because we've stopped buying albums doesn't mean we've gotten over using albums as cultural benchmarks. The albums chart is still expected to be a reliable indicator of what's happening in pop culture at this very moment. If the chart measured strictly *actual* album sales, it would be reduced to music that appeals only to people who still buy music. And then we would have to accept that the apotheosis of popular culture is Adele and Christmas records by dorky vocal groups like Pentatonix.

The pivot away from fetishizing the album experience is reflective of classic rock's decline. The rise of the album coincided with the culmination of classic rock's artistic and cultural influence in the late sixties, and the album format stayed strong as rock remained dominant in the seventies, eighties, and nineties. But as music culture became less rock-focused in the twenty-first century, the significance of the album also decreased.

In classic-rock culture, the album was *it*. A classic album defined not just an artist's career, but also an entire era. Albums marked time in classic rock, creating signposts for when cultural movements rose to prominence and when they crested, after which a new series of albums would arise to signal what was next. If American history is conventionally perceived as a compendium of wars and presidential administrations, rock history is often boiled down to discographies—the ebb and flow of the recorded output by classic rock's most important icons defines the very shape of the music and the culture that music informed. Concerts and interviews are also entered into the historical record, but classic-rock artists are judged first and last by their albums.

What does an album mean to a rapper who made his name putting out free mix tapes loaded with scores of hastily recorded tracks every six months online? Or the DJ who spellbinds dancers by crafting a web of sound that can stretch on for hours on end? Outside of rock, doesn't the album format seem a little old-fashioned? Shouldn't music flow with the speed of culture, rather than be fixed in a traditional, rigid package?

While it's true that pop artists such as Beyoncé and Kendrick Lamar continue to put out albums that are conceived as cohesive statements, the future is probably closer to Drake's 2016 release *Views*, the first album to accumulate one billion streams on Apple Music, in part because its twenty-song track list was constructed to maximize clicks. In 2017, R & B singer Chris Brown did a literal double down on Drake by releasing a forty-three-track record, *Heartbreak on a Full Moon*. Artists are now rewarded for putting out collections of songs that are far larger than traditional albums, because more songs equals more streams, which increases revenue and market penetration. In the future, albums will probably be more like playlists that can be altered after they've been "released," like Kanye West's 2015 LP *The Life of Pablo,* a self-proclaimed "living breathing changing creative expression" that never came out in a physical format.

Perhaps the album just made more sense in the sixties, an era of gurus, cult leaders, and martyred politicians. Back then, listeners expected rock stars to dictate great truths from a lofty perch accented with sweat-stained scarves and cocaine bumps. Bob Dylan famously advised, "Don't follow leaders," but he was outvoted. Dylan's rock-star peers were more than happy to strike messianic notes, whether it was Jim Morrison affecting a Jesus Christ pose onstage or John Lennon growing a Jesus beard (not long after asserting the Beatles' dominance over the original JC) or doomed saviors like Jimi Hendrix crucifying themselves for the sins of a decadent generation.

In classic rock's prime, the album functioned as a truth-delivery device, a perfect document passed down to the public in order to be analyzed, decoded, and enshrined for posterity's sake. Rock magazines fetishized the back stories of how albums were made, and rock radio stations played the songs over and over until they became a shared language. Over time, these stories became legends that listeners passed down to the next generation. And at the core of those legends was the common understanding that music simply mattered more when it was presented in a forty-five-minute bulk divided into twelve songs that sprawled over two sides of vinyl.

Today's gurus aren't rock stars or even pop singers or rap-pers. They're curators—flesh-and-blood algorithms that swiftly sift through reams of sonic detritus and come up with the perfect playlist to make you temporarily forget that jogging is the worst. What curators have done is make a case for playlists representing an evolutionary improvement on the album format.

This case is not without merit. Whereas an album offers a finite number of songs, a playlist can continue forever. While an album inevitably includes filler, skits, spoken-word interludes, and dodgy experiments, a playlist includes only the good songs.

An album is a statement by one artist who may or may not suck, but a playlist contains infinite artists who were decent enough to produce at least one worthy track.

And though I see the validity of this argument, I'll never accept it. I am the product of an era that molded music nerds (particularly *classic rock* nerds) to regard the album as the highest form of musical expression. I don't just revere albums, I revere *concept* albums, the most pretentious LP subgenre, which never make a lick of sense from a storytelling perspective but nonetheless leave me invigorated with their misguided ambition. I even appreciate *bad* concept albums, like Styx's *Kilroy Was Here,* which gifted the world "Mr. Roboto," the closest that rural America ever got to a Kraftwerk record.

While I recognize that playlists are more convenient and versatile, I will never truly believe that playlists are *better* than albums. I like having a finite number of songs. I find meaning in filler and dodgy experiments. I live for plumbing the soul of a single artist attempting to make a singular statement, even if that statement is "Dennis DeYoung is afraid that killer robots from the future will murder rock 'n' roll."

A bundle of interconnected tunes unified by a cover, liner notes, and artistic vision will forever be my go-to truth-delivery device.

My classic-rock education wasn't just handed down from classic-rock radio. I was also schooled by rock critics—Lester Bangs, Greil Marcus, Dave Marsh, and scores of other Caucasian-nerd sages whose bylines live on amid dusty back issues of *Rolling Stone* and *Creem.* Their lessons were burned into my brain and remain indelible all these years later. Classic-rock radio disseminated the music, but what rock critics instilled was a philosophical framework that brought order and meaning to the music. Rock critics not only told me what to listen to, they also articulated the music's larger significance.

Admittedly, I didn't fully understand what exactly Greil Marcus was going on about in *Mystery Train*, a heady magnum opus published in 1975 that expounds on the mythology of Elvis Presley, the rustic fantasies of the Band, the coked-up funk fatalism of Sly Stone, and the acerbic cultural satire of Randy Newman with an academic's precision and an evangelist's passion. I put serious strain on my cerebral cortex trying to absorb Marcus's hybrid of postdoctoral thesis and epic poetry. I'm pretty sure that nobody else at my middle school was thinking about what "Sail Away" communicated about the American slave trade. But I knew better. I knew Randy Newman was *important,* because Greil Marcus told me he was important.

Take this passage from *Mystery Train* about the Band's self-titled 1969 LP:

> The album tells no lies. It touches the size and the age of the country, [and] takes in its fabulous multiplicity . . . every character, every place, every event in the music looms up at once. Crossing the great divide, the Band left community in their wake.

The first time I heard "Up on Cripple Creek," I didn't detect the "fabulous multiplicity" of America in the interplay of Levon Helm's forceful drum kick and Garth Hudson's carnivalesque organ fills. But that was on me, not Greil Marcus. *The album tells no lies.* Marcus promised that *the* truth could be discovered by listening to music the right way, and I desperately wanted some of that truth for myself.

I knew enough to recognize that Marcus felt alienated—inside his own country and even his own skin. And since alienation is the default position of the average teenager, I was captivated by Marcus's ability to use the music he loved to find a place that he could call home. It didn't have to make sense to me or anybody else; *Mystery Train* made sense to *him*. This is what albums seemed to offer—a skeleton key for understanding your own heart.

Cruising the stacks of old *Rolling Stone* issues at my local library was my version of enrolling at Classic Rock University. One day, I uncovered a special issue devoted to the one hundred best albums of the rock era, defined in self-serving terms as starting in 1967 (when *Rolling Stone* was founded) and ending in 1987 (when the issue was published). I had dabbled in various album guides that I found at the library, but I had never before encountered what was essentially a map of the classic-rock canon. Here was something that told you explicitly what the best albums were, and even put them in order. There was a hierarchy! This was crucial information.

I don't know if this was the first time that a major music magazine tried to lay out the essentials of rock music, but *Rolling Stone*'s list was definitely the first big albums list that I encountered, and I've met numerous rock critics over the years who were similarly influenced by that list. It's like the Velvet Underground of list issues—everybody who read it went on to make their own lists.

Here is the top 20 from that *Rolling Stone* issue:

1. The Beatles, *Sgt. Pepper's Lonely Hearts Club Band*
2. The Sex Pistols, *Never Mind the Bollocks*
3. The Rolling Stones, *Exile on Main St.*
4. John Lennon, *Plastic Ono Band*
5. The Jimi Hendrix Experience, *Are You Experienced*
6. David Bowie, *The Rise and Fall of Ziggy Stardust and the Spiders from Mars*
7. Van Morrison, *Astral Weeks*
8. Bruce Springsteen, *Born to Run*
9. The Beatles, *The Beatles*
10. Marvin Gaye, *What's Going On*
11. Elvis Costello, *This Year's Model*
12. Bob Dylan, *Blood on the Tracks*
13. Bob Dylan and the Band, *The Basement Tapes*
14. The Clash, *London Calling*

15. The Rolling Stones, *Beggars Banquet*
16. Patti Smith, *Horses*
17. The Beatles, *Abbey Road*
18. The Rolling Stones, *Let It Bleed*
19. The Band, *The Band*
20. Prince, *Dirty Mind*

Now, as a grown man, I know enough to be skeptical of canons, which are inherently flawed because they're assembled by humans with biases that are hard to set aside. The *Rolling Stone* list was compiled by sixteen people, all of them white men. And it's probably not a coincidence that there's only one woman in the top 20, and only three black artists.

But back when I first started learning about classic rock, I was just grateful that someone was telling me what to think because I wasn't ready yet to think for myself. From *Rolling Stone*, I learned that *Are You Experienced* wasn't merely an album with songs I knew from WAPL, like "Foxy Lady" and "Purple Haze," but also an invitation to follow Jimi Hendrix "into a fourth dimension where his Fender Stratocaster is a paintbrush, where feedback can sing and amplifiers shriek with pain." And while I was aware of *Ziggy Stardust* thanks to two pals who used to sneak out of Sunday school at my church in order to jam on Bowie in the parking lot—I was stuck hearing about Jonah and the whale as those dudes contemplated time taking a cigarette—I relied upon *Rolling Stone* to teach me that Bowie "took rock theatrics and pan-sexuality to a new peak." This was heady stuff.

Rolling Stone sent me reeling to the tape rack that hung nailed to the wood-paneled wall above my bed, which housed my burgeoning music collection. A sizeable portion were greatest-hits albums—a Doors best-of, the blue-colored *Classic Queen* compilation released to cash in on *Wayne's World,* and that Billy Joel tape with the black and white cover where Billy looks like Robert Downey Jr. in *Less Than Zero*. In light of the *Rolling Stone* list, greatest-hits albums now seemed fraudulent. If you wanted to know what a band was *really* up to, you had to do the work and dig into the original albums. For a classic-rock acolyte, putting all of the best songs on the same tape was tantamount to cheating.

I had organized my tapes alphabetically, but now I set about reordering them in terms of artistic legitimacy. That meant the greatest-hits tapes were sent down to the bottom. I also marginalized my leftover tapes from my pre-classic-rock pop period—before long, *Rhythm Nation 1814* and *Forever Your Girl* would be banished from the rack altogether.

This left my precious *Led Zeppelin IV* and *The Dark Side of the Moon*—that neither ranked in *Rolling Stone*'s top 20 made me think that perhaps I had judged them wrong, so they were nudged down slightly. I stole Bruce Springsteen's *Born in the U.S.A.* from my dad and put it near the top of the rack. I flat-out shoplifted the Who's *Live at Leeds* and *Who's Next* from a dive-y record shop near the mall that went out of business a few years later. (My interest in classic rock was rivaled only by my interest in petty crime—thankfully that ended when I got busted for jacking some men's magazines from the bookstore at the mall in eighth grade.) And I bought U2's *The Joshua Tree* with my birthday money—it was only a few years old, but *The Joshua Tree* was already destined for a place of honor in the classic-rock canon.

At the top of the rack was the greatest album ever made, according to *Rolling Stone* and other classic-rock wise men: *Sgt. Pepper's Lonely Hearts Club Band.*

Sgt. Pepper was instantly greeted with ecstatic praise upon its release on June 1, 1967. *Time* called it "a historic departure in the history of music." The *New York Times Book Review* believed *Sgt. Pepper* signaled a "golden renaissance of song." The London *Times* went even further, declaring that *Sgt. Pepper* was "a decisive moment in the history of western civilization."

The Beatles were the Beyoncé of their time—everything they

did was viewed as #flawless. But the response to *Sgt. Pepper* was hyperbolic even by the Beatles' standards. *Sgt. Pepper* was the ultimate truth bomb, a paisley-colored sign of the times devised by the world's best band after months of sequestering themselves from the public. The narrative of *Sgt. Pepper* was that the Beatles had become so popular that they couldn't tour, because pubescent girls screamed so loud that it prevented John, Paul, George, and Ringo from properly hearing their own music. So the Beatles retired from the road, and entered the solitude of a recording studio to craft an immaculate rock masterwork.

The world expected profundity at the end of this process, and profundity is what the world swiftly projected onto *Sgt. Pepper*. Along with the Beach Boys' 1966 release *Pet Sounds*—Paul McCartney's favorite album, and a model for the Beatles' new obsession with studio wizardry—*Sgt. Pepper* was pitched as an unassailable masterpiece made by forward-thinking oracles who wanted you to know precisely how brilliant they were. In retrospect, being hailed as a masterpiece ultimately seems like *Sgt. Pepper*'s raison d'être.

In case it's not already obvious: I'm a lifelong *Sgt. Pepper* skeptic. The first two Beatles albums I ever heard were *Sgt. Pepper* and *A Hard Day's Night*, because those were the only Beatles albums my dad owned on CD. And I thought *A Hard Day's Night* was at least twice as good as *Pepper*. Classic-rock heads tend to severely underrate the early (as in pre–*Sgt. Pepper*) Beatles, but *A Hard Day's Night* is probably the best John album in the Beatles canon, especially if you appreciate his power-pop side—John highlights include the title track, "I Should Have Known Better," "If I Fell," "I'll Cry Instead," "You Can't Do That," and "I'll Be Back." (I would bet that this is the Beatles album that Paul Westerberg likes the most, even more than *Let It Be*.) As I entered my full-blown Beatlemaniac phase, I came to respect *Pepper* but I never played it as much as *Abbey Road*, *Revolver*, or *Rubber Soul*. I even preferred *Magical Mystery Tour*, which has "Strawberry Fields Forever," "Penny Lane," and "I Am the Walrus." Meanwhile the only truly great song on *Sgt. Pepper* is "A Day in the Life." The rest is either pretty slight ("With a Little Help from My Friends," "Lucy in the Sky with Diamonds," "Lovely Rita") or pretty corny ("When I'm Sixty-Four," a song about Paul McCartney's relatively youthful period back in the midaughts). *Sgt. Pepper* is to *Magical Mystery Tour* what *Is This It* is to *Room on Fire*—the first Strokes album gets all the hype but the follow-up that everyone always dismisses as crap is actually stronger. Maybe Julian Casablancas was the walrus all along.

My favorite Beatles LP is 1968's *The Beatles,* better known as *The White Album.* There's very little that's slight or corny about *The White Album.* (Except for the album-closing "Good Night," but that's easy enough to skip.) It's remarkable how much of seventies rock can be traced directly back to *The White Album,* whether it's Sabbath ("Helter Skelter"), Pink Floyd ("Dear Prudence"), Elton John ("Sexy Sadie"), Queen ("Honey Pie"), James Taylor ("Blackbird"), John Denver ("Mother Nature's Son"), the Eagles ("I Will"), Cheap Trick ("Birthday"), Abba ("Ob-La-Di, Ob-La-Da"), Blue Oyster Cult ("Back in the U.S.S.R."), or early Talking Heads ("I'm So Tired"). Even now, whenever a band makes a sprawling double album, *The White Album* remains the model for ambitious excess. Pearl Jam steered its career into a mountain in the midnineties because it stopped making grunge anthems about kids who shoot themselves in the face and started making kitchen-sink masterworks like *Vitalogy* and *No Code* that aped *The White Album.* (Actually, Eddie Vedder topped John Lennon in the "tedious experiment" department with his "Revolution No. 9" rip, "Hey Foxymophandlemama, That's Me.")

Whereas the narrative for *Sgt. Pepper* for the past half century has been "This Is the Greatest Album Ever Made," the narrative for *The Beatles* is "This Is the Most Destructive Album Ever Made." *The White Album* destroyed the Beatles' unity—even sweet Ringo was driven to quit for two weeks by the Beatles' bad mojo. *The White Album* destroyed the sixties dream by becoming a cornerstone of Charles Manson's self-created homicidal Jesus myth. It destroyed the reputation of Maharishi Mahesh Yogi, who John Lennon believed got a little handsy with Mia Farrow when the Beatles retreated to India in 1968, inspiring John to write one of his best songs, the beautifully spiteful "Sexy Sadie." It destroyed the reputation of Yoko Ono, John's new girlfriend, who wouldn't stop hanging around the studio and subsequently caught decades' worth of grief for supposedly breaking up the Beatles when it was really John who put Yoko before the band all along. Above all, *The White Album* destroyed the utopian illusion of brotherhood created by previous Beatles records—out of thirty songs, only sixteen feature all four Beatles, and the estrangement is obvious even when they are playing together. It's a soap opera in the form of a Beatles album. Even when I'm not playing it, I'm thinking about it.

My favoritism toward *The White Album* has at least as much to do with the record's incredible mythology as it does with the songs. No classic-rock band has a better mythology than the Beatles. If they hadn't existed, they would've had to be invented by desperate rock writers. (Or maybe all of the best rock-related metaphors would be applied to the toxic dynamic between Ray and Dave Davies.) The arc of the Beatles' career is perfect and applied constantly to measure the arcs of other bands, who never manage to be as good or interesting as the Beatles were. They started out as mop-topped innocents, they had a middle period in which they discovered drugs and Dylan and baroque instrumentation, and then they turned on each other in spectacularly mean fashion right as the culture at large was going to hell. Obviously, a lot of other amazing stuff happened in between all of that. But I'd have to write a whole book on the Beatles to pack it all in. (And there are already five thousand Beatles books to choose from.)

In 1995, during my senior year of high school, ABC aired the six-hour documentary *The Beatles Anthology* over three nights, attracting more than twenty-seven million viewers. (For comparison's sake, that's a couple mil fewer than a typical episode of *Friends* that year. The Beatles were big but not Chandler Bing–

level big in '95.) The following year, an expanded version that stretched for ten hours was released on home video. Since then, revisiting *The Beatles Anthology* has been a semiannual tradition for me. I don't think I've watched any rock doc more—not even *The Last Waltz, Gimme Shelter,* or *Rush: Beyond the Lighted Stage,* and those movies put together are only about half as long. No other band could justify making a documentary about itself that runs longer than *Shoah.* But the Beatles could—not just because they're still the most popular rock band ever, but also because nearly everything the Beatles did between 1962 and 1970 was momentous.

The White Album has both better songs and a better story than *Sgt. Pepper.* Nevertheless, *Sgt. Pepper* has the superior reputation. Its status as the first rock album that non–rock fans felt compelled to take seriously means that *Sgt. Pepper* is responsible for a lot of rock's intellectual baggage. No other album had a greater influence on how rock is discussed by fans and critics, and how artists conceived of their own albums. There are (at least) three critical clichés that *Sgt. Pepper* codified, which are the most common reasons given for why it's an important record. Subsequently, they became the reasons for why *any* important record is considered as such.

Critical Cliché No. 1: *Sgt. Pepper* Was "Progressive"

Numerous studies have shown that people tend to appreciate music that sounds like music they're already familiar with. Scientists confirmed this by studying the human brain, but it's also readily apparent any time you go to a sporting event and people get fucking jazzed by hearing "We Will Rock You" for the billionth time. However, rock-critical orthodoxy dictates that a band cannot be truly excellent unless it makes decisive changes to its sound with every record. (The exceptions are the Ramones and AC/DC, both of which achieved meathead perfection early on and did not deviate one iota from their meathead comfort zones afterward.) While the unthinking, visceral response to music derives from a sense of comfort, the intellectualized response requires that music be *challenging* and *experimental*. This is where *Sgt. Pepper* lives.

If a band insists on recycling a proven formula, critics will inevitably refer to *Sgt. Pepper* as a counterexample, pointing out that the Beatles went from "She Loves You" to "Norwegian Wood" to "A Day in the Life" in just four years. The implication is that the Beatles were great not simply because they wrote amazing songs, but also because those songs grew appreciably more sophisticated and high-minded over time.

Critical Cliché No. 2: *Sgt. Pepper* Is Personality/Narrative Driven

When it comes to popular music, people like to think that art and celebrity have a binary relationship, but in reality, it's actually a yin-yang arrangement. For a celebrity to matter, she has to make great art. For great art to change the world, it really helps if the artist is already a celebrity. It's not *required*, but in lieu of celebrity, a narrative that can connect the album to something bigger needs to be invented. *The Velvet Underground and Nico* invented punk. *Never Mind the Bollocks* upended arena rock. *Nevermind* killed hair metal. *Sgt. Pepper*, meanwhile, created the idea that an album can be an agent of cultural change even when the songs are about whimsical circus workers and sexy meter maids.

Why did *Sgt. Pepper* become the ultimate sixties avatar and not Love's *Forever Changes* or the Pretty Things' *S. F. Sorrow* or some other classic album from 1967? In terms of artistic merit, *Forever Changes* is twice the record that *Sgt. Pepper* is. The sublime "Alone Again Or" makes "When I'm Sixty-Four" seem as cool as Lawrence Welk. However, the Beatles are ten times more famous than Love. A grand gesture that acknowledged the sea change in pop culture at the exact moment that the sixties became *the* sixties meant more coming from the Beatles than any other band because so many people relied on the Beatles to point the way forward. The impact of the Beatles' fame amplified the impact of *Sgt. Pepper.* For the Beatles, being the best band ever was always intertwined with being the most *famous* band ever.

Critical Cliché No. 3: *Sgt. Pepper* Is Political Without Being Explicitly Political

People who care way too much about music tend to use music as the lens through which they view the world. Inevitably, this requires projecting a political agenda onto art that otherwise has no explicit political message. For all its supposed weightiness, *Sgt. Pepper* is the silliest album the Beatles ever made. It has no overt "message." The Beatles could've said anything they wanted—more than any other rock band, they had the juice to denounce the Vietnam War or to refer to Lyndon Johnson as a puckered asshole. But the Beatles didn't do that. They made a concept album indebted to British music-hall culture, which was probably the *least* relevant thing they could've done. That didn't prevent serious thinkers from gleaning deep messages from the adventures of Billy Shears and Lucy in the Sky with Diamonds.

The political importance of *Sgt. Pepper* had more to do with what it signified than what it actually said. *Sgt. Pepper* is probably the most 1960s thing ever—the music and the iconography encapsulate pretty much everything that those of us who weren't alive at the time have been taught to understand as essential to the era. *Sgt. Pepper* is the prequel to every terrible Austin Powers impersonation. But it's also "meaningful," because people needed it to be.

When *Rolling Stone* declared in 1987 that *Sgt. Pepper*—an LP released just five months before the magazine's first issue—was the greatest album ever, it helped to fix *Sgt. Pepper* as a baby boomer touchstone. And if there's anything that subsequent list makers came to despise, it's baby boomer touchstones.

A backlash against *Sgt. Pepper* was already under way by the late seventies—in the 1979 anthology *Stranded: Rock and Roll for a Desert Island,* Greil Marcus called it a "Day-Glo tombstone for its time" and claimed that *Sgt. Pepper* already seemed played out back in 1968. But anti–*Sgt. Pepper* sentiment really started to pick up steam in the aftermath of that first "greatest albums of all time" issue of *Rolling Stone.*

Now, whenever a magazine or website does a GOAT list, it will either replace *Sgt. Pepper* with another Beatles album (usually *Revolver*) or redraw the parameters to exclude the sixties entirely. *Rolling Stone's* Gen X offspring, *Spin,* has done numerous album lists where the sample goes back only to 1985, the year *Spin* was founded. Self-aggrandizement aside, the purpose is to reframe rock history for a new group of readers, to assure them that they play a central role in the larger narrative and haven't missed anything important before now.

This phenomenon is symptomatic of the generational provincialism that dominates music discussions. Nobody seems capable of judging music purely on its own merits—accumulated historical resentments always get in the way. I'm sure you know the drill: The generation in power asserts its preferences, which inevitably derive from a period when those people were between the ages of sixteen and twenty-four. Eventually, those people are pushed aside by a younger generation that has grown up resenting the generation in power and reflexively believing that what those people like must be overrated. The ultimate example of this occurred in 2012, when *Spin* did a Top 100 guitarists list—normally the purview of *Rolling Stone*—and included emblematic dubstep bro Skrillex, who does not actually play guitar. Not since the cancellation of *thirtysomething* had so many boomers been so scandalized.

This makes charting a comprehensive list of the greatest rock albums ever problematic. Or maybe it doesn't. This is a classic-rock book, and I researched this the analog way—I looked at a bunch of lists, I made note of the albums that appeared with the greatest consistency, and I compiled this unscientific, alphabetized list of albums that are commonly ranked among the best of the best albums ever.

The Beach Boys, *Pet Sounds*

The Beatles, *Revolver*

Bob Dylan, *Highway 61 Revisited*

Marvin Gaye, *What's Going On*

Michael Jackson, *Thriller*

Nirvana, *Nevermind*

Pavement, *Slanted and Enchanted*

The Rolling Stones, *Exile on Main St.*

The Smiths, *The Queen Is Dead*

The Velvet Underground, *The Velvet Underground and Nico*

Even this list is easy to nitpick, if you want to apply the aforementioned critical clichés introduced by *Sgt. Pepper. Exile on Main St.* isn't very progressive, unless the cause happens to be legitimizing heroin addiction. *The Queen Is Dead* doesn't have a strong celebrity hook for anyone who wasn't reading the *NME* in 1986. And *What's Going On* isn't political without being political, it's just straight-up political.

But for the most part, the *Sgt. Pepper* standard holds. Records like *Pet Sounds, The Velvet Underground and Nico,* and *Slanted and Enchanted* are credited with changing the sound of rock 'n' roll. *Revolver* and *Thriller* are enriched by the back stories of their larger-than-life creators. And while *Highway 61 Revisited* and *Nevermind* are lyrically opaque, they were regarded as revolutionary totems reflective of the larger culture in their respective times.

But again—these are critical clichés. Does anybody really love an album because it "changed the sound of rock 'n' roll" or acted as a "revolutionary totem reflective of the larger culture"? Does a record's *significance* really make you *feel* anything? What does any of this have to do with *truth*?

What we're talking about here isn't music but mystique. And mystique isn't organic, it's invented—by music critics, older brothers, and rock documentaries. It comes from someone telling you that something is great and describing it in a way that convinces you that it's great before you even hear it.

I still believe in mystique. And I still care about albums, because I *want* to believe in albums. For any of this to matter, you need to buy in. You have to want to be transformed. To me this is the essential difference between the music listening of my youth—when I lived in a world of albums—and music listening now. Our current world is a place where algorithms help us find an approximation of what we think we want. But the best albums deliver something you never knew you wanted. And it might take years of listening to the same record—over and over, because it hasn't yet quite connected—before you finally get it.

"The Hero Meets the Spirit Guides Who Will Point Him Toward Greatness . . ."

"Bob Dylan's Dream"

NOTES ON TRACK 5: Dylan is one of our main influences. We always try to make albums as good as his, even the bad ones.

Before I became obsessed with Bob Dylan, I was obsessed with becoming obsessed with Bob Dylan.

Dylan albums were among the most sacred in the rock canon. In *The New Rolling Stone Record Guide*—the one with the blue cover, 1983 edition, the only bible that mattered to me as a young classic-rock convert—Dave Marsh described Dylan's 1966 masterwork, *Blonde on Blonde,* as "rock and roll at the farthest edge imaginable, instrumentalists and singer all peering into a deeper abyss than anyone had previously imagined." I took this in and understood that Dylan was at the top of the classic-rock food chain, with the Beatles and the Stones, the one guy above anyone else that I had to figure out. "Bob Dylan is the father of my country," Bruce Springsteen once said, and I was eager to also become a citizen of the United States of Bob.

Dylan albums were totemic items thought to contain valuable

secrets, great mysteries, and profound wisdom. But you couldn't just plunder their riches willy-nilly. You had to *earn* all of the treasure that was inside. You had to work at it, even if it wasn't going to be easy. So I worked for many years.

But for many years I did not become a Dylan fan.

Nothing had prepared me to appreciate his thin, wild, mercury sound. I had heard a few Dylan songs on the radio, but he didn't seem to slot comfortably in any format. Strangely, Dylan songs upended the traditional oldies/classic-rock divide—WAPL occasionally played "Like a Rolling Stone," in spite of that song's coming out in 1965 and therefore residing in traditional oldies territory. Meanwhile, WOGB played "Lay Lady Lay," Dylan's Top 10 hit from 1969's *Nashville Skyline,* which should've represented his classic-rock period. But local radio mostly avoided Dylan—practically nothing was played from *Blood on the Tracks, Desire,* or his other seventies albums, and there was zilch from Dylan's eighties and nineties work. Based solely on radio exposure, I was better acquainted with songs by Jethro Tull and Ted Nugent than Bob Dylan.

Dylan songs were very long and densely coded. Time and again, I would try to engage with the gnarled verbiage and circular logic of the lyrics and fail horribly. Take "Sad-Eyed Lady of the Lowlands," the eleven-minute closer from *Blonde on Blonde.* This song gave me brain damage. Dylan once claimed in another album-closing tune ("Sara," from 1976's *Desire*) that he wrote "Sad-Eyed Lady of the Lowlands" in New York's Chelsea Hotel for his then-soon-to-be-ex-wife, Sara Dylan. But he actually wrote the song during an all-night Nashville recording session in early 1966, scrawling line after line about his sad-eyed lady while some of the finest (and most expensive) session musicians in the world sat around smoking cigarettes and playing cards. A few years later, Dylan admitted that he "started writing and just couldn't stop," presumably because he was zonked out on speed. "After a period of time, I forgot what it was all about, and I started trying to get back to the beginning," he told *Rolling Stone* in 1969.

"Sad-Eyed Lady of the Lowlands" was like a foreign language devised by a man who himself only half-understood all the conjugations. According to Dylan, the sad-eyed lady had "eyes like smoke" and "prayers like rhymes" and a "voice like chimes." The lowlands from whence she came were a place "where the sad-eyed prophet says that no man comes," but how did one get there? Dylan drafted a map that seemed to consist only of dead ends, littered with a "deck of cards missing the jack and the ace" and allusions to "basement clothes" and "warehouse eyes" and "Arabian drums." And that was just in the first two verses. There had to be at least seventeen more verses after that. If Dylan got lost in this song, what hope did I have?

I was raised on the seventh-grade-English-class model of poetry interpretation, in which every line has to be connected to a concrete meaning. But "Sad-Eyed Lady of the Lowlands" offered no easy answers. The only overarching message, in this Dylan song and all the others I tried in vain to decode, was, "You're on your own, kid." Priceless advice, I came to understand, whether you're trying to interpret rock lyrics or just make it through the day.

Some listeners drive themselves insane trying to get to the end of the onion. They refer to themselves as Dylanologists— self-appointed professors in the school of rock's poet laureate. The most famous Dylanologist was a writer, political activist, and stark-raving-mad lunatic named A. J. Weberman. In the late sixties, around the time that Dylan and his family moved from Woodstock to Greenwich Village, Weberman started stalking his idol. Among Weberman's many innovations in the field of Dylanology was something he called garbology, in which he dug through Dylan's trash in order to uncover evidence supporting his crackpot theory that Dylan was a heroin addict who had sold out the political left at a time when activists were gaining traction in stopping the Vietnam War. Along with analyzing Dylan's discarded coffee filters and banana peels, Weberman was a crazy-devoted interpreter of Dylan's lyrics, which he parsed like a World War II code breaker poring over intercepted Nazi correspondence. In 2005, Weberman published a truly demented but endlessly fascinating 536-page tome called *Dylan to English Dictionary*, in which he isolates hundreds of words that recur in Dylan songs and uncovers their "actual" meanings.

In the smoke rings of Weberman's mind, whenever Bob Dylan uses the word "frost," he is really referring to middle-of-the-road twentieth-century poet Robert Frost. When Dylan uses the word "load," he's really referring to drug slang for twenty-five bags of heroin. When Dylan mentions Texas, Weberman argues that Dylan really means Europe. When Dylan says "thick," Weberman surmises that Dylan is referring elliptically to contracting HIV in the late eighties. (Did I mention that another of Weberman's totally unfounded crackpot theories concerns Dylan's being HIV positive? We are truly through the looking glass here, people.)

I can see now that I was listening to Dylan all wrong. The Weberman approach of "solving" Dylan songs is a pointless exercise. Dylan songs are never about the destination. If you love Bob Dylan, you come to wish that the journey would never end, for this is what keeps his music fresh over so many listens. All of the detours in Dylan songs—which lead to other detours, which lead to still more detours—offer limitless possibilities. I wanted something I could put in a box, like all of the other songs I had ever heard, because I hadn't yet fathomed an alternative in which—to quote Harvey Keitel in *Mean Streets*—I could fuck around with the infinite. But that's what "Sad-Eyed Lady of the Lowlands" is—a pathway to the infinite. I came to *Blonde on Blonde* on a mission to get down to the bottom of it, but *Blonde on Blonde* is infinitely better as a record with no bottom.

Hundreds of artists have covered Bob Dylan's songs, but only Bob Dylan can sing his songs a hundred different ways.

It's not just that Dylan changes up his phrasing, or that his voice sounds completely different depending on which decade you happen to be hearing him. Dylan's singular talent as a vocalist is his ability to convey two or three or even four different emotions at the same time. Listen to Dylan sing "Just Like a Woman," and you'll hear cruelty, tenderness, anger, and sorrow. That mess of feelings inside your chest when somebody breaks your heart, which you can't articulate because your brain doesn't know how to reconcile the devastation that's been wrought—that's what Bob Dylan was born to express.

But when I first heard Dylan, his voice just seemed weird and I didn't like it. As an early-nineties alt-rock baby, I was raised to appreciate grating vocal styles—Kurt Cobain's parched howls, Billy Corgan's piercing caterwauls, Polly Jean Harvey's threatening whispers. But Dylan's dust-bowl wheezing, which was subsequently pinched into a needling whine by amphetamines and then lacquered over with a country gentleman's croon during his *Nashville Skyline* era, rubbed my inexperienced eardrums raw. I recall a feeling of relief while watching Eddie Vedder and Mike McCready perform "Masters of War" at Dylan's thirtieth-anniversary tribute concert, televised from Madison Square Garden in 1992. I couldn't make heads or tails of Dylan's version, originally recorded for his second album, *The Freewheelin' Bob Dylan*, when I was fourteen. But thanks to Eddie and Mike, "Masters of War" sounded like an acoustic Pearl Jam B-side, a preview of the quieter numbers from the next PJ record, *Vs.* Pearl Jam made sense to me in 1992. Bob Dylan did not.

When Dylan performed at that Madison Square Garden show, he looked gaunt and disengaged. On "My Back Pages," he was surrounded by a gaggle of adoring classic-rock royalty—Neil Young, Tom Petty, George Harrison, Roger McGuinn—who each took a verse on Dylan's ode to pushing beyond the limitations of your past. The irony of "My Back Pages" that night couldn't have been sadder—here was Dylan, hemmed in by his own legacy, utterly unable to transcend his own back pages, and his discomfort showed. Dylan's voice was even more choked off than usual. He was awkward and stiff amid all the pomp and circumstance in his honor, and seemed incapable of moving his arms or legs more than a few inches. Dylan was practically a wax figure on that stage, fit to be boxed and shipped to a museum.

Three weeks after the thirtieth-anniversary show, Dylan released his twenty-eighth studio album, a collection of folk standards recorded in his garage called *Good as I Been to You*. At the time, the record was treated mostly as an afterthought—reviews were more positive than they had been for 1990's *Under the Red Sky*, one of the most disastrous albums of Dylan's career, but an LP of old folk covers hardly seemed to herald a comeback for rock's most celebrated songwriter.

I came to *Good as I Been to You* many years later, when I had fully converted to the Dylan cult and sought out everything he had ever recorded. I doubt that *Good as I Been to You* has ever been anyone's entry point into Dylan. Like most people, I was first hooked by the peerless invention and youthful fury of his midsixties period. Then I went back to the early-sixties folk stuff, and then fast-forwarded to the midseventies "divorce" records, *Blood on the Tracks* and *Desire*. After that, you start investigating the less heralded records. *Good as I Been to You* falls into that camp.

The seventh track, "Hard Times," also known as "Hard Times Come Again No More," was written by Stephen Foster, often referred to as the father of American music, in 1854. "Hard Times" was a popular parlor song in its day, which means it was the epitome of pop music back in the 1850s. It's a protest song of sorts, imploring listeners to "pause in life's pleasures and count its many tears / While we all sup in sorrow with the poor." But the line that sticks out to me—and maybe it did for Dylan, too—comes next: "There's a song that will linger forever in our ears / Oh! Hard times come again no more."

"Hard Times" lingered long after Foster's death in 1864, having been adopted by folk singers like Dylan more than a hundred years after it was written. It was then carried forward by artists such as Dolly Parton, Emmylou Harris, Johnny Cash, Mavis Staples, Bruce Springsteen, Iron & Wine, and Mary J. Blige and the Roots, all of whom either recorded versions of "Hard Times" or performed the song live well into the twenty-first century.

As a budding Dylanologist, I surmised that *Good as I Been to You* and its companion record, 1993's *World Gone Wrong,* represented another retrenchment by Dylan in the traditions of American music. There's a pattern of rootsy reboots in Dylan's career going back to his "basement tapes" period in 1967, when he hid out with the Band in upstate New York in the wake of a chemical-addled explosion of creativity and pop stardom in 1965 and '66. A decade after that, with his marriage perilously teetering on the edge of oblivion, Dylan retrenched again with the Rolling Thunder Revue, a nightly hootenanny modeled on Dylan's early days as a folkie in Greenwich Village, only now on a rock star's budget. Much later, a couple of decades after returning to folk music on *Good as I Been to You* and *World Gone Wrong,* Dylan would dig into the past yet again by recording a series of albums in the 2010s dedicated to American pop standards popularized by classic crooners like Frank Sinatra and Bing Crosby, the kinds of artists that the parents of Dylan's fans back in the sixties would've enjoyed.

It's a good theory, but Dylan himself has disproved it. Dylan never "returned" to the past, because he never left it. Dylan songs that seemed revolutionary or topical or just strange in the sixties and seventies were nothing new as far as Dylan was concerned. All of his music was part of an unbroken chain. "These songs didn't come out of thin air. I didn't just make them up out of whole cloth," Dylan said in 2015, during an instant-classic acceptance speech for the MusiCares Person of the Year award. "It all came out of traditional music: traditional folk music, traditional rock 'n' roll, and traditional big-band swing orchestra music."

As an alienated kid growing up in the middle of Minnesota iron country, young Robert Zimmerman wasn't all that different from me, back when I was an alienated kid growing up in the middle of Wisconsin papermaking country. When Dylan was a tween, he was drawn to music created long before he was born, just as I was. Dylan has spoken of how, at the age of ten, he serendipitously discovered two important items lying around in the house—a guitar and a mahogany radio with a record player that spun 78s. On the turntable was a recording of "Drifting Too Far from the Shore," a gospel song written by Charles E. Moody in 1923 that's been recorded by Bill Monroe, Hank Williams, Porter Wagoner, and Jerry Garcia, among many others.

Young Bobby Zimmerman felt transformed by this music. It made him feel like he was somebody else—it made him feel like Bob Dylan, the person he had always been deep down inside. Dylan would have similar experiences throughout his adolescence and early adulthood. Dylan learned about the Blue Yodeler, Jimmie Rodgers, a defining country singer of the early twentieth century who died eight years before he was born, from a tribute record by Hank Williams, and it inspired him to start dabbling in songwriting. Hearing the gritty prison songs of Huddie William "Lead Belly" Ledbetter, initially recorded in 1939 by legendary folklorist Alan Lomax, helped to steer Dylan away from rock 'n' roll and toward folk music around the time he graduated from high school in 1959. While briefly attending college in Minneapolis in the early sixties, Dylan read Woody Guthrie's fictionalized autobiography *Bound for Glory* and swiftly became a devotee of the Oklahoma cowboy, whose period of greatest renown had been twenty years earlier.

"For three or four years, all I listened to were folk standards," Dylan said in that MusiCares speech. "I went to sleep singing folk songs. I sang them everywhere: clubs, parties, bars, coffeehouses, fields, festivals. And I met other singers along the way who did the same thing and we just learned songs from each other. I could learn one song and sing it next in an hour if I'd heard it just once."

Dylan's old friend and rival John Lennon once described the blues as a chair. "'Please Please Me' and 'From Me to You' and all those were our version of the chair," Lennon said of the Beatles. "We were building our own chairs." I learned about the chair from listening to Bob Dylan. What I had heard in Led Zeppelin, Pink Floyd, and all of the classic-rock bands I loved—that sense of the past, present, and future happening simultaneously—Dylan had heard in Lead Belly and Woody Guthrie and "Drifting Too Far From the Shore." Dylan has said that to him folk music didn't sound archaic, that it in fact uncovered "how [he] always felt about life." That's how classic rock made me feel.

Dylan passed that feeling of immortality along to me and countless other people by plugging his songs into the same continuum of music that had transformed him. Bob Dylan made me see that the rock mythology I was obsessed with went back further than just rock 'n' roll, and deeper than just the sixties and the seventies. It was also there in Jimmie Rodgers and Lead Belly and Woody Guthrie. It seemed to me like the very backbone of human civilization.

This was nothing less than a spiritual awakening, an ongoing conversation going back centuries between the dead and the living through rock 'n' roll. If you could see yourself in old songs, it kept the voice on that ancient record alive. And it might keep you alive, too, by connecting you to a deathless universal spirit.

The first Dylan album I ever loved wasn't a proper album. It was a bootleg recording of a Dylan concert performed with the Hawks, soon to be known as the Band, in Manchester, England, in 1966, part of the most famous tour in rock history.

This was Dylan's first "electric" tour, in which he performed by himself with an acoustic guitar in the first half of the show and then was joined by backing musicians in the second half. This might seem innocuous now, but at the time it was a major scandal—the folk-scene politics of the time suggested that Dylan was committing sacrilege when he played amplified music. This is what makes the second half of the Manchester tape—mislabeled the "Royal Albert Hall concert" by bootleggers—so dramatic. You can hear the crowd getting more pissed off after each song with the Hawks. The trolls are heckling Dylan, and drowning him out with whistles and slow-clapping whenever he tries to introduce the next number. But they never succeed in stopping Dylan and the Hawks. The musicians just bulldoze over all of the disgruntled punters howling in the darkness. It's like punk rock ten years before the Ramones and the Sex Pistols.

According to legend, Dylan wanted the shows on this tour recorded so he could review them once he got offstage and try to discern why exactly the audience hated it so much. But Dylan could never figure it out. The tapes to him always sounded pretty good. In fact, it was some of the most powerful rock 'n' roll ever recorded.

Before the final song on the "Royal Albert Hall" tape, "Like a Rolling Stone," some turtleneck-sporting dweeb in the audience screams an unholy epithet: "Judas!" Dylan seems stunned. "I don't believe you," he says. "You're a liar!" Then—and you can hear this on the tape—Dylan turns to the band and says, off mic, "Play fucking loud!" A couple of beats later, "Like a Rolling Stone" comes crashing in like an asteroid slamming into planet Earth, initiating the apocalypse. This version is much slower and much, much *harder* than the studio cut. The last word of each line in the chorus is shouted a little louder than the last—*feel, own, hooome, unknooooown, stooooone!* Dylan is drawing out the phrases, injecting extra venom, cultivating surplus spite, making sure that the weight of every accusation is so heavy that it pulverizes. He might also actively be trying to annoy the audience. Either way, it rocks like a son of a bitch.

This concert was finally released via legitimate channels in 1998, and again in 2016 as part of a massive thirty-six-disc box set collecting every recording from the tour. But I first encountered the "Royal Albert Hall" recording back when it was still an illegitimate bootleg, a secret shared by those in the know, which gave the tape a stature that exceeded even the incredible music it contained. This was music that you weren't supposed to hear, music that was actually *illegal* to sell or buy. Illegal music?

I thought that only existed in the world of Rush's *2112*. The "Royal Albert Hall" bootleg was like science fiction to me.

In the twenty-first century, pirated music became a way of life for music fans. But pirated music is different from bootlegged music. Pirated music is music that is supposed to be purchased, whereas bootlegged music isn't even supposed to be released. Live tracks, outtakes, rehearsals, radically different and not wholly successful but still fascinating alternate versions of songs that you already know and love—this is the stuff of bootlegs. It's what you seek out when you already own all of the albums and you're still chasing the buzz you felt before those records were worn out. Bootlegs are like an undiscovered back door to a house that you've lived in for years. They make the familiar seem unfamiliar again.

If albums are the signposts of rock history, bootlegs are a portal to rock's shadow history. In a way, they're just as important to the creation of classic rock mythology, because they were often difficult to track down. The only music greater than the music that moves you is the music you've been told over and over *would* move you *if only* you could hear it.

In terms of album sales, Dylan trails far behind the Beatles, Led Zeppelin, and Pink Floyd. But no artist has been bootlegged more. The first significant rock bootleg was *Great White Wonder*, a mishmash of early Dylan recordings from 1961 and tracks that Dylan recorded at the Big Pink house in upstate New York with the Hawks in 1967, the first flash of what would become known as *The Basement Tapes*. *Great White Wonder* initially appeared in California record shops, though the legend quickly spread among Dylan fans about a whole album's worth of material—perhaps multiple albums—that Dylan was withholding from the public. For hard-core Dylanologists, *Great White Wonder* was like the Dead Sea Scrolls.

Six years later, Dylan's record label, Columbia, finally released a cleaned-up version of *The Basement Tapes*, overseen by Robbie Robertson. In the liner notes, Greil Marcus played up the mythology of the music, comparing *The Basement Tapes* to epochal recordings in music history such as Elvis Presley's "Mystery Train" and Robert Johnson's "Love in Vain." But *The Basement Tapes* included only a fraction of the music recorded by Dylan and the Hawks, and was marred by overdubs that altered the shape of the music. Marcus's words only fueled fans' hunger to hear the "actual" *Basement Tapes,* and bootleggers obliged by compiling a five-volume set that dwarfed the Columbia version. (An official "genuine" *Basement Tapes* box set was finally released in 2014.)

I found the "Royal Albert Hall" tape at New Frontier Record Exchange, a cluttered, cavelike shop downtown that smelled of cigarettes and stale coffee. I started going there in middle school, usually showing up right when the store was supposed to open at eleven A.M., which was forty-five minutes before the store actually opened. I'd stand next to the door and wait for Stan, the proprietor, to pull up in a Chevy Nova. Stan was the most rock 'n' roll guy in my town—he wore flannel shirts and chain-smoked Camels and always looked like he was on the third day of a weeklong bender. (In my memory, Stan resembles Neil Young after a dozen honey slides, that mystical concoction of pan-fried weed and honey that Young consumed heavily during the *On the Beach* sessions.) Stan would see me waiting, wordlessly nod, and wonder why this kid wasn't spending his Saturday morning doing something worthwhile, like underage drinking or sleeping. And then he let me in.

New Frontier first and foremost trafficked in vinyl, even though vinyl had not yet made a comeback in the early nineties. I didn't own a record player, so I mostly just stuck to the small but surprisingly stacked tapes section. I bought a lot of crucial tapes at New Frontier: Neil Young and Crazy Horse's *Rust Never Sleeps,* the Sex Pistols' *Never Mind the Bollocks,* Queen's *A Night at the Opera.* Each time I bought a tape, Stan would just wordlessly nod in approval.

When I finally got a CD player for my fourteenth birthday, I started scanning the CD section, though CDs were more expensive, so I had to be choosier. One time, I saw a double-disc set that

I had read about in books but had never actually touched with my own bare hands—Dylan's "Royal Albert Hall" concert. The discs were $30, way too rich for my blood. But Stan said he would dub a tape for me for $10. I wasn't yet a Dylan fan at that point, but I couldn't pass up this opportunity. I had to act now, or risk never coming across this bootleg ever again. I handed Stan my $10 and made arrangements to return for the tape a few days later.

In those days, I don't think I said more than ten words to Stan. I was too scared. He knew things that I wanted to know, but I was too intimidated to ask. But to this day I am grateful for those tapes. Stan sold me the world.

One of the ironies of Bob Dylan's career is that while his al-bums are considered essential listening for a basic understanding of rock music, the man himself has said time and again that he's not very good at making albums. "My songs always sound a lot better in person than they do on record," Dylan said in 1969, not long after recording some of the most beloved LPs in rock history. Throughout his career, he has spoken of his failures to replicate the sound in his head, though he's never seemed to try very hard to get it.

Here is Dylan explaining his recording method to *Rolling Stone's* Jann Wenner in that 1969 interview: "We just take a song; I play it and everyone else just sort of fills in behind it. No sooner you got that done, and at the same time you're doing that, there's someone in the control booth who's turning all those dials to where the sound is coming in . . . and then it's done. Just like that."

Dylan is a cagey guy, and it's possible that on the day he gave this interview he didn't feel like giving Jann Wenner a more thorough rundown of his creative process. But, clearly, Dylan is not Brian Wilson or Paul McCartney. He wasn't inclined to make his own *Pet Sounds* or *Sgt. Pepper*. He has never been a creature of the studio. Dylan's methods have always been primitive and slapdash compared with the pop geniuses of his time. He gets bored playing anything more than once. He's quick to say "good enough."

"I'm not giving you a hundred percent. I'm not giving *anyone* a hundred percent," Dylan said in the mideighties, when he was making some of the worst records of his life. In 2001, when he was making classic albums again, he admitted that he almost quit recording altogether in the early nineties. "I'd rather play on the road. Recording is too mental," he said.

Apparently, even making a proper track list was "too mental" for Dylan. For years, he routinely left some of the best songs off of his albums—like "Up to Me" off *Blood on the Tracks*, "Abandoned Love" off *Desire*, and "Blind Willie McTell" off *Infidels*. Bootleggers were the first to rescue these songs; they also circulated the "Royal Albert Hall" concert when Dylan held back the release because he didn't think the recordings were up to snuff. It's not an exaggeration to suggest, as scores of Dylan fans have testified, that bootleggers have had better taste in Dylan's music than Dylan himself.

Dylanologists have long wondered: Does Dylan intentionally make it hard for his most ardent followers to hear some of his best material? Or is it possible that he's held back so much music because he honestly believes that the best versions of his songs don't yet exist?

My favorite Dylan song is "Visions of Johanna," from *Blonde on Blonde*. It's his greatest questing tune, full of romance and foreboding, piling on seductive images—heat pipes cough, country music plays soft, all-night girls whisper, a lover's face stares back like a mirror—that evoke spiritual wanderlust with no particular place to go. The narrative ostensibly concerns a love triangle between the narrator, his lover Louise, and another woman, Johanna, whom the narrator secretly pines after. But it's really about yearning for something that's missing, a flaw in the human condition that doesn't go away even when you have everything you could possibly ever need. As long as the unknown exists, the belief that something better is out there is never quite dissuaded.

Using officially sanctioned recordings as well as bootlegs, I've tried to follow Dylan on his journey through this song by compiling a "Visions of Johanna" playlist composed of different versions recorded in studios and concert halls. There's the version on the record, in which Dylan sounds laconic and stoned, approaching the song as a supremely self-absorbed young man who considers Johanna only in relation to his own desires. A similar vibe exists on two outtakes from the *Blonde on Blonde* sessions, including a galloping, sped-up take with the Hawks that recounts the song's emotional ménage à trois with arrogant bravado.

A version culled from the Rolling Thunder Revue tour in 1976 couldn't be more different—here Dylan plays the song accompanied only by his acoustic guitar and sings it in a painful, pleading tone, reimagining "Visions of Johanna" as the mournful lament of a man taking stock of how his wanderlust has wreaked havoc on his family. The song got another dramatic makeover in 1988, when Dylan assembled a three-piece band headed up by *Saturday Night Live*'s G. E. Smith and transformed even his most contemplative numbers into guitar-heavy arena rock. Now Dylan was using "Visions of Johanna" to recharge himself— playing it was an exercise in reminding Bob Dylan how to be Bob Dylan again.

Then there's an odd take from a residency in Minneapolis in 1992, in which Dylan spits out the lyrics rapidly while the music skitters along on a skiffle-like rhythm, a metaphor for middle-aged uncertainty. A version from 1995 is more relaxed and sensitive— Dylan is less concerned with rebooting "Visions of Johanna" than finding his place in the old warhorse now that he's lived many lifetimes with the highway blues. My favorite version, though, might be the one recorded at a gig in Dublin in 2005, almost forty years after it was written. The arrangement is stately and beautiful, and Dylan's vocal is wily and melancholy. You can hear how the perspective has shifted—Dylan has grown up enough to now consider the feelings of Louise and Johanna, and to learn from them.

Could this be the definitive version of my favorite Dylan song? I hope not. I never want to stop being surprised by "Visions of Johanna." It has come to symbolize the significance of Bob Dylan's art in my life. What the narrator in that song goes through is an allegory for being a Dylan fan—if you never stop yearning, the song never ends.

"Hello There" (Live at Budokan)

NOTES ON TRACK 6: We laid this one down on our last tour. Albums are one thing, but playing live is a whole other ball game. You're not a real band if you can't kill it onstage, then briefly leave the stage so people will applaud for you, and then deliver a preplanned encore.

The rock canon was a whole new world that I was eager to explore. But there was another destination beyond the canon that was even more mystical, and for a while much less accessible—the rock show.

If albums were like scripture, the rock show was church. Albums promised truth, but the live show was *reality*. You went to a rock show to bask in the glow of your chosen rock gods and to commiserate with other acolytes. It was the place to drink, do drugs, meet women—all of the activities that most fascinated me and filled me with the deepest dread.

Women scared me the most, because I also wanted to be around them the most. All rockers do. Since the beginning of time, women have been the greatest rock fans. No band has ever formed with the intention of attracting a room full of guys. A guy-heavy audience is the absolute worst for rock 'n' roll—who wants to play for plain, basic, boring-ass dudes? Women dance. Women scream. Women look glamorous when they're sweaty—unlike men, who just look sweaty. Women also have the best taste. Women thought the Beatles were fab long before the intelligentsia did. Women flocked to Led Zeppelin when *Rolling Stone* was panning their albums. Women worshipped Bowie as an extraterrestrial sex god as critics harrumphed over whether he represented a triumph of style over substance. Women will stand by you even if you're considered uncool by so-called experts. They're always the ones you want in your corner.

Women have also inspired some of the greatest classic-rock songs of all time. Many of them are anonymous—the foxy lady, the cinnamon girl, the American woman (and American girl), the long cool woman in a black dress. But some have gone down in history as muses—like Pattie Boyd, who inflamed the normally stoic George Harrison into writing his gooiest love song, "Something," and then provoked Harrison's heartsick pal Eric Clapton into risking his friendship by confessing his unrequited love in "Layla." (Harrison lost the girl but kept Clapton.) Even George Harrison, who surely belongs in the top 1 percent of coolest men who ever lived, is no match for a good woman.

And then there's Pamela Des Barres, a legendary figure in classic-rock lore, who had relationships with Jimmy Page, Keith Moon, Jim Morrison, and Gram Parsons in the late sixties and early seventies. Des Barres is commonly classified as a groupie, a reputation she didn't back away from in her iconic memoir, *I'm with the Band,* basically the X-rated version of *Almost Famous.* But Des Barres was really just a prolific fan who functioned as a street-level music critic back before rock criticism was recognized as an actual profession. (Rock criticism stopped being recognized as an actual profession around 2003.) Few rock fans have ever loved music as much as Des Barres did. It's one thing to admire the eccentricities of an outsider classic like *Trout Mask Replica.* It's another to show your appreciation for the twisted genius of Captain Beefheart by giving him a hand job. Des Barres truly went the extra mile.

As much as I loved classic rock, it was a lonely pursuit. I did all of my listening and reading and thinking about music by myself in my room. None of my friends cared about Zeppelin or Pink Floyd or the Beatles or any other band that predated 1987. (They were too busy listening to the Offspring.) I was a loner by nature, and classic rock fed into my antisocial impulses. But the rock show offered deliverance from all of that. It was a place where I could finally meet members of my tribe. Even better, many of them would be female. I just had to find a way there.

For the first several years of my new life as a rock 'n' roll obsessive, I was too young to go to a rock show. This problem was compounded by growing up in a small Wisconsin town that was at least a four-hour round-trip drive from a city where touring bands visited. I longed to see U2's Zoo TV tour in 1992, but I was still one year away from getting my driver's license. Seeing Bono's ironic rock-star posturing hinged on my ability to convince my mother to drive two hours to Madison and sit with me inside Camp Randall Stadium while a bunch of Irish rockers mocked George Bush. It was, in a word, impossible.

Not that my mother completely resisted the call of the rock 'n' roll wild. She claimed to have seen Huey Lewis and the News back in the early eighties, before *Sports* and *Back to the Future* made them (temporary) superstars. Now, I had reason to question the veracity this story. Number one, she claimed that Huey played a low-rent supper club on the north side of town, which does not seem plausible, even for a white harmonica player named Huey. Number two, my mother has always been terrible with names, especially when it comes to bands. For example: When I was in high school, I asked permission to head down to Milwaukee with friends to see R.E.M. on its arena-conquering *Monster* tour. "I love REO!" she said. My mom thought I was referring to REO Speedwagon, staple of Midwestern county fairs since the dawn of time, whose smash 1980 album *Hi Infidelity* was one of the few tapes that she owned. (We will revisit my mom's love of REO Speedwagon later in this book.)

Since my youth and my mom were squared against me in my early rock years, I had to rely on live albums for rock show experiences. Perhaps that's why I've always held the somewhat contrarian opinion that live albums are awesome.

Rock experts have long dismissed live albums as space fillers in a band's discography. Whenever a live album comes out, it's assumed that the band is either taking too long to finish its next studio record (thus necessitating the rush release of placeholder product) or is trying to fulfill the requirements of an onerous contract without doing any extra work. The eighties college-rock band Camper Van Beethoven summed up the conventional wisdom on live records with the title of its own concert LP: *Greatest Hits Played Faster.*

I don't care—I love live albums. Live recordings were an invaluable resource for me in my pre-concertgoing days. I treasured them for the documentary aspect as much as the music. I still appreciate live albums as historical snapshots for all of the classic-rock bands that I was never able to see in their primes. Studio albums were made for all time, but concerts capture a moment *in time* that would've disappeared forever otherwise.

Years before I became a regular concertgoer, live albums taught me what I liked and didn't like about rock shows. My least favorite rock-show cliché is (and forever will be) the fake encore—that is when the band leaves the stage and pretends that the show is over, and then comes back out to play a few more songs, supposedly because the audience did a really good job of applauding. Even when I was a rock show neophyte, I sneered at the people who fell for this ruse.

Meanwhile, my favorite rock-show cliché is when bands interpolate lyrics from classic-rock songs into their own songs, creating a kind of greatest-hits sandwich that elevates whatever song the band is performing to instant-classic status by association. I don't know who did this first, but the masters of this maneuver were U2 (who did it in *Rattle and Hum* when they played "Bad" and integrated the Rolling Stones' "Ruby Tuesday" and "Sympathy for the Devil") and Pearl Jam (who quoted Pink Floyd's "Another Brick in the Wall" on a number of bootlegs I collected in the early nineties, often during the fade-out of the song "Daughter"). I liked this because it reflected how I was already experiencing rock music, as an art form outside of the normal "past, present, and future" paradigm. I viewed rock the way Matt McConaughey saw time in the first season of *True Detective,* as a flat circle.

The first live albums I heard were the ones popular enough to spawn classic-rock radio hits. Each bit of captured audio revealed an essential piece of information about what I could expect when the stars finally aligned and I could attend my first rock show. From Kiss's "Rock and Roll All Nite" (culled from 1975's overdubbed-to-death *Alive!*), I learned rock 'n' roll algebra—i.e., the value of energy and conviction versus intelligence and taste is inversely proportional to the number of dudes hopped up on Schlitz and weed packed inside Detroit's Cobo Hall. From Cheap Trick's "I Want You to Want Me" (taken from 1979's teen-scream-saturated *At Budokan*), I discovered the virtue of audience participation, particularly when the audience consists of young Japanese girls who can sing pitch-perfect backing vocals. From Bob Seger's "Turn the Page" (drawn from 1976's truck-driver classic *Live Bullet*), I was granted a backstage view, where the crew guys did bumps off the road cases in between switching out guitars for the strung-out musicians under the lights. Those film-noir saxophone wails on "Turn the Page" spoke to me. Seger was as burned out by rock 'n' roll as I was by the eighth grade. I might have been a rock-show virgin, but "Turn the Page" made me feel weary about the road and cynical about never-ending tour cycles.

The live album that got the most encores on WAPL was Peter Frampton's *Frampton Comes Alive!* Released in 1976, *Frampton Comes Alive!* was an unlikely smash for the journeyman Frampton, an ex-member of the English blues-rock group Humble Pie whose pre–*Comes Alive!* studio work had failed to gain much of a commercial foothold. A pleasant-enough guy with long, frizzy blond locks—on the cover of the album he looks a little like Diane Keaton in *Manhattan*—Frampton was the epitome of the unexceptional grinder whose tireless, yeomanlike work pays off when good luck unexpectedly intervenes. For Frampton, the combination of a photogenic cover, some solid pop songs, and supportive radio programmers helped to drive sales of *Frampton Comes Alive!* past the six-million mark in the U.S., making it the year's bestselling LP and one of the most popular live records ever.

Frampton Comes Alive! became a mainstay of seventies suburbia, the classic-rock equivalent of the station wagon or backyard trampoline. It turned the idea of "greatest hits played faster" on its head—"Baby, I Love Your Way" and "Show Me the Way" didn't become hits until they were featured on *Frampton Comes Alive!* And then there was "Do You Feel Like We Do"—when it originally appeared on Frampton's 1973 record *Frampton's Camel,* it clocked in at a relatively economical 6:44. But on *Frampton Comes Alive!* "Do You Feel" ballooned to more than twice that length, affording enough space to accommodate long guitar solos and an even lengthier talk-box solo, finally wrapping up at an ungodly 14:16.

And yet, somehow, *that* was the version that became popular! I later learned that "Do You Feel" became a classic "bathroom break" song for radio disc jockeys. Every jock back in the seventies and eighties required a few extra-long tracks in their arsenal in case they needed to sneak out to take a leak. (Other examples include Meat Loaf's "Paradise by the Dashboard Light" and—this was for especially dire digestive emergencies—the marathon version of the Allman Brothers' "Whipping Post" from 1971's *At Fillmore East*.) As a kid, I just thought the DJs at WAPL *really* liked "Do You Feel Like We Do." (In reality, the jocks were probably just drinking mammoth-sized cups of coffee.) Thanks to the power of repetition (or maybe it was Stockholm syndrome)

I came around on it. All of the elements that I picked up from other live albums existed in this song—the energy, the audience participation, the displays of instrumental virtuosity. But what I liked most about it was the open space—for minutes at a time, the band was just vamping while the audience buzzed like lightning bugs in the distance.

What "Do You Feel Like We Do" captured was the atmosphere inside the arena at SUNY Plattsburgh in Plattsburgh, New York, where the song was recorded on November 22, 1975. Frampton came alive nearly two years before I was born, but this field recording made me feel like I was in the audience catching a contact buzz, brushing up against thousands of anonymous heshers, and absorbing the aura of this nondescript British man who spoke vaguely of "the way."

I wanted to be shown the way, too.

As I wrapped my head around "Turn the Page" and "Do You Feel Like We Do," I understood the central tenet of rock-show mythology: seeing a great band play live is a transformative event that can change the world. But where did this belief come from? What was the big bang (or series of big bangs) that established the rock show as the pivotal ritual for citizens of rock 'n' roll nation? Why exactly do we feel like we do?

As I delved deeper into rock 'n' roll lore, I learned that five rock shows seemed more important than the other tens of thousands of gigs played throughout time. These five shows were spoken about with such reverence that, in my mind, they took on the stature of religious rituals preordained with legendary status. These shows created narratives so deep and profound in rock history that they still influence the language we use to describe iconic live music moments. Even people born decades after these shows took place have a found a way to talk about them, either directly or by proxy, sometimes knowingly and sometimes not.

1. The Beatles on *The Ed Sullivan Show*—
February 9, 1964

Purists might take exception to including this on a list of seminal
live performances. Aside from a few hundred hysterical teenage
girls and assorted gobsmacked crewmembers and confused old
people, the vast majority of the audience for this gig watched it on
television. However, the Beatles on *Ed Sullivan* is a bedrock event
in the creation of the rock-show myth, for this was the performance that established the idea that seeing a band play live rock
music can alter the course of your life.

Watching the performance more than fifty years later, the
electricity of the moment is muted. The audio is muddy, the
visuals fuzzy. The Beatles are presented in their most carica-
tured form—heads bob, choruses "Woo!," and the post-song
bows are formal. The whole band seems stiff in the early going.
The camera fixates on Paul (always the head-bobbiest Beatle)
and Ringo, who can't shake a wide, gawky grin as he bashes out
a workmanlike four-four. You can't even see John, except for
a stolen shot here and there spotlighting his stout half-crouch
stance, like he's ready to open fire with his Rickenbacker. Only
George exhibits any movement, leaning into the guitar solo for
"All My Loving" as he bounces from John's mic over to Paul.
By the time the Beatles start their second song, a cover of the
trite "Till There Was You" from *The Music Man*, it all seems almost . . . *wholesome*. Certainly not very rock 'n' roll by today's
standards.

Of course, postmortems decades after the fact mean nothing
here. Critiquing the Beatles' performance on Ed Sullivan is like
hiring a copy editor to do a once-over on the Declaration of Independence. Supreme historical significance obliterates any petty
nitpicking. In the realm of classic rock, this performance is the
"big bang" creation story for virtually every rock star from the
sixties and seventies.

BRUCE SPRINGSTEEN: "Rock 'n' roll came to my house where there seemed to be no way out . . . and opened up a whole world of possibilities."

TOM PETTY: "The minute I saw the Beatles on *The Ed Sullivan Show*—and it's true of thousands of guys—there was the way out."

BILLY JOEL: "That one performance changed my life . . . Up to that moment I'd never considered playing rock as a career . . . I said: 'I know these guys, I can relate to these guys, I am these guys. This is what I'm going to do—play in a rock band.'"

GENE SIMMONS OF KISS: "There is no way I'd be doing what I do now if it wasn't for the Beatles."

JOE PERRY OF AEROSMITH: "It changed me completely. I knew something was different in the world that night."

You get the idea. If not for the Beatles, Gene Simmons would be selling carpets in Brooklyn.

Now, it could be argued that Elvis Presley's iconic "waist-up" performance on *Ed Sullivan* from seven years earlier—this was when TV censors tried to keep Presley's magical midsection away from the nation's young people by filming only his torso and shit-hot sideburns—deserves to be on this list. Here's why I don't include it: Every rock band that exists right now is on a continuum with the Beatles. Presley remains a foundational artist in American music, but his connection to modern pop stars is less obvious—the line is clearer to Prince or Michael Jackson than to the King of Rock 'n' Roll. But the Beatles model—a four-piece rock band that writes and performs its own songs—is still predominant for rock artists. Which is why any time a band kills it on television, it is usually likened to a "Beatles on *Ed Sullivan*" moment. (For people of my generation, seeing Nirvana's music video for "Smells Like Teen Spirit" on MTV for the first time was a "Beatles on *Ed Sullivan*" moment.)

2. Bob Dylan at the Newport Folk Festival—
July 25, 1965

I've already extolled the virtues of Dylan's "Royal Albert Hall" bootleg from his first electric tour. But here's the official "Dylan goes electric" story in case you haven't already heard it a million times: Dylan decided to perform with a backing band at the world's most famous folk-music festival, where Dylan had performed annually since 1963 to great acclaim. But when Dylan rocked, people got mad and booed.

By the time of his mythical '66 tour a year later, Dylan seemed to get off on the jeers. But when the audience reacted that way for the first time, it naturally freaked him out. He quickly exited the stage in a daze after playing only three songs. That made the audience even more pissed off. Finally, Dylan was coaxed back, and strummed two songs, "Mr. Tambourine Man" and "It's All Over Now, Baby Blue," on a borrowed guitar. After that, he didn't return to Newport for another thirty-seven years.

This moment is credited with changing the course of rock history. Countless documentaries have rehashed the same narrative about how Dylan merged the thoughtfulness of folk with the sound of rock 'n' roll, forever changing both forms of music in the process. Which is true, *I guess*. But the real reason that Dylan at Newport matters in the context of our discussion of epochal concerts is because it established "don't give the people what they want" as an artistic virtue in rock music. Before Dylan, there was a natural inclination for rock performers to please the audience. That's what the Beatles did—they even played show tunes, for crying out loud, because show tunes were popular in the early sixties. But after Dylan, it suddenly became cool to do the opposite of what your audience might want at a live gig, because the opposite of what they want is what they might actually *need*.

When I was raving about the "Royal Albert Hall" bootleg, I credited Bob Dylan with playing punk rock one decade before the official advent of the punk era. I know this sort of thing can be annoying, like when Michelle Pfeiffer tells a class of inner-city students that Bob Dylan is actually a rapper in *Dangerous Minds*. But the connection between punk and Dylan's '66 tour is pretty clear-cut. Dylan played bracingly loud music for an audience that was probably going to hate it. And how did they respond? By booing. If they had also spat on him, Dylan would practically be a Johnny Rotten doppelganger.

3. Jimi Hendrix at the Monterey Pop Festival—June 18, 1967

Hendrix at Monterey is considered the greatest star-making performance ever. At the time Hendrix was living in England, where he became the toast of London's rock-star elite after muddling in obscurity for years as a journeyman guitarist in the United States. Before Monterey, Hendrix's early singles were only available stateside as imports and were known only by hip tastemakers. When he arrived backstage at Monterey, Hendrix was surprised to find that people were ingesting "Purple Haze" acid, named after his first single.

But after Monterey, Hendrix became one of the top rock stars of all time. Unlike the Beatles during their first TV appearance, Hendrix at Monterey still sounds like a motherfucking monster. The endless debate about whether Led Zeppelin or Black Sabbath invented heavy metal instantly becomes irrelevant the moment you hear the quicksilver opening riff to "Killing Floor," a maniacal transformation of the Howlin' Wolf classic into the big bang of guitar shredding. Not only was Hendrix galaxies beyond every other guitarist, he was also a pioneer of guitar technology. Utilizing a battalion of wah-wah pedals and fuzz boxes, Hendrix also wielded an Octavia, which could alter notes by an entire octave, an effect used famously on "Purple Haze." Onstage at Monterey, Hendrix created undulating waves of sound that seemed to melt into one another, a perfect soundtrack for a sea of undulating, melting minds.

Hendrix was also amazing *to look at*. He played guitar with his teeth, behind his back, with his crotch, with his amp, and finally with a can of lighter fluid and a match. For the mythically minded, Hendrix's performance was a pornographic adaptation of the Christ story—mysterious birth, blessed life, violent death, and glorious resurrection. His musical influence on subsequent hard-rock and metal acts is incalculable, but his showmanship truly set him apart as a rock god. Any time a band blows shit up onstage, it's a callback to Hendrix offering his guitar as a fiery sacrifice to the dark lords of rock.

Incredibly, lots of people tried to argue that Hendrix actually sucked at Monterey. "A psychedelic Uncle Tom," sniffed Robert Christgau in *Esquire*. "Not the great artist we were told," insisted Jann Wenner in *Rolling Stone*. Pete Townshend—who had argued with Hendrix backstage about the Who doing its own destructo-shtick right before he went on—hypocritically dismissed Hendrix's "gimmicks" as "crass."

Hendrix internalized this criticism and came to view theatrics as the opposite of art. He took to shredding while standing in one place onstage, a butterfly suddenly nailed to the wall. Fortunately, subsequent generations of arena rockers went on to blow shit up unabated.

4. Woodstock—August 15–18, 1969

As a member of Generation X, I was trained by my peers to hate Woodstock; there was no greater symbol of baby boomer hegemony. Whenever my generation tried to have our own era-defining music event—Live Aid! Farm Aid! Woodstock '94!—it would inevitably be compared in a negative light to the original three days of peace and love at ol' Yasgur's Farm in upstate New York. "We had Hendrix, Sly, and CSNY! What do you losers have? A piss-poor Zeppelin reunion? John Cougar Mellencamp? Freakin' Green Day?"

I resented this. Worse, it made me feel jealous, just as it surely made other people my age jealous. Woodstock wasn't the first major rock festival—we just never talked about Newport and Monterey. But Woodstock stands as the defining example of an idealized communal experience at a massive rock show. It matters because it was the first big concert where the audience mattered more than the artists, an impression due in large part to the interminable eponymous documentary released the following year.

For nearly four hours, Michael Wadleigh's *Woodstock* dwells on every burnout, bong, and buttock packed into the muddy concert grounds, presenting the festival audience as an insta-nation-state with its own laws, creeds, and social mores. While the music is exhaustively documented, the film's cameras are actually pointed more at the audience—the fans are invited to talk at length about their lives and share their thoughts on the era's youth culture, and are ultimately glamorized as romantic dreamers. *Woodstock* is a celebration of hippies doing hippie things set against a groovy soundtrack. When the film became a counterculture hit, it showed that boomers were as interested in watching themselves as watching musicians.

The celebration of self at Woodstock has echoed through every other subsequent mass musical gathering, no matter the genre. It's possible that the Grateful Dead would've had a much shorter career if people hadn't felt the need to re-create a mini version of Woodstock at each of the band's shows. The Dead played Woodstock, though you can't see them in the movie. But more than any other sixties band, the Dead came to personify the Woodstock ethos: show up, do what you want, *take* what you want, don't worry about the consequences.

And so it goes for the myriad music festivals that take place every summer—the Coachellas, the Bonnaroos, the Lollapaloozas, and their many, many knockoffs. The biggest complaint about music festivals—by "biggest," I mean "most often voiced by segments of the music media"—is that the headliners are interchangeable. There's typically a reunion by a band from the seventies or eighties, one or two famous and still vital-ish groups from the nineties and early aughts, a gaggle of midlevel indie bands that get covered by the right midlevel indie websites, and a shit-ton of DJs. But the music at these festivals is beside the point, which is why they sell out before the lineups are even announced. What people want is an excuse to get wasted in a field with their friends, just like the denizens of Woodstock back in '69. The audience is always the top-billed star at any music festival.

5. Altamont—December 6, 1969

Altamont is *The Empire Strikes Back* to Woodstock's *Star Wars*— and we all know that *Empire* is better, right?

I know it's unseemly to frame Altamont—the designated "death of an era" moment for the sixties—as anything other than a tragedy. Because four people died, including Meredith Hunter, an eighteen-year-old man who was stabbed to death by the Hells Angels. (Though four people also died at Woodstock.) Because sociopathic bikers were hired to work security. (Though those hippies messed with the Angels' hogs.) Because the Stones abdicated responsibility when the concert went sideways. (Though the Stones played *incredibly* that night, perhaps because Hells Angels kingpin Sonny Barger—allegedly—kept a pistol trained on Keith Richards during the entirety of the gig.)

At the very least, Altamont is an excellent satire of Woodstock. What was bucolic at Woodstock—the flower children, the free acid, the piles of dung, promoter Michael Lang's impish perpetual smirk—seemed grossly irresponsible and menacing at Altamont. It underscores the sheer luckiness of Woodstock; repeat a lawless, drug-fueled scenario ten times, and you're going to get a lot more Altamonts than Woodstocks.

Altamont's legacy is defined by *Gimme Shelter*, the Maysles brothers' concert documentary from 1970. The film famously ends with Hunter's murder, which occurred as the Stones played "Under My Thumb." *Gimme Shelter* is the most terrifying rock documentary ever made, a reminder that a rock show can devolve into chaos and actual life-or-death peril. This is also what makes *Gimme Shelter* one of the most *seductive* rock movies. If you believe that the rock show experience should include an element of danger—because the fear of being around older, tougher, and potentially lethal grown-ups is what animated your initial excitement to venture into shadowy, smoky places to hear live music—Altamont signifies the logical endpoint of that danger.

In his 2010 memoir, *Life,* Keith Richards tries to downplay Altamont's archetypical "evil to end all evil" reputation. "In actual fact, if it hadn't been for the murder, we'd have thought it a very smooth gig by the skin of its fucking teeth," Richards writes, adding that escaping Altamont via helicopter "was no hairier than getting out of the Empress Ballroom in Blackpool." He seems to regard Altamont as exceptional only because the Stones played "Brown Sugar" for the first time to a live audience that night, an incredible statement that seemingly confirms Keef's warped sense of reality after a half century inside the Stones' bubble.

But maybe Keith Richards is *also* right—the Stones cultivated an air of loosely supervised, "anything goes" anarchy at their shows throughout the sixties, and that has been the de facto rock-show vibe ever since. The best you can hope for at any gig is Altamont-like spontaneity where nobody happens to get killed.

In 1994 I finally made it to my first big rock show: the Rolling Stones at Madison's Camp Randall Stadium, during the Voodoo Lounge tour. I was two weeks from turning seventeen—still mostly ignorant of all the fabulous/frightening vices of adulthood, I was hoping this concert would commence my formal education.

I entered the stadium with a head full of Altamont trivia. I knew that singer Marty Balin of Jefferson Airplane was punched out by the Hells Angels during the Airplane's set. I knew the stage that day was only two feet high, which enabled pretty much anyone who wanted to walk onstage to walk onstage, assuming they could plow past a phalanx of bloodthirsty bikers. (In

Gimme Shelter, you can see somebody's German shepherd pace back and forth in front of Jagger as he does his "Brothers and sisters, please cool out!" act to an increasingly unruly crowd.) I had heard the stories about yellow acid laced with strychnine that was handed out at Altamont by CIA agents tasked with discrediting the hippie movement, a conspiracy theory straight out of Thomas Pynchon.

"Mick Jagger had long pretended to be the devil. Then one night he threw a party and the real devil showed up. The Stones have never recovered," Rich Cohen writes in his 2016 book, *The Sun and the Moon and the Rolling Stones,* summing up the accepted Altamont narrative. Like me, Cohen came to the Stones later on, when they lost all sense of danger and settled into a decades-long groove as a nostalgic hit machine. "When I watched them, I knew it was a fantasy," he writes—"it" being whatever the Stones once signified as a harbinger of orgy-fueled apocalypse. I guess I knew it, too, going into that Voodoo Lounge show.

I had assumed that the Stones would probably be finished after this tour—after all, Mick Jagger had recently turned fifty, and it was inconceivable in the midnineties that a rock star could continue much longer after that. I actually thought *Voodoo Lounge* was pretty decent when it came out, especially the Keith songs. (The deeply haggard "Thru and Thru" was later used to great effect on *The Sopranos.*) But my expectations were low—the nineties were hardly a golden age for new Stones tunes, and the band was more or less spent creatively. (The best Stones song of that decade is Sheryl Crow's "If It Makes You Happy.") I went in expecting to see a band play out the string. But when the Stones came out—I could barely see them, as I was sitting in literally the last row of a college football stadium—something unexpected occurred as they kicked into the Bo Diddley stomp of "Not Fade Away." Time stopped. The space around me turned in on itself. My brain blacked out and suddenly I was back to the late sixties. Incredibly, the Stones didn't resemble middle-aged gazillionaires; they were the Stones of my imagination, the outlaws who played like motherfuckers as murderous bikers turned Northern California into a medieval battleground.

At the concert's midpoint, Jagger queued up "All Down the Line," one of the tastiest deep cuts from *Exile on Main St.* On the record, "All Down the Line" is the rare track to jump out of the murk rather than revel in the sleaze. If you've ever had to rouse yourself awake at three A.M.—for an early flight, for a crying baby, for another beer at an all-night rager that you'll surely regret in four hours—that's what "All Down the Line" feels like. So much of *Exile* exudes exhaustion, with its drugged-out tempos, blurry guitars, and Jagger's slurred vocals. But "All Down the Line" captures the brief high of that unexpected third wind that comes a few hours before you finally slip into a coma. On *Exile,* the Stones attack "All Down the Line" as a matter of survival. Without that third wind, the Stones wouldn't have been capable of standing upright.

Live, "All Down the Line" sounded both slicker and slower than the *Exile* version. Charlie was spot-on as always, but Keef and Ron Wood didn't have the tension that distinguished Richards's interplay with Mick Taylor during the Stones' glory years. As players, Richards and Wood bantered like drinking buddies, turning "All Down the Line" into a more conventional party song rather than the desperate push to maximize your inner reserves from *Exile.* The Stones in their prime were strong enough to allow themselves to appear weak. The 1994 version of the Stones wasn't willing to risk that level of exposure.

But if "All Down the Line" no longer affected the Stones the same way, it hit me with the seriousness of an Old Testament sermon. When Jagger wailed, "I need a sanctified mind to help me out right now," I felt classic-rock mythology open up and make a space for me. I no longer was an observer of ancient history. I was there, bearing witness, *with the motherfucking Rolling Stones,* in real time.

Did the Stones sound good? I guess so? My hero worship was so blinding that I honestly can't say for sure. The Stones transported me to a place beyond my classic-rock fantasies. A quarter mile separated me from the band, but I was still technically sharing space with the Glimmer Twins—and even from my distant orbit, the feeling was intoxicating.

Every subsequent rock show I've attended—hundreds upon hundreds of shows over the course of almost twenty-five years—has been about chasing that feeling.

"My Love Will Not Let You Down"

NOTES ON TRACK 7: We opened for the Boss back in '85. Nice guy. Bruce always empties the tank. He let us gas up his '69 Chevy.

The greatest live performer has always been Bruce Springsteen. I realize that I am not the first forty-year-old white guy to make this argument. Nevertheless, I believe it to be true.

Every Springsteen show is a capital-E Event like Woodstock, and nearly as long. A Springsteen gig promises to be transformative like the Beatles on Ed Sullivan, confrontational like Dylan at Newport, and theatrical like Jimi at Monterey. It's less dangerous than Altamont, because bikers at his shows like to get drunk and dance to "Hungry Heart." But a Springsteen show has the same level of excitement. Even Bruce's sidemen sound like Marvel superheroes—the Mighty Max, Professor Roy Bittan, Miami Steve, the Big Man. (Garry W. Tallent doesn't have a cool nickname—his superpower is *talent*.)

Jon Stewart summed up the mythos of the Springsteen rock

show at the 2009 Kennedy Center Honors. A tanned and impossibly fit Bruce was in the house that night sitting next to President Obama. When you're a politician in America, it's always a good idea to keep your friends close, but Bruce Springsteen closer. Stewart hit the usual Boss beats in his speech—he talked about Jersey, and the Jersey Turnpike, and how when Springsteen's music fills even the shittiest car, it feels like you're rumbling down the highway in a '69 Chevy with a 396, fuelie heads, and a Hurst on the floor.

The crux of the speech addressed Springsteen's live prowess: "Whenever I see Bruce Springsteen, he empties the tank," Stewart declared. Emptying the tank—or, in the parlance of our subject, "proving it all night"—is the nut graph of the Springsteen legend. When Springsteen released a live quadruple record at the height of his popularity in the mideighties, he mostly avoided accusations of self-indulgence because for Springsteen fans four discs of live music is a *minimum* requirement. For true believers, a three- (or even four-) hour Springsteen show can never overstay its welcome. If you feel like leaving after the first encore, well, you just aren't listening close enough to the *narrative* of the set list, in which the youthful optimism of "Backstreets" leads to the disillusionment of "Racing in the Street" and finally the spiritual meltdown of "Johnny 99." Look, let me pull out this bootleg from the *Born in the U.S.A.* tour in '84 and allow me to explain—hey, where are you going?

Nobody has ever wanted to be great more than Bruce Springsteen—his drive to be immortal was fueled by boundless, neurotic intensity. A sane man does not sweat his ass off for more than 180 minutes in front of 50,000 people every night when he already has millions in the bank. This is the act of an individual with an unquenchable desire to prove himself, over and over again, even when he's already beloved as a national treasure. How this ambition affects your perception of Springsteen is the most important factor for determining whether you're a fan. It either gives his work a heightened sense of urgency (what I would refer to as "stakes") or weighs his songs down with overwrought, self-important baggage (what someone else might refer to as "pretension").

Those inclined to view Springsteen as a corny windbag will argue that no other rock legend is as self-conscious about tending to his public persona. Springsteen, after all, hired a rock critic, Jon Landau, to be his manager and record producer. Those who don't like the Boss have long theorized that Springsteen's seemingly inexhaustible appeal among rock critics stems from this pact with one of their own—it's like a beauty pageant contestant marrying a guy who looks exactly like the people judging the contest. For a Springsteen-loving rock critic, fantasies about being the person who acts as the man's most trusted confidante don't seem so unrealistic.

This argument is persuasive only if you've never seen Springsteen live. But once you've witnessed a Springsteen concert, all you want to do is see as many Springsteen concerts as possible. Sometimes, it doesn't even have to be an actual concert. In 2012, I waited ninety minutes inside of a cavernous convention hall to hear Springsteen give the keynote address at South by Southwest in Austin. Bruce would not be able to "prove it all night" on this day—Springsteen was speaking at noon, so at best he could "prove it through the lunch hour." But it was still an opportunity to bask in the man's presence, which is all that mattered to me.

The speech (of course) concerned the value of having a good live show. Play every gig like it's your last. Leave it all on the stage. Empty the tank. "Your handshake is your ticket," declared Springsteen, the grizzled rock 'n' roll Horatio Alger.

The core components of the Springsteen rock show are energy, grit, and the sort of grandiosity that only a performer professing the selfless humility of the "workingman" can get away with. Decades into his stadium-rock period, Springsteen still presents himself as the consummate bar-band professional. "I was signed as an acoustic singer-songwriter, but I was a wolf in sheep's clothing," Springsteen said at South by Southwest. "I had nights and nights of bar playing behind me, to bring my songs home."

But Springsteen is also a perfectionist—he's not one to simply plug in and blast away recklessly. His obsessiveness in the studio is well documented—watch any of the documentaries on the making of *Born to Run, Darkness on the Edge of Town,* or *The River,* and you'll find an ongoing narrative about a restless man writing five songs for every one deemed worthy of inclusion on a record; an obsessive-compulsive who orders his drummer to hit his drum for weeks in the studio in search of that magic Phil Spector Wall of Sound *boom*; a goddamn lunatic who wants garage-rock messiness and soul-band professionalism simultaneously.

But Springsteen was also insane about having the right live sound. This psychosis intensified during the *Darkness* tour in 1978, when the E Street Band took his most furious collection of songs ever and blew them up in basketball arenas and hockey sheds far beyond Springsteen's traditional stronghold in the Northeast.

It was one thing for Springsteen to demand that every show be a three-hour battle royale for the souls of spiritually tortured young men and women wandering in the metaphorical dark of Candy's hall. But he also required that his band play for hours *before* the show. It was then that any mistakes from the previous night were addressed, and new songs were brought up and quickly learned. Even Springsteen's song introductions were practiced and perfected, so that his onstage storytelling would seem spontaneous and yet improbably well crafted. And then (according to Peter Ames Carlin's 2012 biography, *Bruce*) he would prowl every row and aisle of the arena, "microphone in hand, listening for gaps in the amplification, drum tone, or worst of all, echo," in an impossible effort to fine-tune the sound in buildings built for athletic competitions.

After the gig . . . well, there was no such thing as "after the gig" for Bruce Springsteen in the seventies. Everywhere else in the rock world, rock stars still dated fourteen-year-olds and dabbled in black magic and engulfed themselves in blizzards of cocaine. Springsteen meanwhile was a monk by comparison—even on the road with his band, he was a man alone with his pen, paper, and outsized drive to be the greatest rocker of his generation. He sequestered himself on the "quiet" bus, working out his latest songs and imagining the next night's gig, while his saxophone player, "the Big Man," Clarence Clemons, oversaw the postshow carousing on the tour's other, resolutely not-quiet bus.

What happened behind Bruce's back stayed behind Bruce's back. But if he caught the E Street Band acting out, his disapproval could be swift and severe. Carlin relates a story from the *Darkness* tour involving two unidentified members of the E Street Band, one of whom was caught by Springsteen holding a coke spoon to the other guy's nose in the dressing room before showtime. Bruce exploded: "If. I. Ever. Fucking. See. This. Again. I don't care who it is. They're *gone*. On the *spot*. I'll fire them," Springsteen seethed.

Later, Bruce was pressed about the incident by the band's road manager. Surely he wouldn't fire a member of the E Street Band, already becoming an important piece of the Springsteen legend.

"Absolutely," Springsteen shot back. "I could replace any of those guys in twenty-four hours."

Springsteen's aversion to drugs and alcohol, along with the other self-destructive trappings of rock stardom, kept him insanely well preserved as he entered middle age. That all-consuming fastidiousness back in the seventies has functioned as a fountain of youth in the twenty-first century. When you see Bruce now, you don't have to squint so hard to see the guy who was on all those old album covers. If anybody is going to live forever, it's Bruce Springsteen. I refuse to believe otherwise.

Every hero's journey needs a period of intense adversity. Odysseus ventured into Hades. Luke Skywalker lost his hand. The Beatles played for drunken Germans in Hamburg. For Bruce Springsteen, the sojourn in hell occurred in the nineties.

Springsteen has described the mammoth success of *Born in the U.S.A.* in the mideighties as "destabilizing," but the aftershocks didn't really register until the next decade. Bruce had scaled down from *U.S.A.* with 1987's *Tunnel of Love,* a synth-y tone poem of romantic desolation conceived in the midst of his crumbling marriage to actress Julianne Phillips. Bruce then scaled down even more by breaking up the E Street Band and recording two albums, 1992's *Human Touch* and *Lucky Town,* with top studio players.

When Springsteen released *The Ghost of Tom Joad* in 1995, delivering cinematic character studies about migrant workers and petty criminals in a raspy stage whisper, he was still trying to figure out how to be just another guy, as opposed to the national mascot that he had become after *Born in the U.S.A.* But as Springsteen humanized his persona, he also diminished the cultural stature of his art. Think *Superman II,* when Superman temporarily gives up his superpowers and learns what it's like for a mortal to get his ass kicked. Getting your ass kicked is not fun.

Tom Joad put Springsteen at a crossroads—he could revive himself as the all-American He-Man of the arena-rock circuit, or carry on as just another fortysomething white male singer-songwriter. Going the latter route wasn't completely fruitless—Springsteen won an Oscar in 1994 for "Streets of Philadelphia," and the following year he briefly re-formed the E Street Band for a couple of mournful new tracks recorded for a greatest-hits album. But overall, this was by far the worst time to be a Springsteen fan.

I have loved Bruce Springsteen since I was six years old. *Born in the U.S.A.* made Bruce seem as approachable and kid-friendly as Huey Lewis, my other favorite rock star in kindergarten. I couldn't grasp the politics of "Born in the U.S.A." or the bottomless desire of "I'm on Fire." But Bruce's herky-jerky strut in the "Dancing in the Dark" video was just the ticket for white boys from the Midwest who would never learn how to moonwalk. From then on, Bruce would be a fixture in my life.

During the grunge era of the nineties, however, Bruce was an anachronism. The rise of Nirvana didn't just make hair metal unfashionable—it also signaled the decline of heartland rock. Kurt

Cobain sought to dismantle the very mythology that Springsteen had guilelessly fortified on *Born to Run*. Instead of pulling out of your town full of losers in order to win, rock stars in the nineties gave up on winning and reveled in loserdom. Soon, the days of stand-alone white male rock stars also being *pop* stars were over, unless you were willing to rebrand as a country singer or license your songs for pickup commercials.

When MTV advertised an *Unplugged* special timed with the release of *Human Touch* and *Lucky Town*, I had to play down my Springsteen love in front of my friends. Springsteen apparently still had some juice with the music network, as they actually let him play with his new, post–E Street backing band made up of anonymous L.A. session players. But the MTV audience, save for stalwarts like me, had abandoned Springsteen. My buddies would heckle Bruce whenever commercials for his *Unplugged* popped up incongruously between Soundgarden and Toad the Wet Sprocket videos. Like Peter denying Christ, I said nothing.

How did the hero come back? Most people time it to the E Street Band reunion tour that commenced in 1999. If the nineties proved anything to Springsteen, it's that the members of the E Street Band are not as replaceable as he once thought they were. The support they provided—musically, morally, symbolically—was crucial to sustaining the mythology of Springsteen's music. Moving back to New Jersey after a stint in Los Angeles was another step in the right direction. In L.A., Springsteen had taken to wearing leather vests with no shirt underneath; this Bon Jovi cosplay spoke to his overall artistic confusion. But in New Jersey, he was in his natural habitat—it was back to jeans and plaid shirts and leather jackets, just like on the cover of *Darkness on the Edge of Town*.

I buy into the theory (originally forwarded by my former boss Bill Simmons, of the Ringer fame) that Springsteen was actually reborn a few years earlier, at the 1997 MTV Video Music Awards, when he performed "One Headlight" with one of the world's most popular rock bands of that time, the Wallflowers. When you watch the video of the performance, you can see Bruce

Springsteen learning how to be Bruce Springsteen again. At the beginning of the clip—as unlikely as it might seem now—it's clear that the Wallflowers are doing Springsteen a favor. Bruce seems tentative as he strums his Fender Esquire; he hasn't really *rocked* in a while. Plus, he has a goatee, which is weird, like we're actually seeing his less impressive and somewhat tepid twin brother, Barry Springsteen. On the chorus, Springsteen joins Jakob Dylan on backing vocals. You expect that distinctive Springsteen bark to drown the other guy out, but Dylan is out-singing Springsteen. Again, it seems inconceivable. But look it up on YouTube. I swear it's true.

On the second verse, a sense of relief is apparent on Springsteen's face. He's made it this far and everything sounds pretty good. Dylan cedes the microphone and generously invites Bruce to take over, and suddenly it's apparent that "One Headlight" is secretly the best Springsteen song of the nineties. Looking back, Jakob Dylan's most crucial contribution to rock 'n' roll was providing a placeholder for Bruce Springsteen in the culture when the man himself wasn't at his strongest. "One Headlight" was a massive radio hit in the late nineties; it proved that there was still an audience out there for wild and innocent story songs about girls named Cinderella. For twenty years, Springsteen had owned songs like that, but he had ceded his kingdom in order to make muted records about AIDS victims and Mexican migrant workers. Fortunately, Dylan kept the brawny midtempo rock anthem alive just long enough for Springsteen to catch a second wind in his career.

Then Bruce plays a smoking guitar solo, like he's still trying to prove that he's the fastest gun in Asbury Park. It's now official: "One Headlight" has officially been taken over.

Bruce wrangles the third verse away from Dylan—he's no longer a guest on this song, he has declared squatter's rights and taken possession. Now Bruce is all you can hear and look at and care about. On the outro, Bruce tries to trade solos with the Wallflowers' guitarist but the poor guy's hands can't move. (I'm serious, watch the video, the man is stunned in the presence of the Boss.) So, Springsteen just tears out a few more dirty licks until the song ends.

Then the sounds of glorious victory: A hail of "Bruuuuce!" chants reigning down from the audience, a Greek chorus welcoming our hero back to greatness.

It's been argued that the biggest beneficiary of Springsteen's wilderness period in the nineties was Garth Brooks. Music critics had to come up with something to account for how a mediocre potato-faced white man with a weakness for black hats, tight Wranglers, and multicolored shirts became the decade's bestselling artist, eventually shipping more than 160 million units worldwide. Being a music critic in the nineties was like being a scientist from Loch Ness who specializes in large aquatic monsters. You had one job, and that was to explain the unexplainable dominance of Garth.

So why not pin it on Bruce's low profile? Country music essentially annexed heartland rock in the nineties, after pop music kicked it to the curb as grunge and gangsta rap took over youth culture. Garth was granted custody of the earnest singer-songwriter wing of heartland rock, and Shania Twain put a pop spin on the Def Leppard–AC/DC jock jams wing with the assistance of her husband, the producer Robert John "Mutt" Lange, the enigmatic sentient mullet who manned the boards for *Back in Black* and *Pyromania*.

It's a good theory, except heartland rock didn't completely disappear in the nineties. While Bruce suffered through a rare uncool period, there was one roots rocker who benefited directly from Springsteen's decline at the start of the decade, and then seemingly suffered once Springsteen surged back at the end of the decade.

I refer to none other than Tom Petty.

There was no malevolence or, ahem, *pettiness* on Tom's part.

He was simply following the heartland-rock line of succession. In the hierarchy of eighties heartland rock, Bruce Springsteen was president, Tom Petty was vice president, John Mellencamp was speaker of the house, Bob Seger was president pro tempore, and Bryan Adams was (I guess?) secretary of leather jackets. If Bruce ever faltered, Tom was constitutionally required to step up.

In the eighties, the established power structure was ideal for Bruce and Tom. Bruce definitely wanted to be at the top of the heap, and Tom was happy being the guy below the top guy. (Mellencamp meanwhile stewed that the "Cougar" era undermined his long-term credibility and cost him the election.) I say this with love, as someone who owns every Tom Petty record, even the duds, like *Let Me Up (I've Had Enough)*: Tom did not burn with the same desire to be great that Bruce does. He just didn't have that uptight East Coast thing, where he was driven to torment himself over every aspect of his career. Tom was a laid-back Floridian— built for comfort, not for speed. And I adore that about him! I couldn't handle it if my relationship with Tom was as intense as my relationship with Bruce. Tom Petty was casual and easy. And loving him was always casual and easy.

Tom Petty could always be counted on to be just good enough. Recording three or four perfect singles and then padding the rest of the album with jangly, expertly performed filler is just good enough. Rhyming "some place to go" with "Joe Piscopo" is just good enough. Tom did not have to prove it all night. He was fine knocking off at around eleven P.M.

I'm sure Tom would've been happy being the scrappy Avis to Bruce's world-conquering Hertz forever. But then the nineties happened, and everything that once favored Bruce in the eighties shifted and now favored Tom. Turns out there were three things that Tom did better than Bruce, and they all mattered a lot in the new decade. One, Tom was better at making solo records. His two best LPs of this period, *Full Moon Fever* and *Wildflowers,* were credited to Tom Petty, rather than Tom Petty and the Heartbreakers, and they made him a much bigger star than he had been as a mere bandleader. Now, what's weird is that most of the Heartbreakers play on those records, including the two most crucial members of that band, guitarist Mike Campbell and keyboardist Benmont Tench. Bruce went through the ritual of ditching the E Street Band, whereas Tom merely got rid of giving his band equal billing. Score one for the wily Southerner over the arrogant Yankee.

Two, Tom was surprisingly good at making music videos. He was even awarded MTV's Michael Jackson Video Vanguard Award, which is the one thing that Tom Petty, Britney Spears, and Rihanna have in common. Tom Petty has more memorable music videos than you probably assume that he does—there was that *Mad Max*–style clip for "You Got Lucky," the *Alice in Wonderland* homage for "Don't Come Around Here No More," the "Take on Me" rip-off that is "Runnin' Down a Dream," and the video for "Into the Great Wide Open," in which Johnny Depp gets into a catfight with Faye Dunaway. Springsteen made a big deal out of hiring superstar directors like John Sayles and Jonathan Demme, but he never did anything interesting with them. The concept for Bruce Springsteen videos was always "make Bruce look like an unglamorous mook." The worst was when he hired Brian De Palma to make the "Dancing in the Dark" video, and he didn't allow the master of bombastic suspense cinema to film him burying a chain saw into Nils Lofgren's skull.

Third, and most important of all, Tom was better than Bruce at not trying too hard. Trying too hard was good in the seventies and eighties and also good in the aughts and the 2010s, but not so good in the nineties. It was the only decade in which Bruce's extreme work ethic made him seem suspect. And it was very easy to make fun of Springsteen during the alternative era. His persona— the raspy voice, the chiseled body, the marathon concerts, the big anthems about America—made him a target for caricature by a generation of ironists. But how could you make fun of Tom Petty? What was there to exaggerate? You can't really talk slower or act more stoned than Tom Petty. That sideways grin of his deflected any jokes—Petty seemed preemptively amused that you might care enough to criticize him, a classic nineties move that Petty perfected in 1979. At a time when Bruce seemed woefully out of place on MTV, Petty fit in perfectly as an aloof forty-year-old grunge superstar.

By 1997—the same year Bruce rediscovered his mojo with the Wallflowers at the VMAs—Petty had retreated to a chicken shack in Northern California, where he shot smack and licked his wounds after a series of personal tragedies, including the end of his twenty-year marriage. Fortunately, Tom pulled himself out of the blackness of heroin addiction and rebounded in the twenty-first century with one pretty good album (*Highway Companion*), several okay albums (*The Last DJ, Mojo, Hypnotic Eye*), and lots of excellent tours with the Heartbreakers. (He wrapped a triumphant tour honoring the fortieth anniversary of the start of his recording career just one week before he died in 2017.) After a glorious run in the nineties, Petty was back to being the No. 2 guy on the heartland rock chart, right where he was always meant to be.

As Springsteen entered the twenty-first century, he fortified himself against old age by bulking up his arms and chest and slimming down his waist and legs. In his twenties, Springsteen was skinny, even scrawny. In his thirties, he started working out, getting jacked like an eighties action star during the two-year stadium tour for *Born in the U.S.A.* By the time he was in his sixties, Bruce had Popeye's physique, with big arms, a barrel chest, and wiry legs wrapped in miraculously tight jeans.

Springsteen worked himself out creatively, too—starting with *The Rising* in 2002, he got back to putting out new records every two or three years. And they were *good* records. My favorite is 2007's *Magic*, which stands as Springsteen's best attempt at finding a middle ground between his classic sound and something a little more modern. By this time, Springsteen was awash in coolness points after years of indie bands name-checking him in interviews. Many of the era's most significant rock bands were influenced by late-seventies Springsteen (the Hold Steady), early-eighties Springsteen (the National), and mideighties Springsteen (the Killers). With *Magic*, Springsteen set out to compete with those bands directly. The foundation of *Magic* is built on the interplay of Springsteen's guitar, Max Weinberg's steadfast drums, and Clarence Clemons's nostalgic sax wails. But there are also unexpected nods to the Magnetic Fields (the sublime "Girls in their Summer Clothes," because Bruce clearly was jamming on *69 Love Songs* during that first E Street reunion tour) and Arcade Fire (the steely "Devil's Arcade," which suggests that Springsteen studied 2007's *Neon Bible* to teach him how to rip off his own classic eighties heartland-rock sound.).

Still, the concert stage is where Springsteen has made his most aggressive stand against time. He tours as much as ever, even as the people at his side have fallen. I remember seeing Bruce on St. Patrick's Day in 2008—Danny Federici was MIA, sick with cancer and not long for this life. (He died the following month.) Clarence Clemons sat off to the side of the stage whenever he wasn't blowing his sax—his knees and hips had been replaced, and he didn't stand except for when Bruce called for "Badlands" or "Jungleland." (Clemons died in 2011.) As for Bruce himself, he was still built like a Cadillac, and he revved his impeccably maintained engine for more than three hours. Relentlessly prowling the stage, then the entire arena, he strutted among his followers with an emperor's swagger. When he ran out of arena floor, he let the audience raise him up and crowd-surf him back to the stage. I lost my breath just watching him, but Springsteen never missed a lyric.

More than his albums, Springsteen's story is told via his live shows. Each tour has a theme: In '75, it was "prove yourself." In '78 it was "great vengeance and furious anger." In '80 it was "coronation." In '84 it was "domination." In '88 it was "dissolution." In '92 it was "confusion." In '95 it was "shut the fuck up, my 'intimate' theater tour requires silence."

In the new century, Springsteen's narrative settled on a singular theme: resilience. He is more overtly political than ever—lyrical metaphors and commercially dubious character studies no longer cut it for Bruce. He has seized upon his position as a figurehead, not just for rock 'n' roll but for a kind of populist humanism that had evaporated from politics. Whenever disaster struck in America, Springsteen appeared to restore dignity: 9/11, the Iraq War, Hurricane Katrina, the housing crisis, Hurricane Sandy. Police brutality and transgender rights also entered his purview.

Meanwhile, in his songs, he beat the drum for perseverance—come on up for the rising, bring on your wrecking ball, we shall overcome. In concert, Springsteen's body became his central metaphor—he battered himself every night with the demands of his marathon concerts, and emerged renewed. The promise of a Springsteen live show is that Bruce will never fold, never break, never not be there for an audience that has watched seemingly every other national monument crumble into smoking ash.

In late 2015, Springsteen announced that he would be touring with the E Street Band behind the *Ties That Bind* boxed set celebrating his 1980 double album, *The River*. Atypically, he would be playing essentially the same set every night—twenty songs from *The River*, plus a dozen or so hits and scattered deep cuts. Talking to *Rolling Stone*, Springsteen claimed to be energized by the challenge of the tour's rigidness, while also admitting that *The River* was an odd choice for the arena-rock treatment.

"It ends on a strange note with 'Wreck on the Highway,' where it's just a guy and his thoughts," he told David Fricke of *Rolling Stone*. "The album starts with the pursuit of connection and community, the desire to find out where you fit in, and ends up with this guy in a bedroom with the person he loves and his thoughts."

At first it seemed like another resilience tour—a tribute to the power of *The River* after all these years. As the tour commenced, resilience would remain the theme, but for different reasons. As Springsteen crisscrossed the country, rock stars kept dying. He would pay tribute to them all. The River Tour was now known as the mourning tour.

First it was David Bowie, who died two days after releasing his final studio album, *Blackstar,* at the beginning of 2016. A spooky meditation on the transition to the afterlife, *Blackstar* also exhibited Bowie's creative restlessness—Bowie's primary musical influence was Kendrick Lamar's jazz-rap masterpiece *To Pimp a Butterfly*—which carried on unabated even as he battled liver cancer in the final months of his life. Bowie's death was genuinely shocking—there had been rumors that he'd been ill for years, due to his seclusion from the public in the years after his final concert tour in 2004. But Bowie never seemed human, much less mortal. How could a space oddity die?

Bowie was an early Springsteen fan, recording a cover of "Growin' Up" for his 1973's covers album, *Pin-Ups,* though the song wasn't officially released until 1990. (Bowie later covered another early Springsteen track, "It's Hard to Be a Saint in the City," recognizing the glam rock in lines like "I could walk like Brando right into the sun / Then dance just like a Casanova.") Springsteen never forgot Bowie's support back when he really needed it. For Bowie, he played "Rebel Rebel" in Pittsburgh, the tour's opening date.

Then it was Prince, whose passing was somehow even more shocking. Unlike Bowie, Prince kept a regular presence in pop culture in the years before he died. In 2014, he did a weird cameo on the Fox sitcom *New Girl* and performed a dazzling mini-set on *Saturday Night Live.* Prince didn't go down like Elvis or Michael Jackson, once-beautiful creatures who deformed themselves before suffering untimely deaths. He still looked *good.*

Prince also seemed like something other than human—he had apparently stopped aging after 1989, and still sang and danced as well as he ever had. And yet, one morning in April, he was found slumped in an elevator at his Minneapolis-area headquarters,

Paisley Park, dead from an overdose of prescription painkillers that he took to soothe a body battered by years of grueling performances.

The peak of Springsteen's stardom coincided with Prince's pinnacle during the summer of 1984, when *Purple Rain* dueled with *Born in the U.S.A.* for chart supremacy. Bruce held the top spot for four weeks in July, and then Prince proceeded to take over for the remaining twenty-two weeks of the year. Back then, Springsteen and Prince were giants benevolently sharing the same planet. Now, only one remained. For Prince, Bruce played "Purple Rain" at both Brooklyn shows.

The one awkward tribute was for Glenn Frey—Bruce and the Eagles had always stood on opposite ends of critical esteem in the seventies, and this naturally bothered the Eagles. When *Rolling Stone* reported that Springsteen sold out two nights at the L.A. Forum on the *Darkness* tour, Eagles manager Irving Azoff called to point out that, no, this was not true, Springsteen had not sold out the Forum, but the Eagles had. Nevertheless, Bruce played "Take It Easy" in Chicago for Frey.

Springsteen was uniquely qualified to soothe bereaved rock fans. He has always leaned into the neediness of his audience for a hero, playing a hybrid of drinking buddy and father figure for the millions of people who have formed a codependent relationship with Bruce Springsteen records. My own Springsteen neediness is borderline unhealthy. He's not merely my favorite rock star—my emotional ties are far messier than that. I'll put it this way: if you made a Venn diagram of Springsteen fans and people who have weirdly poisonous relationships with their fathers, I would be sitting dead center with enough other sad sacks to fill Giants Stadium for a three-night stand. Bruce didn't get along with his dad either, and like Bruce, we've all used Bruce Springsteen songs to work out our feelings about the old man.

Bruce's toughest song about his dad was 1978's "Adam Raised a Cain," which paints a brutal picture of a resentful paternal presence who "walks these empty rooms looking for something to blame." Around the same time he wrote his greatest father song, "Independence Day," where Bruce accepts that his father is never going to be the man he needs. These are not comfortable feelings to express in pop culture. The push to normalize dysfunctional parent-child relationships is overwhelming; most songs, films, and TV shows promise that reconciliation is possible if you try hard enough. That's the message of *The Royal Tenenbaums*, the *Star Wars* movies, and that stupid Mike + the Mechanics song. But in "Independence Day," Bruce accepts that his father won't change, and that the only thing he can do to maintain sanity is walk away. Millions of sons and daughters have been forced to make that difficult decision, but "Independence Day" is the rare work of art to acknowledge it.

After "Independence Day," Springsteen's stance toward the father figures in his songs noticeably softened. On 1982's acoustic masterwork *Nebraska*, Springsteen raged against Reagan's economic policies but empathized with the dad in "Used Cars," a pitiful figure who is humiliated in front of his children by a patronizing car salesman. And while Springsteen preemptively mourned the end of his marriage on *Tunnel of Love*, he did share fond memories of his dad in the wedding-day song, "Walk Like a Man," singing tenderly, "All I can think of is being five years old following behind you at the beach / Tracing your footprints in the sand / Trying to walk like a man."

For those of us who have never had a good father-son talk with our real dads, these are more than songs—they're the closest things we have to patriarchal advice about how to be a grown-up. Bruce Springsteen songs have supplanted many of the experiences I've had with my actual father because the results with Bruce are so much more satisfying.

When the River Tour was announced, I immediately bought tickets for the shows in St. Paul and Milwaukee. A month later, shortly after Bowie died, I bought a ticket for the Chicago date.

I was suddenly feeling extra-protective of my favorite classic rockers.

Now, you could point out that paying hundreds of dollars to see multiple shows on a tour where Springsteen planned to play the same songs every night made little sense. Not only was the set list fixed, but so were the between-song patter and Springsteen's seemingly spontaneous stage moves. But, again, this argument only makes sense to the unconverted. I'm a man who *needs* to see Springsteen shows.

The River Tour would always start with the throwback Spector-esque pop of "Meet Me in the City," an outtake from the boxed set and the only "new" song in the entire show. Springsteen would wave to the crowd, motion to the band, maybe chuckle a little into the microphone, and then count off—*ah-one, ah-two, ah-one, two, three, four!*

Before the final verse, Bruce would tell whichever city he was in that he was happy to be there. "What I want to know is, are you ready to be *transformed*?" he would say. "Are you ready to be *transformed*? Are you ready to be *transformed*?" This was a hypothetical question, of course. We were at a Springsteen show. Transformation was the whole point.

After that, the show settled into a push-pull rhythm between bar-band rockers and gut-wrenching ballads. "Sherry Darling" and "Hungry Heart" were naturals for crowd participation. "Two Hearts" was a showcase for the ritualistic mic sharing between Bruce and Miami Steve that symbolizes friendship and efficient use of amplification technology. The bleakest moments somehow segued seamlessly into breezily dumb rock songs—Bruce contemplated an endless abyss on "The River" and "Point Blank" and chose instead to head out to "Cadillac Ranch." But all the while the show would shrink, from a feeling of community to the guy lost in his own head in "Wreck on the Highway."

The repetition of those *River* shows didn't lessen the experience of seeing Springsteen for me. Rather, it made me see my life through the lens of Springsteen's music. During those two months, I felt like I was living inside *The River*—or maybe I was reminded that I had been living there all along.

For the concert in Chicago, I drove six hours by myself, a classic Springsteen-ian adventure on the open road. In my mind, I imagined peeling out in the lonely cool before dawn, out of my town full of losers and toward certain victory. I would sit tight, take hold, and stop for gas and pork rinds before tearing off down Thunder Road.

Once I got into town, I hooked up with my friend Keith and drank about forty-five beers before the show. We talked about our families and our jobs—neither of us worked in factories but our cushy media jobs nonetheless felt like working at a *content* factory. And then Bruce came out with the band, and my heart leapt into my throat. There he was, *still alive!* Judging by the concert recordings from this tour that I downloaded later, Chicago was easily the worst show I saw, in terms of things like polish and not fucking up the intro to "No Surrender." But in terms of fun and rock 'n' roll–ness, it was easily the most enjoyable night of my mini-*River* run. (This was my "Two Hearts" show.)

In St. Paul, I went to see Bruce with my wife, and since the show was only twenty minutes from our front door, the journey wasn't epic, it was domestic. Out of solidarity with my wife, who we were 90 percent sure was pregnant, I watched Bruce sober. I also agreed to leave right as the band kicked into "Tenth Avenue Freeze-Out" in the encore, because she was experiencing early-stage morning sickness. Or maybe she was just tired because Bruce had already played almost three and a half hours. But we were crossing our fingers for morning sickness! (This was my "I Wanna Marry You" show.)

For the Milwaukee show, I was back on the road for another long road trip. But it was less carefree than the Chicago trip—my wife really was pregnant. And she was really feeling sick during her first trimester, and it had gotten worse in the days since the St. Paul gig. I felt guilty about leaving her alone with our son, who was in the midst of a grumpy spell, so I could go off and get drunk at another Springsteen show six hours away. I decided to cope with my guilt by getting *very* drunk at the Springsteen show, which sort of worked until I texted my wife during "Jungleland," and my wife responded by sending me a video of our son throwing a tantrum after waking up in the middle of the night.

As Jake Clemons revived the spirit of his late uncle with a passionate performance of the classic "Jungleland" sax solo, I did not feel uplifted, I felt the distance between the fantasy of a Springsteen show and the reality of my familial responsibilities. Ironically, I needed a Springsteen show to point this out to me. (This was my "Stolen Car" show.)

When Springsteen was a young man, the dried-out riverbed from *The River*'s title track functioned as a metaphor for adult disappointment. Dryness equals impotence, lack of motion, a failure to get to that place where you really wanna go and can walk in the sun. In 1980, Springsteen wasn't far off from the freewheeling drifter at the center of *The River*'s best-known track, "Hungry Heart." The guy in that song likens himself to "a river that don't know where it's flowing"—there's freedom in that life, but constant displacement was also starting to lose its appeal for Springsteen.

As a much older man in 2016, Springsteen revisited *The River* after having had a few wives and three children. The family life that he'd previously only imagined had become real, but it was now largely in his rearview. If Bruce still equated himself to a river, he had traveled far enough to see the ocean that eventually swallows all tributaries.

I liked *The River* in my teens and twenties, but it wasn't until my thirties that I realized that I had been too young to truly understand it before. Before I had a family of my own, I could only appreciate a song like "Wreck on the Highway" as an aesthetic by-product of Springsteen's fascination with country music. Springsteen took the title from a Roy Acuff song, but whereas Acuff's song is like a PSA about the dangers of drunk driving ("There was whiskey and blood all together / Mixed with glass where they lay"), Springsteen focuses on a man who witnesses a car accident, and how it reminds him that the love he has for his girlfriend—like everything else in life—will not last. This is not something you can fully grasp when you're twenty-one. When I first heard "Wreck on the Highway," it seemed merely morbid. But at forty, I understood that Springsteen was talking about the same existential fear that lurks inside my heart whenever I watch my wife and children sing songs together over Lego blocks and dry Cheerios. How can I hold on to something that mortality is slowly stripping away from my grasp?

My hope is that Bruce Springsteen can continue to guide me forward.

"Turn the Page"

NOTES ON TRACK 8: Life on the road is tough. Sometimes you tell the day by the bottle that you drink. And times when you're alone, all you do is think. Wait, did we just quote Bon Jovi's "Wanted Dead or Alive"? Yes, we think we did.

Great art often encompasses contradictory ideas simultaneously. Bad art does this, too, though only by accident. In Night Ranger's "Sister Christian," for example, drummer Kelly Keagy lectures a young woman on the dangers of premarital sex ("Don't give it up / Before your time is due"). However, in the only other Night Ranger song that I used to hear on WAPL, "Don't Tell Me You Love Me," guitarist Jack Blades informs an unnamed lady, "I've got a pistol for action," and "I love the way that you use me," while also making it clear that he's merely "a kid on the run." At no point does marriage come up in the conversation.

This is what you call a "mixed message." Mixed messages are the lingua franca of classic rock—it's what provokes Judas Priest fans to shotgun beers in parking lots outside of arenas and believe that Satan is telling them to shotgun themselves in the face at home.

The most contradictory classic-rock trope is the "life on the road" song. This subgenre of the power ballad is typified by Bob Seger's "Turn the Page," an epic wallow in rock-star self-pity that I've already discussed in detail in chapter 6, but I feel compelled to bring up once more because here I am, on that classic-rock road again, there I am, up on that classic-rock-analyzin' stage.

The closest rival to "Turn the Page" in the annals of "life on the road" songs is Creedence Clearwater Revival's "Lodi," in which John Fogerty covers all of the essential bases: the monotony of touring, the unfulfilled dreams of fame and fortune, the specter of substance abuse, the unappreciative audiences in dead-end towns, and the feeling that you'll never escape this exhausting lifestyle. You can hear variations of these themes in subsequent "life on the road" songs, whether the tone is tragic (Loudon Wainwright III's "Motel Blues"), semitragic (Kid Rock's "Only God Knows Why"), or tragicomic (Tenacious D's "The Road"). Then there's Jackson Browne's *Running on Empty,* the best "life on the road" album in the classic-rock canon, because it was actually recorded onstage, backstage, in hotel rooms, and on the tour bus. Browne was like a Method actor when it came to "life on the road" songs— when he sings about drinking coffee in the morning and snorting cocaine in the afternoon, you can almost hear the sniffing sounds in the background.

My favorite song on *Running on Empty* is "The Load-Out," a sad ballad about how hard it is to be one of Jackson Browne's roadies. "They're the first to come and the last to leave," Browne sings. "Working for that minimum wage." Intellectually, "The Load-Out" doesn't hold up to scrutiny—putting Jackson Browne's guitar back in its case every night can't be that hard. Emotionally, however, Browne's sensitive tenor always makes me ache with road-weary sympathy pains.

(Honorable mention goes to the second-best "life on the road" LP, 1972's *Everybody's in Show-Biz* by the Kinks, in which Ray

Davies offers up a series of definitive anthems about how bad backstage catering was in the early seventies.)

Conceptually, the "life on the road" song is supposed to present an authentic (i.e., depressing) depiction of rock stardom as a series of occupational hazards. You could even describe these songs as cautionary tales, except "life on the road" songs in fact do the opposite of discouraging future rock lifers. (If anything, songs like AC/DC's "It's a Long Way to the Top (If You Wanna Rock 'n' Roll")" function as de-facto instruction manuals for wannabes.) I doubt Joseph Campbell ever listened to Bob Seger, but if he had, I'm sure he'd agree that "life on the road" songs make life on the road seem like a hero's journey. "Turn the Page" doesn't disavow the drudgery of the humdrum rock life but romanticizes this kind of existence—ridin' sixteen hours with nothin' to do sounds awful until you add a cinematic sax wail and a husky, whiskey-coated vocal. The sort of quests described in a "life on the road" song might seem insurmountable, but they clearly were *surmounted,* or else these people wouldn't have become famous enough for the rest of us to hear this song.

What first set me off on romanticizing life on the road? It has to be *The Last Waltz,* Martin Scorsese's classic 1978 documentary about a farewell concert performed by the Band and a supporting cast of iconic rock legends at Winterland Ballroom in San Francisco.

The Last Waltz is most remembered for its musical performances, captured with supreme elegance by Scorsese—Bob Dylan and the Band tearing into "Baby Let Me Follow You Down" with the same fire they had on the '66 tour, Neil Young dueting with Joni Mitchell on "Helpless" with a rock of cocaine hanging from his nostril, and, most spectacularly, a portly purple-suited Van Morrison doing high kicks at the climax of a never-better "Caravan." But when I was a teenager and watched my VHS copy of *The Last Waltz* approximately fifty-seven times, I was just as transfixed by the scenes *between* the musical performances, in which Scorsese interviews the members of the Band. In the shorthand of the film, each guy is turned into an archetype, sort of like a classic-rock version of the Seven Dwarves. There's Arrogant (Robbie Robertson), Salty (Levon Helm), Sweet (Rick Danko), Tragic (Richard Manuel), and Quiet (Garth Hudson). We see these guys smoke cigarettes, shoot pool, shoot the shit, and generally come off like the coolest individuals to ever grow beards and wear wide-brimmed hats.

Critics of *The Last Waltz* complain that Scorsese focuses too much on Robertson at the expense of the other members, particularly Helm, Danko, and Manuel, who for many fans represent the true soul of the band. Those guys sang all of the songs, and they were imbued with a gritty sensitivity that was simultaneously tough and emotional without seeming affected. Robertson, meanwhile, seems incapable of doing anything without affectation.

Scorsese's focus on Robertson is felt most acutely in the interview segments, where Robertson often talks over his bandmates, who mostly just sit in the background while looking glamorously intoxicated. "The road was our school," Robertson intones gravely in one scene. "It taught us all we know. There's not much left that we can really take from the road. You can press your luck. The road has taken a lot of great ones. Hank Williams. Buddy Holly. Otis Redding. Janis. Jimi Hendrix. Elvis. It's an impossible way of life."

As it's presented in *The Last Waltz*, the Band decided to break up in order to save themselves from the hard, decadent life of touring musicians—that same "strung out from the road" feeling that Bob Seger sings about in "Turn the Page." But the graceful departure from rock 'n' roll craziness depicted in *The Last Waltz* is not the whole story. In reality, only Robertson wanted to break up the Band. Just five years after the film was released, the other members decided to reunite. Only then, without Robertson, they were back to playing the sort of dives that the Band had left behind after they took up with Dylan and became famous.

The most outraged critic of *The Last Waltz* was Helm, who complained bitterly in his caustic 1993 memoir, *This Wheel's on Fire*, about how (in his view) Robertson and Scorsese railroaded the rest of the Band. "I didn't want any part of it," Helm writes. "I didn't want to break up the band." According to Helm, he only went along with the movie because the Band's management made it seem as though he didn't have a choice. Besides, Helm assumed that the Band's retirement would be similar to farewells by Frank Sinatra and David Bowie, who eventually returned to touring after brief hiatuses in the seventies.

The central argument of *This Wheel's on Fire* is that Robertson unfairly seized control of the Band, which started out as a utopian collective in which all of the members freely collaborated without concern for songwriting credits. By all accounts, Robertson was the most responsible and conscientious member of the Band, and over time he assumed the role of leader and principal songwriter, which entitled him to a larger cut of the royalties. But in Helm's mind, his experiences as the group's only American were paramount in their lyrics and iconography.

Along with feuding over money, Helm hated Robertson's unilateral decision to take the Band off the road. For Helm, Robertson's self-mythologizing in *The Last Waltz* about not wanting to end up like Hank Williams or Elvis Presley was straight-up egotism. Helm believed the whole point of being in a rock band was to *ramble*. "I'm not in it for my health," Helm writes in *This Wheel's on Fire*. "I'm a musician, and I wanna live the way I do."

In his younger years, Helm lived hard—he drank, smoked, shot heroin, and snorted blow. Whatever it took to keep going down the road. "I'm not in it for my health" became Helm's epitaph—a 2013 documentary called *Ain't in It for My Health* documents his final years as a touring musician, before he died of throat cancer in 2012 at age seventy-one.

Helm's book did a lot to deconstruct the narrative of *The Last Waltz*—if Robbie Robertson is now commonly perceived to be one of the biggest jerks in rock history, it's mainly due to Helm's cold-blooded character assassination in *This Wheel's on Fire*. But *The Last Waltz* nevertheless was the culmination of Robertson's effort to put himself front and center in the Band—it's still the most famous document of the Band's music and legacy, and Robertson is in it way more than all of the other members.

That Manuel (who committed suicide in 1986 at forty-two) and Danko (who died of heart failure in 1999 at fifty-five) also perished after years of declining health brought on by years of down-and-out tour living might be used as evidence that Robertson was right to walk away from the Band when he did. But what's romantic about his perceived prescience? Even as a statement of fact, "Robbie Robertson was right" has never been inspirational in any context.

Part of loving classic rock is regarding the road as a fearsome yet romantic metaphor for living a life of absolute freedom outside of normal society—precisely the kind of life that most of us will never live. We want our heroes on the stretch of concrete, enduring one blackout night and hungover morning after another, because it enables us to witness the very extremes of human existence from a safe vantage point. Levon stayed on the road. He went down swinging. All Robbie did was talk about it.

All "life on the road" songs are conflicted about the agony and ecstasy of touring. But no road song has deeper contradictions than "Ramblin' Man" by the Allman Brothers Band, the greatest and most cursed Southern-rock group of all time. Few classic-rock bands relished life on the road as much as the Allmans, or understood as well just how torturous staying on the road at any cost could be. And you can hear it all in "Ramblin' Man," so long as you know what to listen for.

Released as a single at the tail end of the summer of 1973 and written and sung by the band's feisty guitarist Dickey Betts, "Ramblin' Man" is the Allmans' biggest hit; it peaked at No. 2. Unlike the muscular blues rock and jazzy improvisations that distinguished past Allman Brothers albums like *At Fillmore East* and *Eat a Peach,* "Ramblin' Man" is an airy blast of pop-country joy, in which Betts's reedy tenor amiably relates a story about a ne'er-do-well who was "born in the backseat of a Greyhound bus," a fatalistic biographical footnote that the narrator uses to justify an existence of endless carousing.

"Ramblin' Man" is a spiritual cousin to two other rambling-man songs that derive from the country tradition. Hank Williams Sr.'s 1951 ballad "Ramblin' Man" is a doom-laden lament about a perpetual drifter who is driven to pull up stakes whenever he hears a train whistle blow. Like Dickey Betts in the Allmans' "Ramblin' Man," Williams frames his song as a warning to a potential lover to not get too close, lest he break her heart. (Pee-wee Herman expresses similar sentiments in his "I'm a loner, Dottie, a rebel" speech in *Pee-wee's Big Adventure.*) Ultimately, both the Allmans and Williams view ramblin' as a lifestyle that one is predisposed to live, be it by God or perhaps something more nefarious lurking in one's damaged psyche. They can try to explain the lure of this lifestyle in a song, but at best they can only "hope you understand."

The other crucial precursor to the Allman Brothers' song is Ray Pennington's swaggering 1967 tune "I'm a Ramblin' Man," later covered by Waylon Jennings on his excellent 1974 LP *The Ramblin' Man.* Whereas Williams's "Ramblin' Man" is forlorn and lachrymose, Pennington's "I'm a Ramblin' Man" is frisky and lascivious, reveling in the pleasures of roaming from town to town and leaving scores of one-night stands in your wake. Pennington also positions his rambling song as an ostensible warning, but it just feels like an extended come-on, a flirtatious game of hard-to-get that the protagonist knows will get him laid by the end of the night. "You'd better move away / You're standin' too close to the flame," Pennington drawls. "Once I mess with your mind / Your little heart won't beat the same." It's one of the greatest humblebrags in country-music history.

The Allman Brothers Band managed to take the darkness of

Hank Williams and the lightness of Ray Pennington and fuse them together into the greatest "Ramblin' Man" of them all. Granted, the darkness is only in the song's subtext. If you heard it on the radio without knowing anything about the Allman Brothers, all you would feel is delight, particularly during the final two minutes, when Betts plays off Chuck Leavell's virtuosic piano licks before launching into a celebratory solo that flutters warmly, like the last rays of sun at dusk.

To get at the heart of darkness at the center of "Ramblin' Man," you have to be aware of who you can't hear in the song—the band's founding guitarist, Duane Allman, who died in a motorcycle crash not long after turning twenty-four in 1971. By the time "Ramblin' Man" became a hit, the Allman Brothers Band's original bassist, Berry Oakley, would also be dead at age twenty-four. Oakley perished in a different motorcycle crash in 1972, one year and thirteen days after Duane died, at an intersection just down the road from Duane's accident. One of Oakley's final recording sessions was for "Ramblin' Man," which went on to become the most popular song he ever played on.

The deaths of Duane Allman and Berry Oakley—and the Allman Brothers' determination to stay together in spite of those tragic losses—form the core of the band's legend. A cursory listen to "Ramblin' Man" seems to suggest that the Allmans carried on because life on the road was too fun to quit prematurely. Its sound is as inviting as a pitcher of lemonade on a hot July afternoon. But the song's lyrical theme, that one is born to ramble and therefore fated to exist in a constant state of dislocation, is decidedly less enticing. By the end of the song, before that wondrous instrumental break, Dickey Betts's repeated exhortation of the chorus—"Lord, I was born a ramblin' man"—takes on a twinge of desperation.

The popularity of "Ramblin' Man" pushed the Allman Brothers Band to the greatest heights of its career. For a brief spell in the midseventies, it was the highest-grossing touring act in the country. But like Robert Johnson forty years earlier, the Allman Brothers Band appeared to have struck a Faustian bargain for its success. That's the portrait painted by teenage rock journalist Cameron Crowe in his mythical *Rolling Stone* profile of the band from 1973, which later provided much of the inspiration for Crowe's valentine to the classic-rock era, *Almost Famous*.

Crowe opens the story cinematically on the band's long-haired singer, Gregg Allman, sitting by himself in a lonely hotel room in San Francisco a few hours after a triumphant concert at Winterland. Allman stares at a flickering TV set playing an old horror movie as Crowe asks him how the Allman Brothers found the wherewithal to hold it together after losing two members in quick succession. "I've had guys come up to me and say, 'Man, it just doesn't seem like losing those two fine cats affected you people at all.' Why? Because I still have my wits about me? Because I can still play?" Allman asks Crowe rhetorically. "Well that's the key right there. We'd all have turned into fucking vegetables if we hadn't been able to get out there and play. *That*'s when the success was, Jack. Success was being able to keep your brain inside your head."

The other famous road song in the Allman Brothers catalog, "Midnight Rider," has the same high-lonesome feeling as that *Rolling Stone* profile. That melancholy also haunts Hank Williams Sr.'s "Ramblin' Man," which paints wanderlust as both a coping mechanism and a debilitating mental condition. "I've got to run to keep from hiding," Gregg Allman sings at the start. If he doesn't keep moving, whatever demons he's running away from—drug addiction, grief, his brother's ghost—will eventually find him. Which is why he's "bound to keep on riding."

In "Midnight Rider," there is no joy in rambling or playful lust for "them Delta women" down in New Orleans like there is in "Ramblin' Man." When Gregg sings, "The road goes on forever," it's not celebratory. He sounds scared out of his wits. For Allman, rambling is a rote exercise motivated by fear and paranoia. All that's left is the chase for the sake of the chase. "I've gone by the point of caring," he sings near the end. "But I'm not gonna let 'em catch me, no."

I'm sure Gregg Allman wasn't *just* full of dread when it came to touring. He surely also enjoyed it. After all, Allman kept on playing until almost the very end of his life in 2017, three years after the Allman Brothers Band played its final gig at the Beacon Theatre in Manhattan. Even as the recurrence of liver cancer compromised his quality of life, Allman appeared to be genuinely engaged in performing live. Playing the best possible version of "Statesboro Blues" or "Stormy Monday" remained a constant goal. Music was his vocation and sanctuary, as well as the only constant in a life filled with so much loss. The losses never stopped—he was married seven times and endured the premature deaths of two more bassists, Lamar Williams and Allen Woody. Four months before Allman died, founding ABB drummer Butch Trucks shot himself, ending his life at age sixty-nine.

The archetype of the Allman Brothers Band as a stalwart road band was created by "Midnight Rider" and *At Fillmore East,* and bolstered by the band's perseverance in the face of losing Duane Allman and Berry Oakley, which is personified by the lighthearted sound of "Ramblin' Man." A strain of tragic fatalism runs deep in the Allmans' music, as does an indomitable will to keep on ramblin' in spite of the consequences.

In the iconography of the Allmans, the road is a place where you try to make a livin' and do the best you can, and a symbol for the grind of human existence amid omnipresent hardship. When I hear "Midnight Rider" and "Ramblin' Man," I'm inspired by the Allman Brothers Band's determination and chilled by the underlying darkness of what awaits when this hero's journey reaches its end. Because in spite of what the song says, the road does not go on forever.

"Draw the Line"

NOTES ON TRACK 9: This is not a pro-drug song. It merely describes an awesome experience that coincidentally involved the ingestion of massive quantities of pills, booze, and cocaine—as all the best rock songs do.

When I wrote my first book, *Your Favorite Band Is Killing Me,* I wanted to travel to different cities to do book events, in part, because I yearned to be a character in a Bob Seger song. When my publisher declined to pay for my travel, I looked at this setback as the first verse of my woeful tale of touring hardship. ("When you pull into the bookstore / Having paid your last cent / You wonder if it was worth it / My readers look kind of spent.")

But overall, my limited tour experience was neither as terrible nor as epic as "life on the road" songs had led me to expect. The only interesting thing that happened during my promotional tour occurred when I was at home and booked to appear via phone on an L.A.-based radio show cohosted by Jillian Barberie.

If you don't know who Jillian Barberie is, here's a quick rundown of her résumé:

- She is best known for delivering weather reports on Fox's NFL pregame show back in the midaughts.
- She has appeared in *Maxim* twice.
- She is the former cohost of *Good Day L.A.*, a morning show known to non-Angelenos for the hilarious clips on YouTube of Barberie acting insane.

I was invited by the show's producer to appear on Barberie's radio show because my first book includes a chapter on Prince, who had died a few days earlier. I was told that Barberie and her passive male cohost wanted to talk about Prince's legacy, which seemed fine to me, for I am officially A Man with Published Opinions About Prince.

However, this is not *really* what Barberie wanted to talk about. What we actually talked about was Gene Simmons, who had just gotten in trouble for saying that David Bowie's death was "tragic," because he died from cancer, while Prince's death was "pathetic," because it appeared to be drug-related. Barberie agreed with Simmons, and wanted to know if I also agreed with Simmons.

Have you ever had a conversation in which you wish you were sitting in an ejector seat? So you could just pull the handle and immediately launch yourself out of some awful situation? Talking with Jillian Barberie was like that. At that point Prince's cause of death was unconfirmed. His dependency on painkillers was also still unconfirmed. Nobody knew anything. More important: Who cares? Moralizing over Prince's death seemed offensive, and also unnecessary—why lecture a dead genius on the dangers of his personal peccadilloes?

A recording exists of exactly what was said during my brief conversation with Jillian Barberie, but I refuse to listen to it. This is how I remember it.

"Prince was pathetic," she said.

"No he's not," I said.

"Yes he is."

"No he is not."

"Is."

"Is not."

[Loud noises from Barberie.]

[Loud noises from me.]

Somewhere amid all of the chaos—I think they call it "good radio"—Barberie likened Prince's drug use to drunk driving. This caused my brain to melt. I started shouting uncontrollably.

"You are a bad person! You are a lunatic!"

You would think I would've been kicked off by that point. But I was not. I had broken the handle of my ejector seat and was now trying to pry myself loose with my teeth.

The cohost tried to shift the topic to the Rolling Stones.

"They did a lot of drugs, you probably hate them, too," I replied. That comment is what got kicked me off the L.A. airwaves. Thanks again, Mick and Keef.

Let's rewind to the part before my brain melted. The argument made by Simmons and Barberie has become common in our decadence-averse times—if you use drugs and alcohol in your lifetime, you will be diminished in death, because it's "your fault" that you died. This very non-classic-rock idea has taken hold in these very non-classic-rock times. A core tenet of classic-rock mythology is that using drugs and alcohol forges a pathway to understanding what it means to be alive, even if it kills you. Maybe *especially* if it kills you.

If I'd had more time—and if my brain had not melted—on Barberie's show, I would've calmly pointed out that while drugs did not kill David Bowie, they could have back in the seventies. And I would've said this not in a judgmental way, but out of admiration, for Bowie had perhaps the greatest drug period in rock history. Yes, I am a person who ranks drug periods in rock history. You can take Gene Simmons. I'll ride with William Blake.

The drug period to which I refer took place from approximately early 1974 to the end of '75, and encompasses the albums *Diamond Dogs, Young Americans,* and *Station to Station,* as well as Bowie's Plastic Soul and Thin White Duke personas. When people talk about Bowie in the seventies, this era is often overlooked. It's a valley between his glitter-rock era in the early seventies and the Berlin era of the late seventies. Between those iconic bursts of creativity, Bowie turned to cocaine after learning that his manager, Tony DeFries, had ripped him off and left him in financial dire straits. And for a brief period, David Bowie transformed into a subterranean homesick alien in his daily life.

You can catch glimpses of this Bowie online. On *The Dick Cavett Show* in late '74, he is a terrifying amalgamation of gray skin, red hair, and conspicuous sniffs. His nose resembles one of those porcelain horses that little girls keep on their bedside tables, but the rest of Bowie is no less brittle. In the BBC documentary *Cracked Actor,* a definitive portrait of Bowie during this time, he talks nonsensically while riding in the back of a limousine careening around Los Angeles. He listens to Aretha Franklin and does massive pulls from a bottle of milk. His body is so emaciated, he looks like an unexceptional Little Leaguer.

Deep Purple bassist Glenn Hughes, who hosted Bowie at his Beverly Hills mansion in the summer of '75, has recalled that Bowie spent his days watching Nazi-era propaganda films, another dose of poison for an already wrecked mind. But for Hughes, Bowie's cocaine psychosis had an artistic purpose. Hughes believed Bowie was making himself suffer for his art.

The defining album of this period is 1976's *Station to Station,* a hymn to Bowie's profound sense of dislocation and his growing homesickness for Europe. It's one of my favorite Bowie records, though Bowie himself did not remember recording it. For the first time, he entered the studio without songs; what Bowie did have was a huge bag of coke, which he placed on the mixing board like Tony Montana during his last stand. The drugs subsequently took Bowie outside of himself.

It was Bowie's custom to unify songs into a thematic whole

on his albums. While he might have changed dramatically *between* records, he tended to follow a single narrative thread *within* each record, whether it was the sci-fi theme of *Ziggy Stardust,* the ironic R & B of *Young Americans,* or the mechanical iciness of *Low.* But *Station to Station* is all over the map. The album's hit single, "Golden Years," was a callback to *Young Americans.* The man-machine groove of "TVC 15" looked ahead to the Berlin albums. The epic prog-rock title track located the unlikely sweet spot between James Brown and the pioneering Krautrock group Can. The album ends with the torch ballad "Wild Is the Wind," originally recorded by Johnny Mathis in 1957.

Bowie was experimenting musically, but he was also conducting scientific experiments on his nervous system, all the while carefully measuring the toll on his body and spirit. Drugs affected his appearance, his voice, and his approach to art. He sang like Dracula with post-nasal drip, and made music that was both ominously dark and sinuously funky, a unique mix that does not exist in the non-exhausted mind. As Ziggy Stardust, Bowie had reveled in the fakeness of his alien rock star persona. But as the Thin White Duke, Bowie was no longer a man. He was a sentient line of blow.

The belief that drugs and booze can help achieve higher con-sciousness, provide the energy to play great shows on the road, and instill ironclad coolness is now commonly viewed as dangerously self-indulgent—or "pathetic," to quote noted sex addict Gene Simmons. After his death, Bowie was excused for his cocaine years because they took place in a distant past that was largely forgotten. In retrospect, Bowie's drug abuse is one of the few things about him that now seems regressive.

Shifting cultural attitudes about chemicals—and their role in classic-rock mythology—were most readily apparent in the reaction to the first and only season of HBO's *Vinyl,* one of the most hyped and expensive bombs in TV history. Spearheaded by Martin Scorsese and Mick Jagger, *Vinyl* depicts the record business of the early seventies, centering on a hard-partying executive named Richie Finestra (Bobby Cannavale), who is improbably connected with every significant act of the time. Richie negotiates record contracts with Led Zeppelin, predicts future greatness for the Velvet Underground, and plays golf with Alice Cooper. Even Bowie (who died one month before *Vinyl*'s premiere in 2016) shows up in Richie's orbit. Richie is like Zelig with chest hair.

The opening scene of the pilot establishes *Vinyl*'s aesthetic. Richie scores cocaine (he calls it "sugar") from a dealer who has obviously studied Harvey Keitel in *Taxi Driver*. (*Vinyl* is populated by actors who emulate how New Yorkers behaved in Scorsese's seventies films, as opposed to the genuine neighborhood characters that Scorsese captured in those movies.) Richie then wanders into a seedy seventies New York rock club outfitted with the requisite debauched accoutrements—heroin needles on the floor, blow jobs performed out in the open, naked fat guys wandering around with impunity. It looks like a Lou Reed–themed TGI Fridays. Onstage is the New York Dolls, a band that *Vinyl* seems to regard as being more popular than they were. (Later in the season, Richie's big discovery, the Nasty Bits, opens for the Dolls, and the gig is treated as a make-or-break star-making moment, despite the Dolls' never being all that successful, except when it came to killing their drummers.)

"I had a golden ear, a silver tongue, and a pair of brass balls," Richie declares in a deeply Scorseseian voice-over. "But the problem became my nose and everything I put up it!"

The most eloquent hater of *Vinyl* was Emily Nussbaum of the *New Yorker*, who directly connected the show's heavy-handedness to classic rock's outmoded hedonist ideology. "Naturally, Richie is piggish and moody; he's a cokehead who keeps relapsing. But, in the tired algorithm of cable drama, his failings are tragic, because he's more sensitive than the goons and weasels who surround him," Nussbaum wrote. "This is TV's own version of rockism, the presumption that any drama about a genius-thug with a sad wife and a drug habit must be a deep statement about America."

Vinyl was predicated on the assumption that a white guy doing drugs and working with rock bands is both undeniably awesome *and* inherently important. And that's the last thing you can assume now about modern culture. In a different time, living a decadent lifestyle truly was viewed as a "deep statement about America." It meant you were an outlaw challenging the morality and social mores of the establishment. But we no longer live in a world where people will just understand intuitively that a character like Richie is heroic and not merely an asshole. You must put it in the proper context, add a layer of Ron Burgundy–like irony, and tweet a preemptive apology. And even then, people will probably think your show is obnoxious.

Speaking of assholes, the man most responsible for the hoari-est strains of rock 'n' roll mythology related to decadence as a path to wisdom and power is none other than Mr. Mojo Risin' himself, Jim Morrison. Which means Morrison is also (at least partly) to blame for all that time I spent in my twenties staring vainly into barroom mirrors while I drank and drugged myself into oblivion. By then, I should've known better. But the Lizard King was too ingrained in my psyche. I wanted to ride the snake, man, and got off on watching myself break on through to the other side.

Like so many impressionable, backward-looking Gen Xers in the early nineties, I had a Doors phase. And, like so many people's Doors phases back then, mine was inspired by Oliver Stone's 1991 biopic, conveniently titled *The Doors*. When Doors cofounder and keyboardist Ray Manzarek declared that Stone depicted Morrison "as a violent, drunken fool," he meant it as a criticism. (Manzarek particularly hated the scene in which a soused Morrison locks his girlfriend, Pamela, in a closest and sets it on fire, an act nearly as egregious as the fourth Doors album, *The Soft Parade*.) But to my teenage eyes, "violent and drunken" seemed like higher ideals. As portrayed by Val Kilmer—a.k.a. Iceman from my childhood favorite *Top Gun,* a character who abhorred recklessness in fighter pilots and T-shirts on volleyball players—Stone's version of Morrison is a warrior-hedonist inhabited by the spirit of a dead Indian chief and several snifters of cheap scotch. He's marked for righteous death and for dirty sex, and not necessarily in that order. Above all, Morrison is shown to be a visionary when it comes to embracing the fascism of rock stardom—he was among the first rock stars to understand the artistic possibilities of provoking large audiences.

If I had read more in middle school, I might have worked my way through the syllabus of adolescent decadence: Nietzsche, Blake, Kerouac, Bukowski, Sartre, Rimbaud, Baudelaire. Perhaps I would've eventually found my way to *The Varieties of Religious Experience,* in which William James writes that "sobriety diminishes, discriminates, and says no; drunkenness expands, unites, and says yes." But I didn't need those books, because along with *Hammer of the Gods* I had *No One Here Gets Out Alive,* the definitive biography/deification of James Douglas Morrison by Danny Sugerman and Jerry Hopkins. For a budding Doors fan, *No One Here Gets Out Alive* was a very heady "trip"—as I surely would've called it back then.

No One Here Gets Out Alive was a crucial resource for Stone as he worked on *The Doors.* (On the film's DVD commentary track, Stone refers to it simply as "the book.") But as with *Hammer of the Gods,* the veracity of *No One Here Gets Out Alive* has been called into question. Doors associate B. Douglas Cameron has called the book a "fantasy" and labeled Sugerman, the band's former manager, "a groupie who took advantage of a situation and wormed his way into the organization." No matter the factual details of Morrison's life, however, *No One Here Gets Out Alive* crystallized the myth of Jim Morrison that lived on for decades after the man himself perished in a Paris bathtub in 1971.

Morrison was a perfect subject for a bombastic polemicist like Oliver Stone. As a filmmaker, Stone yearns to play John the

Baptist for various Christ figures, and Jim Morrison is the only sixties icon more Jesus-like than John F. Kennedy. From the beginning of the Doors, Morrison consciously conceived the band's iconography as an extension of the besotted philosophers he grew up reading. Years before he was famous, Morrison envisioned his earliest songs (including "Hello, I Love You" and "The End") in the context of an imaginary concert that played on a loop in his head. As a student at Florida State University, Morrison took a class on the psychology of crowds and came to see himself as an expert in "diagnosing" massive groups of people. Later, in the *New York Times,* Morrison famously likened the Doors to "erotic politicians" who "make concerts sexual politics." How did this work? "The music we make goes out to the audience and interacts with them," Morrison explained. "They go home and interact with the rest of reality, then I get it back by interacting with that reality, so the whole sex thing works out to be one big ball of fire."

Now, if you're over the age of fifteen, this probably sounds ridiculous. However, my Doors phase occurred right before that, when I was fourteen, so I thought Morrison was profound. To me, Morrison was a sage because he had done all of the things that I associated with the grown-up world. I'm not referring to activities such as paying taxes or holding down a job you hate so you can support people you love. I mean sex, drugs, philosophy, antiauthoritarianism . . . really, just sex. I was an easy mark for the lurid stories related by Sugerman and fine-tuned by Hopkins, a veteran music journalist who had previously written about one of Morrison's biggest heroes, Elvis Presley. As far as I knew, sex really did involve literal balls of fire.

The most memorably gross/"awesome" anecdote from *No One Here Gets Out Alive* takes place at the Alta Cienega Hotel, a rathole located near the Sunset Strip where Morrison drank and romanced underage girls.

Jim was in Room 32 on the second floor, sprawled across the green chenille spread that covered the lumpy double bed. A thin girl of seventeen or eighteen stood near the small television set, her back to the tiny bathroom.

Jim drained a beer and threw the can at a plastic trash basket next to the blond dresser. He missed, knocking a book to the floor: *The Origins and History of Consciousness*.

"Fuck it," Jim belched. He looked at the girl. He moved his chin upward, signaling her to come to the bed. She was a pickup from the night before; he got her whole life story, then he "butt-fucked" her, and now he was bored.

Sugerman and Hopkins maintain that this problematic behavior was required for the Doors to create great art. For instance, when the Doors were making *Strange Days*, Morrison asked his girlfriend Pamela to go down on him while he was recording the vocal for "You're Lost Little Girl," purely for procedural reasons. He wasn't merely a hedonist. He was an explorer of the sexual and chemical underworld, and his experiences in the nether regions beyond sanity and common decency were fed into the Doors' music. Or something like that.

Over the years, the Doors have inspired me to delve deeper into the literature of decadence—by which I mean other books about the Doors. In his 2005 book, *Jim Morrison: Life, Death, Legend*, Stephen Davis (also the author of *Hammer of the Gods*, and the J. R. R. Tolkien of sleaze rock) once again exhibits an ability to describe harrowing rock 'n' roll debauchery in journalistic detail while also not-so-subtly glamorizing that debauchery.

Davis writes that Morrison "could put away two dozen shots of whiskey and a couple of six packs of beer without showing it. But then one more drink could suddenly turn him into a stumbling, psychotic drunk, shouting 'Nigger!' in the streets, pissing in public, and disgracing himself. It was a scandal, and no one had the faintest idea what to do about it."

Clearly Jim Morrison could be a world-class, grade-A monster. Joan Didion observed as much when she dropped in on the

Waiting for the Sun sessions with her husband, screenwriter-producer John Gregory Dunne, who was interested in casting Morrison for his upcoming film *The Panic in Needle Park*. (The part eventually went to Al Pacino.) Morrison rolled into the session very late and very drunk, and accompanied by (in Davis's words) "a slutty-looking teenager." Didion hoped to interview Morrison, but instead she was forced to observe the dreadfully boring things musicians do when they're in a recording studio and too wasted to work.

> Morrison sits down on the leather couch again and leans back. He lights a match. He studies the flame for a while, and very slowly, very deliberately, lowers it to the fly of his black vinyl pants. Manzarek watches him. There is the sense that no one is going to leave this room, ever. It will be some weeks before The Doors finish recording this album.

I know this story should make me like the Doors less, but when you're fixated on rock mythology, it has the opposite effect.

One of the most remarkable rock memoirs I've ever read is Sugerman's *Wonderland Avenue: Tales of Glamour and Excess*. Sugerman started working in the Doors' business office when he was only twelve. Probably not coincidentally, Sugerman also developed a pretty serious drug problem at a young age. But as the title of his book suggests, *Wonderland Avenue* isn't exactly a cautionary tale about the dangers of youngsters smoking weed while fetching groceries for legendary rock bands.

Sugerman's depiction of Morrison in *Wonderland Avenue* is fawning, to put it mildly. ("He felt dangerous," Sugerman writes in one characteristically worshipful passage. "He was still in his black leather pants but with a blue pea coat, collar up. His hair was the longest I'd ever seen. And as much as I was embarrassed to admit it, he was beautiful.") But Sugerman sees Morrison as more like a big brother than a rock star. He writes about how Morrison guided him through one of his first acid trips—and also how he encouraged him to do his homework. When Morrison leaves L.A. for Paris, where he will die soon after, he gives Sugerman a copy of his book of poetry, *The Lords and the New Creatures*. Inside, Morrison writes the following inscription: "See ya at the big rock concert in the sky. Your brother of laughter and freedom, Jim."

Sugerman's book captures a crucial part of the Doors' appeal: it is a big-brother band for naïve teenagers curious about the scariest and most alluring parts of adulthood. The Doors' band name is an allusion to Aldous Huxley's famous quote about "the doors of perception"—but when you're a kid hearing this music for the first time, it might as well stand for the doors that stand between kids and adults. "Hello, I Love You" is a stupid (but good) song about sex, but if you've never had sex (or learned that "Hello, I love you, won't you tell me you name?" will never get you laid), it's suggestive of a deeper excitement you're not allowed to experience yet, like lying in a bed at night and staring at the beams of light coming from a grown-up party on the other side of the door.

In that moment, a drunken man in leather pants who sings in a low, manly croon seems to point the way out.

If the Doors are to blame for instilling so many of the clichés about the value of rock 'n' roll decadence, who is responsible for ushering those clichés out?

I blame Aerosmith.

When I discovered Aerosmith in the late eighties, I didn't know they were a classic-rock band. The first Aerosmith song I ever heard was the band's collaboration with Run-DMC on "Walk This Way," which I didn't even realize was a cover at the time. Based on the music video, I was under the impression that Aerosmith and Run-DMC lived next door to each other and became friends after Steven Tyler crashed his microphone stand through the wall, prompting a spontaneous duet on the first-ever rap-rock song.

The subsequent tunes I heard were the big, glitzy pop hits from 1987's *Permanent Vacation* and 1989's *Pump* that WIXX spun constantly—"Dude (Looks Like a Lady)," "Angel," "Love in an Elevator," "Janie's Got a Gun." It wasn't until I started listening to WAPL that I discovered Aerosmith's not-so-secret past back in the seventies as purveyors of sub-Stonesian sleaze in the form of the original "Walk This Way," "Sweet Emotion," "Dream On," and "Back in the Saddle," among other classics.

In a way, I wasn't wrong when I thought that late-eighties Aerosmith was a new band. While Aerosmith has somehow retained all of its original members since the seventies, the group did a total reboot after flaming out at the end of that decade. And the most important change involved the band's drug abuse. Aerosmith in the seventies was one of the most chemical-addled bands of the arena-rock era. But Aerosmith in the late eighties built a new reputation on the redemptive powers of rehab.

As someone who bought *Pump* on cassette many years before he fully understood the shameless innuendos of "Love in an Elevator," I've always had a soft spot for Aerosmith's MTV era. But once I heard the band's drug-era albums, it was no contest. I was all over 1975's *Toys in the Attic* and 1976's *Rocks* as the "true" Aerosmith records. This wasn't just due to my immature "romantic slob" biases—those albums are actually better musically, too. Getting into early Aerosmith is like meeting the father of every unsavory, big-haired glam-rock dude that you've ever pretended not to love. Guns N' Roses, Mötley Crüe, Poison, even Nickelback—any band that's mastered the art of the disreputable arena-metal jam has studied those seventies Aerosmith albums as if they're a pornographic instruction manual.

Less mystical than Zeppelin and more vulgar than the Stones, Aerosmith appealed to seventies kids by playing blues rock with zero concern for taste or authenticity. It was designed for an audience resistant to dry lectures about Robert Johnson and the

Mississippi Delta, because for them blues music started with "Whole Lotta Love."

The other distinguishing characteristic of Aerosmith's "Blue Army," the nickname given to the band's denim-clad fan base, was prodigious drug use. This is captured in Richard Linklater's *Dazed and Confused,* which takes place in the summer of 1976 and is framed by scenes in which teenagers jam out to "Sweet Emotion" and head out on a road trip to buy Aerosmith concert tickets. The kids in *Dazed and Confused* smoke pot from sunup to sundown purely for the sake of getting high—any ideology about "enlightenment" had fallen away for the typical midseventies teenage stoner.

But the philosophical framework about drugs' being a creative tool was still there for Joe Perry. In the definitive oral history *Walk This Way: The Autobiography of Aerosmith,* cowritten by (who else?) Stephen Davis, Perry claims that the riff to *Rocks'* cataclysmic opening track, "Back in the Saddle," was written while he was high on heroin. Apparently, Perry and Tyler, the so-called Toxic Twins, were using horse throughout the *Rocks* sessions, along with cocaine, alcohol, and whatever else was thrust into their faces. In *Walk This Way,* Perry says he "started studying the folklore of opium as a sacrament and really got into it. It helped me concentrate on my work and became a good writing tool for me at the time . . . before it turned into this fucking monster."

Drugs indeed "turned into this fucking monster" for Aerosmith by the time of 1977's *Draw the Line,* which was recorded at a renovated convent located on a hundred acres in a remote part of upstate New York. Dubbed the Cenacle, this clandestine getaway was ideal for a band with an appetite for destruction—the members of Aerosmith drove and crashed expensive sports cars on the secluded grounds, fired guns in the attic, and ingested a small fortune in chemicals. Whereas on *Rocks* Perry had regarded opioids as a "sacrament," by the time of *Draw the Line* he was no longer capable of being creative or even functional while under the influence.

A story related by Aerosmith guitarist Brad Whitford in *Walk This Way* is indicative of Perry's state of mind at the time: When Perry was asked to record a slide-guitar part for *Draw the Line*'s title track, he couldn't keep it together, and after ten minutes he staggered to the bathroom "and puked his guts out," Whitford says. "Then he came back, played for an hour, went back to his room, and we didn't see him for five days." In the end, Aerosmith spent half a million dollars on an album that signaled the end of its glory years.

By the early eighties, Aerosmith was limping along in a haze of addiction with a fraction of its audience. Aerosmith even released an album, 1982's *Rock in a Hard Place*, without Perry, the soul of the band. At that point, the old Aerosmith died. The new Aerosmith, whose sales figures in the late eighties and beyond would dwarf the band's success in its wayward prime, reemerged with Perry back in the fold and a completely different mythology.

Now Aerosmith was celebrated for overcoming its decadent past and living the "right" way, a dominant narrative for reformed rock stars in the eighties. Bowie, Townshend, Jagger, Keith Richards—the biggest libertines of the sixties and seventies professed to be living clean and sober at this time. Even Lou Reed, the writer of "Heroin," was a spokesman for the eighties-era sobriety campaign Rock Against Drugs.

But the greatest rehab story of all was Aerosmith. A 1990 *Rolling Stone* profile sums up the band's media-friendly comeback story: "Aerosmith is that rarest of creatures—a rock band that's hitting its creative and commercial peak twenty years into its career," journalist David Wild writes in a profile titled "The Band That Wouldn't Die." "Our story is basically that we had it all, and then we pissed it all away," Tyler tells Wild, who contrasts the band's former party-hearty lifestyle with the "new and improved, clean and sober, happily married Aerosmith," an ideal morality tale for the "Just Say No" Reagan-Bush years.

The "rehab as magical career rejuvenator" story line took an absurd turn during sessions for 1993's *Get a Grip,* when four out of five band members were sent away for treatment—even though none of them were currently using drugs. The idea was to "recharge," which the band's management felt was necessary given that Aerosmith had been working for several months and hadn't yet come up with a surefire hit song. If rehab had worked for *Permanent Vacation* and *Pump*, perhaps it would also work to fix *Get a Grip*. "The disease is back. The new addiction is money," bassist Tom Hamilton recalls Aerosmith's manager saying in *Walk This Way*.

What saved *Get a Grip* wasn't rehab, however, but rather the other big secret to Aerosmith's late-career success: outside songwriters. Getting clean was one thing, but using well-known fixers like Desmond Child (who cowrote "Dude (Looks Like a Lady)" and Diane Warren (who wrote all of 1998's "I Don't Want to Miss a Thing," Aerosmith's only No. 1 hit) was a topic that the members of Aerosmith did not care to discuss publicly. But the band's resolve to write songs without input from proven hit makers grew weaker after they signed a deal with Sony in 1991 worth $30 million, the most tangible spoils of their hard-won sobriety.

To justify that kind of payoff, Aerosmith had to move even further away from the drugged-out seediness of its past. Instead, Aerosmith produced three country-tinged power ballads for *Get a Grip* that sounded virtually identical: "Cryin'" (written with Nashville songwriter/producer Taylor Rhodes), "Crazy" (with Child), and "Amazing" (with Richie Supa, who later worked with Pink and Richie Sambora). The songs were promoted with a popular trilogy of music videos on MTV starring Alicia Silverstone (and occasionally Tyler's daughter Liv), about a young girl's dalliances with BASE jumping and lap dancing and Stephen Dorff. *Get a Grip* went on to sell seven million copies.

Aerosmith might've quit narcotics, but they never stopped with excess. Instead of doing too many drugs, they overdosed instead on rehab in the nineties. But it paid off—not only did the members survive, but they expanded their audience by playing their current "good" image off of their discarded "bad" image. When decadence no longer had cachet, Aerosmith pivoted and thrived with a "clean" version of decadence in which money was the most powerful vice. As the biggest recovery addicts of all time, Aerosmith cooked sobriety on a spoon and injected it into their veins.

"The Hero Is Corrupted . . ."

"Mr. Crowley"

NOTES ON TRACK 10: From our misguided Satanic phase. We hoped that Satan would do for us what he did for Robert Johnson. Instead, we were depicted in an unfavorable light in *The Decline of Western Civilization Part II: The Metal Years*.

Any discussion regarding mystical rationalizations for bad behavior in rock 'n' roll would be incomplete without Aleister Crowley, the most diabolical part-time mountaineer in the history of evil and an eternally corrupt influence on some of the biggest rock stars ever.

It's tempting to declare Crowley the world's first rock star, if only "rock star" were adequate to sum up Crowley's frankly insane life. Crowley referred to himself as "the great beast"; the press dubbed him "the wickedest man in the world"; in rock-star terms, he was like GG Allin, if more than three hundred people had ever cared about GG Allin. During Crowley's lifetime—which somehow lasted seventy-two years, from the late nineteenth century to just after World War II—he was known as a writer, painter, magician, and occultist. He was a seeker who constantly sought out new and unusual experiences—the more taboo, the better.

And then he wrote prolifically about what he did, filling dozens of books with vulgar and contrarian screeds that were unapologetically sexist, racist, and generally antihuman. But Crowley was also a nonconformist who galvanized other nonconformists, professing his belief that the only way for man to achieve his full potential was to live without moral or ethical constraints. Naturally, this way of life appealed to the long-haired hedonists who took over the music world twenty years after he died.

After a spiritual quest to Egypt in 1904, Crowley founded his own religion, which he called Thelema. He claimed that a demon spirit called Aiwass dictated to him *The Book of Law*, the bible of Thelema. In accordance with the dream logic that guided his life, inventing his own religion after meeting a demon was no big deal for Crowley. The rest of us might consider a life-changing encounter with the supernatural to be extraordinary, but for Crowley it was merely another Tuesday.

The cornerstone of Thelema is the pursuit of one's True Will, which Crowley believed was an individual's higher calling in life. True Will is not something you can consciously discover, Crowley argued, but rather it must be revealed by eliminating all of the baggage—including psychological hang-ups, petty earthly conflicts, and conventional morality—that keeps individuals from communing with the universe. Only once those things have been set aside can a person realize the infinite power of the divine.

Crowley's method of realizing his own True Will was living a life of unchecked decadence. As biographer Gary Lachman notes in *Aleister Crowley: Magick, Rock and Roll, and the Wickedest Man in the World:*

> Crowley had to have a lot of sex and it had to be wild; the women he had it with had to be seething with "forbidden lust" of the kind associated with the Marquis de Sade or the poet Baudelaire, and the men he had it with had to humiliate him and bend him to their will. He had to have a lot of drugs; famously, by the end of his life, he

was taking enough heroin to kill a room full of nonusers. He had to have a lot of drink; he was known to hold an eye-watering amount of alcohol. And he had to have a lot of experiences. Crowley's life was one long hunt for "experiences."

Years before Jim Morrison was demanding blow jobs in recording booths for the good of his art—and not merely because he enjoyed blow jobs—Crowley lived in the gutter because he believed it was a "higher" form of existence. At least that was his ideology. Scholars have subsequently debated whether Crowley truly believed any of his BS.

Lachman offers his own withering assessment, writing that Crowley was a "selfish" and "insensitive" man who "lacked imagination" and "suffered from a kind of autism." Crowley's self-importance derived from the belief that his behavior was an affront to mainstream moralists. Like so many rock stars after him, he needed people to be offended by what he was doing in order for his behavior to have any greater meaning. Without disapproving conservatives, his supposed religious code would have collapsed in on itself.

Coincidentally, before he became known as an occult expert, Lachman was a founding member of the seminal new-wave band Blondie, and was subsequently inducted in the Rock and Roll Hall of Fame. Lachman came of age in the sixties, when Crowley was reborn as a hip avatar of the era's free-love ethos. Both the Beatles and the Rolling Stones dabbled in Crowley esoterica— Crowley showed up on the cover of *Sgt. Pepper*, and his sensibility informed the Stones' classic late sixties and early seventies period, which kicked off with the devilish anthems "Jumpin' Jack Flash" and "Sympathy for the Devil." (Crowley's most-quoted maxim, "Do what thou wilt," would've worked as alternate title for *Sticky Fingers*.)

A few years later, Crowley's name appeared in the first line of David Bowie's "Quicksand," from 1971's *Hunky Dory* ("I'm closer to the Golden Dawn / Immersed in Crowley's uniform / Of imagery"—Golden Dawn was an occult organization that Crowley infiltrated at the turn of the twentieth century). Later, when Bowie was in the midst of his coked-out midseventies L.A. period, Crowley became the worst kind of role model, provoking an interest in black magic that drove the Thin White Duke to extreme behavior. As a hobby, Bowie's black-magic dalliance went from "casual" to "insane" to "storing bottles of his own urine in the refrigerator" to "exorcising his backyard pool because the magic powder exploding inside of his nostrils told him it was haunted." Fortunately, Bowie eventually escaped L.A. and absconded to Berlin with Iggy Pop and Brian Eno, channeling his demons into making synthesizers sound like extraterrestrial farts on classic albums like *Low* and *"Heroes."*

No rock star was as publicly devoted to Crowley as Jimmy Page. When Page bought Crowley's infamous Boleskine House on Loch Ness in the Scottish Highlands, it was assumed that he was communicating with the damned in order to write *Houses of the Holy* deep cuts. How else was Led Zeppelin able to poorly mimic a reggae shuffle on "D'Yer Mak'er" and still have it come out sounding awesome? Robert Plant was a great front man, but Jimmy's true copilot had to be Satan.

"I feel Aleister Crowley is a misunderstood genius of the 20th century," Page said in 1978. "Because his whole thing was liberation of the person, of the entity, and that restrictions would foul you up, lead to frustration which leads to violence, crime, mental breakdown, depending on what sort of makeup you have underneath. The further this age we're in now gets into technology and alienation, a lot of the points he's made seem to manifest themselves all down the line."

People in the seventies were more forgiving of pro-Crowley talk, similar to how rock stars at that time were more brazen about hanging out with underage groupies. (Jimmy Page was into that form of black magic as well.) Later in his life, Page was conditioned to keep quiet about his adherence to Crowley-style mysticism. When Page was profiled for *GQ* in 2014, he shut down the interview after writer Chuck Klosterman asked whether his interest in the occult was "authentic." Page might've already been perturbed by the previous question, which concerned whether Page's half-decent 1993 album with David Coverdale "was an attempt to annoy Robert Plant." I'm going to assume the answer to both questions is yes.

No matter Aleister Crowley's renown in the underground rock world of the sixties and seventies, his name didn't become familiar to millions of middle-American stoners until 1981, when Ozzy Osbourne included the sorta-tribute "Mr. Crowley" on his multiplatinum solo debut, *Blizzard of Ozz*.

"Mr. Crowley" is notable in Ozzy's canon for two reasons:

1. **It was the first and last time that Ozzy used the word "polemically" in a song.**
2. **"Mr. Crowley" seemed to imply that Ozzy was into worshipping Satan.**

"Mr. Crowley" wasn't really pro–Satan worship, insisted Bob Daisley, Ozzy's longtime bassist and the song's lyricist. "It was about standing back and looking at someone like Aleister Crowley and saying, 'What sort of life is that?'" Daisley said in 2002. That might very well be true—in the song's lyrics, Daisley concludes that Crowley's life "seemed so tragic" and suggests that he was a charlatan. But it's probably not a mistake "Mr. Crowley" was so widely misread, as it's vague enough to welcome differing interpretations. My favorite lyric in "Mr. Crowley" is, "Mr. Crowley, won't you ride my white horse? / Mr. Crowley, it's symbolic, of course." Daisley wanted to make it clear that he was making *a symbolic* allusion to one of the steeds driven by the Four Horsemen of the Apocalypse in the Book of Revelation, not an *actual* steed that Ozzy would've surely been too intoxicated to mount in the early eighties. The anti-Satan-worship stance ultimately taken by Ozzy (and Daisley) in "Mr. Crowley" is reasonable, but also uninteresting; keeping the true allegiances of "Mr. Crowley" a little fuzzy allowed Ozzy to troll God-fearing parents without putting his soul at risk for eternal damnation.

I can't say if "Mr. Crowley" sounded menacing in '81, but it's the opposite of menacing now. The instrumental fanfare that opens the song—a schlocky church organ riff that emits "spooky" synth swooshes ripped off from the *Halloween* soundtrack—is as terrifying as plastic vampire teeth. Nevertheless, fearing Ozzy Osbourne was customary for middle Americans also dreading the onset of phony Satanism in every other corner of eighties suburbia, from Dungeons and Dragons to the Eagles' "Hotel California" to supposedly pro-Lucifer messages imprinted on Styx (!) and Electric Light Orchestra (!!) records. "Mr. Crowley" fed into that fear.

But Ozzy Osbourne wasn't an actual Satanist—he wasn't even a spiritual-minded hedonist in search of True Will. He was just a guy who loved to get fucked up for the sake of getting fucked up. Ozzy's True Will was blotto.

My favorite Black Sabbath album, 1972's *Vol. 4*, ranks with Bowie's *Station to Station* as one of the greatest cocaine albums in rock history. Black Sabbath bassist Geezer Butler estimates that the band spent $75,000 on blow in '72—that's fifteen grand more than the cost of recording *Vol. 4*. It's no wonder Black Sabbath originally wanted to call the album *Snowblind*.

"We were all fucked up bad," Osbourne told biographer Mick Wall. "Dealers coming round every day with cocaine, fucking Demerol, morphine—everything coming round the fucking house." Osbourne also tried LSD for the first time during the *Vol. 4* sessions, which took place in an L.A. mansion rented from millionaire philanthropist John du Pont. (If you've seen the 2014 movie *Foxcatcher*, du Pont is the murderous pseudo–wrestling coach played by Steve Carell.) Ozzy soon took to swallowing handfuls of acid tabs on the regular, though he was the opposite of a chill acidhead. Once, the band visited the beach after dosing, and Ozzy wound up swimming in the sand rather than the ocean.

By the time Ozzy was fired from Sabbath in 1979, he was viewed by his bandmates as a slobbering buffoon who couldn't be relied upon, even given the band's lax "slobbering buffoon" standards. (According to Wall's *Symptom of the Universe,* the final straw came when the band discovered Ozzy passed out in the studio, sleeping in a pool of his own piss.) Black Sabbath replaced Ozzy with the diminutive Ronnie James Dio, who actually looked like Satan, if Queens were a borough of Hades. Dio later pioneered the iconic "devil horns" hand sign known to metalheads everywhere, a fact that Dio pointed out in pretty much every interview he ever conducted until his death in 2010.

Incredibly, Osbourne went from being fired from Black Sabbath for being a pee-stained screw-up, to the most enduring superstar in the history of metal. And this was due almost entirely to his underrated sense of professionalism—or, rather, the professionalism of his wife and manager, Sharon Osbourne. From the eighties onward, Ozzy Osbourne always found a way to adapt to whatever the changing times demanded of him.

On early solo albums like *Blizzard of Ozz* and 1981's *Diary of a Madman,* Ozzy dabbled in cartoon devil worship over the neo-classical guitar wizardry of Randy Rhoads. It was like Van Halen for guys who hated seeing girls at Van Halen concerts. Ozzy even dyed his hair that David Lee Roth shade of blond, but he otherwise kept himself ugly for street-cred purposes.

When I became familiar with him in the nineties, Osbourne had entered his "mature" phase with 1991's *No More Tears,* an album released one month after Metallica's *Black Album* and one week before Nirvana's *Nevermind,* and aligned musically and philosophically between those poles. The big hit from *No More Tears* was the power ballad "Mama, I'm Coming Home," a song I'll always associate with my high school buddy Marc, who tearfully jammed on "Mama" in his pickup the night his girlfriend

Alana dumped him. Try doing that to "Nothing Else Matters" or "Something in the Way"—those tracks just don't work for post-breakup wallowing like "Mama, I'm Coming Home" does.

Again, Ozzy made himself useful, this time as rock's unlikeliest elder statesman. At a time when every other remnant of eighties metal was being swept into the dustbin of history, Osbourne scored one of his bestselling albums because he convinced people that he was a more distinguished version of Alice in Chains.

Flash forward another ten years, and Ozzy had pivoted to another new guise. Ozzy was now the imbecilic patriarch of *The Osbournes*—perpetually confused, mentally compromised, and shaking with apparent post-addiction tremors, the Prince of Darkness was reduced to calling out for Sharon like a helpless child stranded in a high chair whenever he couldn't work the remote control.

This version of Ozzy was born many years earlier, in Penelope Spheeris's monumental 1988 documentary *The Decline of Western Civilization Part II: The Metal Years*, in which Ozzy is interviewed in his bathrobe as he makes breakfast. In the film, Ozzy looks a little like Bette Midler after twelve hours of Jägermeister consumption—his hair has been cropped into a spiky porcupine helmet, which covers a haggard dome done up in light makeup. At one point, Spheeris includes an insert of Ozzy attempting to pour orange juice in a glass and mostly splashing liquid on the kitchen counter. But for the most part, Ozzy is funny and smart in *The Decline of Western Civilization Part II*—a proud survivor comfortable in his own skin as a self-aware cautionary tale.

On *The Osbournes*, this self-awareness curdled into Ozzy's making himself the semiwitting butt of the joke. *The Osbournes* played like a potty-mouthed PSA: *this* is what happens in the aftermath of abusing cocaine, fucking Demerol, morphine, and everything else back in the seventies. Everything that had once been sexy and dangerous (but in a good way) about rock 'n' roll was now viewed as simply destructive and sort of funny. Ozzy Osbourne allowed himself to be cast as the ultimate rock 'n' roll casualty because, as a show business lifer, he must have known that debasement was what the job now required.

Perhaps Ozzy's old enemies in Satan-fearing suburbia viewed this as the man's bill finally coming due, an earthly humiliation acting as mere prelude to the endless punishment that awaited him down below for the crime of selling his soul. But, against all odds, Ozzy has kept on spinning his career forward.

Ozzy even got back together with Black Sabbath—first in 1997 for a co-headlining spot at Ozzfest with Ozzy's solo band, and then sporadically over the next twenty years. This time, Ozzy was clearly the man in charge—his old partner and onetime nemesis, guitarist Tony Iommi, had toiled fruitlessly for years under the Black Sabbath name with a series of post-Dio front men—Ian Gillan, Glenn Hughes, Tony Martin—who only made Ozzy seem irreplaceable. In 2013, the original lineup of Black Sabbath (minus poor Bill Ward, the band's drummer and preferred target for practical jokes and general emotional abuse) released a decent reunion album, *13*, featuring a gently trolling single, "God Is Dead?," for the scattered religious fundamentalists still bothering to pay attention.

When I saw my first Black Sabbath concert in January 2016, I presumed it would also be my last, and not just because it was part of the band's The End tour. The men of Sabbath had lived long enough to contend with the same old-age stuff that normal people deal with. In 2012, Iommi was diagnosed with lymphoma, and Sabbath was forced to arrange tour dates around his cancer treatment, finally deciding that Iommi's health necessitated this being the final Black Sabbath tour.

At Black Sabbath shows in the seventies, Osbourne was known to scream at the audience, *"Are you high?! Well, so am I!"* But when I finally had my chance to see Sabbath, I went out of my way to *not* be high. I didn't want to miss the band. Saying you're at a Black Sabbath show for the songs and musicianship sounds like a variation on the old joke about reading *Playboy* for the articles. But that was honestly the case for me. Shortly after I entered the arena, I could hear the band revving up to the opening strains of "Black Sabbath," and I cursed the people in front of me in the beer line for ordering umpteen cocktails. Ordering cocktails at an arena show is like requesting beluga caviar at a baseball game. Beer, wine, or get out—that should be the rule.

By the time I finally shuffled to my seat, Sabbath had commenced the second song of the night, "Fairies Wear Boots," from *Paranoid*. I was sitting on Geezer Butler's side of the stage, and I quickly realized that I had never contemplated the dexterity of Butler's playing. But the man was a beast—I say that as a person who's only passingly familiar with both beasts and the mechanics of bass players. But whatever Geezer was doing, it certainly *seemed* impressive.

Of course, only other bass players go to Black Sabbath concerts to stare at Geezer Butler. The main attractions are Ozzy and Iommi, the dark underbelly of the singer-guitarist dynamic typified by Mick & Keith and Plant & Page. Iommi bullied Ozzy as a kid, and then bullied him some more once they reconnected—not as *grown-ups*, just when they were older—during Sabbath's prime back in the seventies. But then the power balance shifted once Ozzy's fame as a solo artist eclipsed that of the band that had fired him. Now the value of the brand depended largely on whether revisiting Sabbath was convenient or advantageous for Ozzy.

Onstage together that night, however, Ozzy and Iommi were equals. Sabbath couldn't be Sabbath without both of them—no disrespect to Dio, who is eternally flashing the devil horns in heaven. After so many years of peak decadence, Ozzy and Iommi's True Will was playing these fantastically sinister songs together. So they carried each other: Ozzy's gregariousness emboldened Iommi to move his slight frame with extra oomph, and the monstrous riffs careening with impossible loudness from Iommi's Gibson SG seemed to shrink the size of Ozzy's gut.

Black Sabbath's ability to endure while also projecting fragility suited them. Finally, you couldn't take these guys for granted. Back when Sabbath was at full strength in the seventies, they never got any respect. "Like Cream, but worse!" was Lester Bangs's assessment, and he was more inclined than most rock critics to appreciate Black Sabbath. The first edition of *The Rolling Stone Record Guide* grants one star out of five to each of Sabbath's classic Ozzy-era LPs—with the exception of *Paranoid,* which received two stars. "The would-be English Kings of Heavy Metal are eternally foiled by their stupidity and intractability," reads Sabbath's brief blurb. "Time has passed them by." I could tell you the name of the critic who wrote that, but you wouldn't know him. Black Sabbath, meanwhile, is a name that still means something in the new century.

What offended the first wave of rock critics was that Black Sabbath seemed to have no political consciousness. Sabbath was among the bands blamed for reducing the utopian idealism of the sixties down to mindless parking-lot hedonism. Even Aleister Crowley had an ethos—the kids who toked up to "Sweet Leaf" didn't seem to believe in anything.

That this criticism of Sabbath ignores "War Pigs"—surely one of the three or four greatest antiwar songs in rock history—is beside the point. Black Sabbath *did* have a political consciousness, but that's not what makes it great or important. Black Sabbath is great precisely because it transcends transient stuff such as politics. *Vol. 4* will never be tied to a particular year or ideology or set of passing trends. You put it on and it just sounds like rock 'n' roll. And to me, rock 'n' roll has always been the clearest path to a higher power. Sex and drugs are amazing, but they'll only get you so far. Sex and drugs signify something else to me now than they did when I was nineteen. But *Vol. 4* feels *exactly* the same.

I can put on *Vol. 4* this very instant and know that its hyper-driven bluesy sludge sounds as thick and menacing and eternal as it did when I was a teenager. And I'm sure it sounds that way to people who are teenagers now. Being a teenager today isn't all that different from being a teenager in 1972, or a teenager back when

Aleister Crowley first started fantasizing about filth in the 1890s. Decadence will always be irresistible to young people, because decadence is sexy and fun, and also because doing what you want is the most visceral way to live. But once you're older, and the buzz of sin wears off, the pursuit of being alive starts to matter more than the prizes you spend most of your life chasing. You see that you're on the same road as your ancestors, and your offspring are following you. And the closer you get to the icons who put you on this path, the more vulnerable they seem. But at least they have each other to lean on.

"So Bad"

NOTES ON TRACK 11: This one comes from one of our lowest periods. But we think it's underrated. What some might describe as "bad" we would rather classify as "alt-good."

n 2016, I was walking into an arena in downtown Minneapolis to see Paul McCartney on his One on One tour, and it was taking a superlong time because the man in front of me in line was walking very slowly. The man was so slow that I could feel the people behind me brush against my back. He was so slow that I could imagine myself missing the concert, even though it wasn't scheduled to start for another half hour (and wouldn't actually begin for another ninety minutes). He was so slow I could envision dying in this line as Paul bid adieu after playing "Hey Jude." I was only behind this guy for about twenty seconds, but in that time I managed to perform my entire repertoire of impatient-asshole line behavior: I sighed, I swore, I stared at my nonexistent watch, and I burned a gaping invisible wound in this man's skull.

Then I looked down and noticed that the man only had one leg.

I quickly surmised that he lost the leg because either (1) he was in a war, or (2) he was very, very old, and when you get very, very old, sometimes parts just fall off of your body. Either way, it looks like I'll be spending an eternity in hell for my sins. And my hell will entail being stuck in line behind this man for at least one million years.

As someone who attends a lot of classic-rock concerts, I'm used to sitting among audiences who are, shall we say, *advanced* in age. I suspect most classic rockers are self-aware about being entertainment for codgers. My favorite parts of Donald Fagen's awesomely cranky 2013 memoir, *Eminent Hipsters*, are whenever he makes a bitter joke about how old Steely Dan's audience is. "So this, now, is what I do: assisted living," he writes. Later in the book, Fagen semi-ironically wishes that he could set his fans on fire. The man is a prince.

Euphemisms don't do the audience for that McCartney concert justice—these people were ancient. McCartney was just a few months shy of his seventy-fourth birthday when I saw him, so he was no kid, either. But McCartney is a billionaire rock star who surely has access to highly secret, extremely dangerous but apparently effective antiaging remedies. McCartney has been playing stadiums since 1965, as long as any rock star ever. He's older than most stadiums. Macca needs constant upkeep. I bet he's been injecting unicorn blood on a weekly basis since the late nineties so he can convincingly perform "Helter Skelter."

When McCartney finally came out shortly before nine P.M., the grandmothers all screamed as Paul and his impeccable backing band—rounded out by four relatively boyish forty- and fiftysomethings—launched into "A Hard Day's Night." A few songs later, "Can't Buy Me Love" elicited a similarly rapturous response. From there a pattern was established for the rest of the night: The early moptop-era Beatles hits got the best reactions, whereas the response to anything released after 1966 typically ranged from mild enthusiasm to bemused confusion.

For many of the people in my immediate vicinity, it was clear that the Beatles (to say nothing of McCartney's solo career) ceased to be a going concern once the Summer of Love commenced. Anything in the set list that was even mildly psychedelic—"The Fool on the Hill," "Being for the Benefit of Mr. Kite"—went over like Timothy Leary at the 1968 Republican National Convention. Apparently, there are still people for whom *Sgt. Pepper* is a radical—perhaps *too* radical—musical experiment. This wasn't a classic-rock-radio crowd, it was an oldies-radio crowd.

I, too, was hoping to hear my favorite Beatles hits. But I also secretly wished that McCartney would play "Temporary Secretary," one of the battiest tracks from one of his battiest solo albums, 1980's *McCartney II*. I believe that "Temporary Secretary" is a legitimately great song, even if it is totally bonkers. "Temporary Secretary" sounds like a businessman discussing his staffing practices while also imitating a car alarm. It's genius! But the main reason I wanted to hear "Temporary Secretary" is because I knew that it would confound all of the boomers in the house who stopped following Paul McCartney's career after he wrote "Michelle."

Apparently, Paul McCartney and I were on the same wavelength that night, because five songs into the set, he played a number that only a small, demented fraction of the audience wanted to hear. And yet there he was, jamming on "Temporary Secretary," seemingly oblivious to the mass confusion created by the song's mind-bending mess of synth bleeps and slashing acoustic guitar and McCartney's robo-ranting about needing a woman who can be a belly dancer but not a true romancer. I loved it, and I loved how the people around me *didn't* love it.

I'm guessing that other McCartney fans under the age of forty at that show reacted similarly. Like a lot of McCartney's solo work, *McCartney II* is beloved by McCartney fans who were raised on indie rock, and ignored by McCartney fans who were raised on McCartney's songs with the Beatles. This dynamic is common among different generations of classic-rock listeners—albums by sixties greats that were released and ignored by boomers in the seventies and eighties tend to be most ripe for rediscovery by Gen Xers and millennials later on. But this phenomenon is most pronounced for McCartney lovers.

The experience of discovering an artist after he's built a body of work is much different than following an artist as that work is created in real time. For people who grew up with McCartney, it's the hits that matter, because those are the songs that soundtracked your life. But if you come to an artist later, after all that music was released and initially assessed, the perspective often skews away from hits, which seem overfamiliar, and toward the lesser-heralded gems, which are fresher. Sometimes, latecomers even embrace albums that were widely considered to be bad. This is the lane in which an LP like *McCartney II* resides.

As is the case with all of *McCartney II*, "Temporary Secretary" was recorded entirely by McCartney himself in 1979, during a period in which he was losing interest in his highly successful post-Beatles band, Wings, and instead dabbling in synthesizers and listening to the era's new-wave music, particularly Talking Heads. The first song to come out of these sessions was the infamous holiday tune "Wonderful Christmastime," in which McCartney repeats the chorus about Christmas and how wonderful it is approximately four thousand times over the course of three minutes and forty-five seconds. Like "Temporary Secretary," "Wonderful Christmastime" sounds like it was somehow recorded *before* it was written. Depending on your point of view, this is what makes "Temporary Secretary" and "Wonderful Christmastime" either delightful or dreadful.

McCartney II was an international hit in the summer of 1980, and the album's most Talking Heads–like song, "Coming Up," did well on the pop charts in the U.S. and UK. But among contemporary music critics, *McCartney II* was considered an artistic disappointment. *Rolling Stone* deemed it "strident electronic junk music" composed of "aural doodles designed for the amusement of very young children," which sums up the critical reaction not only to *McCartney II,* but to most of McCartney's post-Beatles work at the time.

In the seventies, McCartney took the worst beating of any ex-Beatle from music critics, in part because it was assumed that McCartney would have the best and most successful solo career. But in the immediate aftermath of the Beatles, McCartney seemed the least sure of how to move forward. McCartney later admitted that he felt adrift, as though he had outlived his usefulness. He retreated with his family to a farm in Scotland and took to drinking whiskey out of the bottle every morning while still lying in bed.

On his first few solo records, McCartney favored a spontaneous, ragged, and semiamateurish approach that extended from his original ambitions for the Beatles' final album, *Let It Be,* which was supposed to present a "warts and all" depiction of the Beatles as a live band before Phil Spector was hired to lard the tracks with string sections and church choirs. On his own, McCartney went out of his way to downplay the mythology that came with being in the Beatles. Early albums like *McCartney, Ram, Wild Life,* and *Red Rose Speedway* are heavy on instrumental jams and lyrics so simple they verge on baby talk. Anyone inclined to argue that McCartney was a genius for writing "Eleanor Rigby" and "Penny Lane" now had to contend with the likes of "Kreen-Akrore" and "Bip Bop."

The consensus on McCartney in 1973 was that either his brain was rotted by marijuana (a view favored by Robert Christgau, among other critics) or he no longer had the will to be great. (Linda McCartney seemed to buy into that theory, classifying *Red Rose Speedway* as a "non-confident record.") McCartney finally redeemed himself critically and commercially that year when he released *Band on the Run,* and settled into a series of successful arena-rock albums like *Venus and Mars* and *Wings at the Speed of Sound.* From then on, McCartney regained his commercial mojo, making sure to chase occasional curveballs like *McCartney II* with a slam-dunk duet with Michael Jackson or Stevie Wonder.

But for people who discovered McCartney later on, it's those maligned, amateurish albums from the early seventies that have bolstered his retroactively hip reputation as a solo artist. For people accustomed to the slackness of indie rock, McCartney's solo LPs seem prescient. To that audience, *McCartney II* and *Ram* don't sound lazy, they sound like Pavement and Guided by Voices. This surprised no one more than McCartney himself. "A while ago, one of my nephews, Jay, said, '*Ram*'s my all-time favorite album.' I thought it was dead and gone, stinking over there in the dung pit," McCartney confessed to *Rolling Stone* in 2016.

McCartney II has similarly attained cult status among indie fans and artists who regard it as forward-thinking avant-electronica. But those people didn't hear *McCartney II* in the context in which it was released. The album came out four months after McCartney spent nine days in a Japanese jail for possession of 219 grams of weed while on tour with Wings. The band fell apart after the tour was canceled, prompting McCartney to release his solo recordings as *McCartney II*. It's not difficult to understand why McCartney was perceived at the time to be sort of dumb and perpetually stoned, and how this perception influenced the opinion that *McCartney II* was mere folly, rather than visionary genius.

I think the truth about *McCartney II* is somewhere in the middle. I love the album because the songs are good and weird and utterly unlike anything else in McCartney's catalog. But I also love it because the dumb/stoned aspects of the record are inextricable from the visionary-genius aspects. *McCartney II* is good because it's good, and good because it's bad.

When I was a writer for the AV Club, I attempted to explain a concept I called a good "bad" record, which is a record that you talk yourself into loving after you've grown tired of all the acknowledged masterpieces and respected second-tier releases in a legendary artist's discography.

Every hard-core record-head does this. It's the only way to

discover "new" music if you're into classic rock—you must dig into the albums that people tell you that you won't like, and you must listen to them many, many times until you find a way to like them. Because you will inevitably tire of *Pet Sounds,* and when that happens you will come around to *Love You* and marvel over the daffy synth sounds in "Johnny Carson," and speculate over whether Brian Wilson's state of mind makes this song an intentional classic or an act of unintentional "outsider art" brilliance. Over time, you might even convince yourself that *Love You* is better than *Pet Sounds*—but, really, it's just that liking *Love You* is more interesting, because music critics haven't told you how to feel about it for fifty years. *Love You* doesn't contain better music than *Pet Sounds,* but it does offer more in the way of discovery and surprises.

Here's how I defined a good "bad" record for the AV Club:

> It's a record where the creators are clearly not fully engaged with the project, which is reflected in the degraded quality of the songwriting and musicianship and an overall feeling of boredom, detachment, or extremely undisciplined self-indulgence that's palpable in the music. That makes it "bad." But instead of making the record less enjoyable, this "badness" actually makes the album more fascinating—so long as the artist in question is a genius—because it provides insight into what makes the artist's "great" records great, and demonstrates how functional he or she is even when operating on a lower level of artistry/sobriety.

The idea for good "bad" records stemmed from my love of the Rolling Stones album *Black and Blue,* which came out in 1976, between 1974's *It's Only Rock and Roll* (respected second-tier release) and 1978's *Some Girls* (acknowledged masterpiece). If you apply the standards normally associated with good music—cogent songwriting, competent musicianship, actively giving a shit about what you're doing—then *Black and Blue* can't be considered a good album. The Stones had just lost the most technically skilled guitarist they would ever have, Mick Taylor, and were about to hire the friendliest guitarist in Stones history, Ron Wood, to replace him. Between Taylor's departure and Wood's entrance, the Stones held cattle calls for a new guitarist, and they incorporated recordings from those auditions into *Black and Blue*. Only half of the songs on the album feature Wood—two other guys, Harvey Mandel and Wayne Perkins, play on the other half, which includes what are arguably the strongest tracks: "Hand of Fate" (the most underrated "great" song in the Stones' catalog), "Memory Motel" (which is slightly overrated but still good), and "Hot Stuff" (which is kind of great and kind of garbage).

The Stones themselves didn't even bother pretending that *Black and Blue* was something greater than it was. ("Rehearsing guitar players, that's what that one was about," Keith Richards confirmed later.) I knew this when I bought *Black and Blue*, but I didn't care, because after plowing through *Exile on Main St.* and *Sticky Fingers* and *Beggars Banquet,* I really wanted a new (old) Stones record.

This is the first phase of the good "bad" album experience: completism.

At first, I hated *Black and Blue*. Even now, I'd argue that the album's best-known song, "Fool to Cry," is the dullest track the Stones ever recorded. There's an old story—I don't know if it's true, but I've chosen to *believe* it's true—about how Keith Richards literally fell asleep onstage in Germany while playing "Fool to Cry" on the Stones' '76 tour. Perhaps you could blame that on heroin, but I prefer to credit Jagger's smarmy falsetto.

Over time, however, I realized that everything that made the text of *Black and Blue* subpar—Mick's boredom, Keith's addictions, the lack of fire and inspiration in the playing and songwriting— made the subtext of the record fascinating to me. Whereas *Sticky Fingers* presented everything I loved about the Stones in a sexy, indestructible package, *Black and Blue* illuminated the Stones' greatness by offering a contrasting example of this band I love at their worst. I liked how you could hear the Stones trying to find inspiration in the jammy, funk-drenched grooves and not finding it. In lieu of discovering greatness, they just kept plugging away, propelled forward by the perpetual motion of their past and whatever chemicals were within easy reach.

This is the second phase of the good "bad" album experience: grudging appreciation.

What's strange is that I can no longer relate to having a grudging appreciation of *Black and Blue*, because now I just straight-up love that record. The funk grooves are tasty. The ballads are wrenching. I'll even sit through "Fool to Cry." If the Stones put out a record like *Black and Blue* now, I would probably end up wildly overrating it and putting it in my top five favorite Stones albums ever. I don't know if *Black and Blue* was secretly great all along, or if it was a matter of my successfully talking myself into liking it. Either way, "Hand of Fate" slays.

I've repeated this process with virtually every major classic-rock artist and band that I love. I am now fully versed in the post-sixties work of the Kinks, even the double-album rock operas that go on for forty-two hours. I enjoy at least one Doors album, *An American Prayer*, that was completed and released seven years after Jim Morrison died. I will defend not only both Page & Plant albums, but also the Page & Coverdale record. I own albums by every iteration of Crosby, Stills, Nash and Young, and will argue that Crosby & Nash is in fact better than CSNY (though not CSN). I'm still not crazy about nineties Springsteen, but I will listen to *Human Touch* and *Lucky Town* when I don't feel like playing *Darkness on the Edge of Town* or *The River* for the ten thousandth time. Come to think of it, *Lucky Town* is in fact much better than most people (even myself) give it credit for.

Herein lies the third phase of the good "bad" album experience: brainwashing.

I am currently staring at a CD copy of *Earth,* **a live album that** Neil Young released in 2016 that augments concert recordings he made while on tour with the band Promise of the Real with live animal noises. For instance, on the song "My Country Home" (originally released on the great 1990 LP *Ragged Glory*), the familiar sound of Young's battered black Gibson rubs up against cawing crows and mooing cows. Young described *Earth* as an "ear movie" that allows you "to feel the difference of everything that's going on on the planet. There's really no judgment on it. It's just there."

At the moment, staring at the CD seems preferable to listening to it. Here is an album by an artist whose music I have loved for most of my life. And yet I'm procrastinating because even an eternally patient Neil Young fan has his limits, and mine might very well be a farmyard Neil Young record.

Maybe the problem is that *Earth* didn't come out thirty years ago. It's possible that thirty years from now, I will have enough space from *Earth* to appreciate it. That's basically what has happened for me in regard to Neil Young's eighties period, one of the most legendary good "bad" periods for any artist ever. This was the decade when Young was sued by the president of his own record company, David Geffen, for not making records that sounded like Neil Young records. Geffen had a point—in the eighties Neil Young flitted from one insane genre experiment to the next. He did intensely personal synth rock (1982's *Trans*), passive-aggressive rockabilly (1983's *Everybody's Rockin'*), anachronistic AM country (1985's *Old Ways*), and beer-commercial blues (1988's *This Note's for You*). Neil Young truly wasn't making Neil Young records; Neil Young in the eighties was like an even more insane version of Ween.

The eighties in general were a rough time for the stars of sixties and seventies rock. For aging artists who had defined their era by constantly innovating, the eighties represented the inevitable point when technology and fashion finally surpassed them.

Young's biggest rival for good badness in the eighties is Bob Dylan, whose quintessential bad eighties album, 1988's *Down in the Groove,* includes inexplicable cameos by Kip Winger, Steve Jones of the Sex Pistols, future *American Idol* judge Randy Jackson, and the producer of Ratt's *Out of the Cellar.* (Dylan later likened himself during this period to an "old actor fumbling in garbage cans outside the theater of past triumphs" in his 2004 memoir, *Chronicles.*) The conundrum for classic rockers in the eighties was that rock stars had never been *so old* before. Now we're conditioned to understand that a seventy-year-old man can stand onstage with a guitar in front of twenty thousand people without its being inherently ridiculous. In the eighties, however, people were still trying to wrap their heads around *forty-year-olds* being rock stars.

Classic rockers faced an impossible choice in the eighties: either service a changing pop marketplace (as Grace Slick did when she appeared with Starship on the *Mannequin* soundtrack) or cater to music critics and their constant craving for novelty (which might be why Joni Mitchell made a new-wave record in 1982). A few artists successfully evolved: Leonard Cohen remade himself into a sexy, gravel-voiced vampire on his synth-pop masterpiece *I'm Your Man,* while David Bowie capitalized on the music video format, which he revolutionized in the seventies, on *Let's Dance.* Meanwhile, classic soul stars fared a lot better than their ex-hippie counterparts: Marvin Gaye, Stevie Wonder, Tina Turner, and Aretha Franklin all recorded big hits in the eighties. When Young was fucking around with "Computer Cowboy (aka Syscrusher)," Gaye was instigating actual fucking with "Sexual Healing."

Neil Young somehow forged a third path that both alienated audiences and confounded critics. His most notorious eighties album, *Trans,* can be broadly described as an attempt to make a "modern" record centered on the sorts of synthetic sounds that were in vogue at the time. But that doesn't really do justice to how bizarre *Trans* is. In no way is it a pop record that was designed for mass consumption; it is a total novelty, but it is so outside what anyone would want or expect from Neil Young that it almost seems intentionally designed to be misunderstood by music critics.

At its core, *Trans* is so personal that it can probably only be understood fully by Young himself. The album's point of view— Young was inspired to distort his vocals electronically by his son, Ben, who was born with cerebral palsy and was unable to communicate—is a specific expression of Neil Young's circumstances with little accommodation made for listeners. This is what people say they want out of art—unfiltered and uncompromised personal expression—but music is rarely as unfiltered or uncompromised as it is on *Trans*.

In a way, it's probably not fair to describe *Trans* as a good "bad" record, because unlike the Stones when they made *Black and Blue*, I don't think Neil Young has ever *not* been fully engaged with a project. Sometimes he has fantastic ideas, and sometimes he has terrible ideas. But no matter the quality of his latest brainstorm, the level of commitment from ol' Neil is always the same—he's all in, no matter what. This is what revisionist critics tend to appreciate most about *Trans*—no matter what else can be said about it, *Trans* is a thoroughly honest and authentic expression of Young's headspace at the time he made it. "His voice is masked beyond recognition, but the pulse—steady and wild—is unmistakably his own," *Pitchfork* observed in a sympathetic reappraisal of *Trans* published thirty-five years after the record was largely panned by critics.

Neil Young's career was eventually revitalized in the nineties, when he was declared "the godfather of grunge," a title that seems more dated with each passing year. But he truly did make himself part of the contemporary rock scene in a way that no other rocker of his generation did. Even Bob Dylan, who made a major comeback with 1997's Grammy-winning *Time Out of Mind*, positioned himself outside of pop music, as a kind of laconic gunslinger figure. In the eighties, Dylan tried haplessly to sound modern. But on *Mind*, he collaborated with Daniel Lanois, the most heavy-handed producer of his career, who steeped Dylan's songs in reverb and film-noir foreboding, a deliberate invocation of an old-timey, sepia-tinged version of America that probably never existed. Neil Young, meanwhile, truly seemed like a nineties artist. He recorded with Pearl Jam, toured with Sonic Youth, and wrote a song about Kurt Cobain's death (after Cobain quoted "Hey Hey, My My" in his suicide note). Young's records were noisy and abrasive in a way that conformed to alt-rock norms. It's still one of his best eras.

In the aughts, Young continued to integrate himself in pop culture, though the results were more mixed—he wrote an awful song about 9/11, "Let's Roll"; he recorded a medium-awful album about the Bush administration, *Living with War;* he recorded a surprisingly not-awful album about the need for electric cars, *Fork in the Road.* With Lanois, he made *Le Noise,* which sounded like chillwave, the trendy-for-a-second indie-rock subgenre that aspired to the fidelity of worn-out VHS tapes. With Jack White, he made *A Letter Home,* a near-unlistenable collection of covers recorded in a sixty-five-year-old Voice-O-Graph vinyl recording booth.

I can find things to admire in all of these records from the 2000s, but "music" isn't one of them. The only Neil Young album I really like from this century is *Psychedelic Pill,* which is also the last album he's recorded this century with Crazy Horse, his reliably worn-in backing band from the old days. Otherwise, Young's ability to maintain immediacy is more admirable than, you know, *good.* But I'm willing to be persuaded.

With *Earth,* I might get there earlier than I expected. When I finally put the CD on, I'm surprised to find that I sort of dig the animal sounds. When the wild bees come out on "Seed Justice," they keep time at least as well as Ralph Molina. On "My Country Home," the crows bother me less than the congas. Even the title song from *The Monsanto Years*—the 2015 album I still haven't forced myself to play yet—won me over, despite the Auto-Tune on

Neil's voice and backing singers who sound like they're crooning a toothpaste commercial.

This gives me a surge of hope, because I feel like the badness of Young's other recent records just might become a salve for me, in a distant time when I'm hovering around retirement age and living in a world where new Neil Young albums no longer exist.

"Dog Eat Dog"

NOTES ON TRACK 12: This one features our new drummer. Our first drummer died. The new drummer replaced our third drummer, who's in prison for assaulting our second drummer. To be fair, our second drummer is an asshole, which is why we fired him and hired the guy who's now in prison.

Before classic rockers died of old age, they died *before* they got old. Or they quit their bands to start less successful solo careers, a fate worse than death if you happen to be David Lee Roth. Either way, a lack of sentimentality regarding changing membership has been required to keep many of the biggest bands in classic rock afloat. If someone goes down in your stadium-filling supergroup, you simply hire somebody else and keep moving forward. That's the classic-rock way, even when you lose your biggest star. And, as fans, we accept this, because the alternative requires giving up something we hold dear. It's just easier to believe that, no matter what, the show must go on.

It's kind of amazing how many classic-rock bands carried on successfully after the departure of a lead singer—Black Sabbath, Pink Floyd, Van Halen, Deep Purple, Genesis, Iron Maiden, and Journey are the most notable examples. Typically, these bands survived because the singer didn't have as much power in the band as the public assumed. Over time, it was revealed that the true leader was the bassist (Pink Floyd), the drummer (Genesis), or in most cases the guitarist.

No band transitioned more successfully after losing a lead singer than AC/DC. If you are even a casual listener of classic rock, you surely know the story: In the seventies, AC/DC's singer was Bon Scott, a denim-clad Scottish-born Australian who spent his youth getting thrown out of reform schools—not just because he was a bad seed, but also because he was doing research for future rock classics like "TNT" and "Dirty Deeds Done Dirt Cheap." One of the all-time rock 'n' roll tough guys, Scott was the rare SOB who could stride onstage without a shirt and appear dignified. Even when he sang about engorged testicles, Bon Scott projected undeniable gravitas.

In 1979, when AC/DC was riding high with what was then its bestselling LP, *Highway to Hell*, it would have been impossible to imagine the band without Scott. And yet, when Scott died in early 1980 at the age of thirty-three—he was found dead in his friend's car after a night of heavy drinking, seven months before John Bonham of Led Zeppelin died in similar fashion—AC/DC opted to move forward with barely a moment's thought. And that's because Scott didn't occupy the power center of AC/DC—the band's guitarists, Angus and Malcolm Young, did.

Angus and Malcolm were never conventional guitar heroes—they weren't flashy showboats who demonstrated awe-inspiring technical skill like Hendrix or Eddie Van Halen. They instead worked hard to *not* stand out, least of all from each other. Study AC/DC albums closely, and you'll notice that Angus plays lead and Malcolm plays rhythm. Perhaps you'll pick out a Gibson SG soloing over a chugging Gretsch Jet Firebird and a drum thud that's slightly behind the beat, along with lots of double entendres that are classified as single entendres in most Southern states. But AC/DC records aren't designed for close listening; they're meant to be heard in stadiums. And in those cavernous spaces, AC/DC sounds like an impenetrable monolith. AC/DC is towering, AC/DC is imposing, AC/DC will take you over, and you will never, ever break AC/DC down into component parts.

The Young brothers were single-minded about maintaining AC/DC's innate AC/DC-ness. Everything about this band has always been on brand—the sound of the guitar is codified, the subject matter of the lyrics is codified, even AC/DC's apparent lack of fashion is itself a fashion statement. The dress code of the band is strictly jeans and T-shirts, all the better to highlight Angus's schoolboy outfit.

What makes AC/DC unique in rock history is this disciplined uniformity. The band perfected its sound on its full-length debut, 1976's *High Voltage,* and then proceeded to make the same album over and over again for the next forty years. And this was deemed perfectly okay. AC/DC is like that corner dive bar that's been around forever even though the bartenders are ugly and the beer selection consists only of Budweiser, Miller Lite, and Michelob. Imagine if AC/DC had decided to record a power ballad in the eighties, or hired a rapper to drop rhymes over their rhythm section in the nineties, or enlisted Skrillex to give them an EDM makeover in the 2010s. It just seems . . . *wrong.* The Young brothers understood instinctively that people who love AC/DC don't want AC/DC to be revamped or modernized. They want AC/DC to be ugly and stocked with limited options.

This discipline helps to explain why AC/DC became an even bigger band once Bon Scott was replaced by Brian Johnson, who joined the band as it was recording *Back in Black,* which went on to sell about fifty million copies worldwide. While clearly inspired by Scott—and allegedly cowritten by him, if you believe the myth about the band drawing on Scott's journals for lyrics after his death—*Back in Black* signaled the sturdiness of the AC/DC machine against even the toughest of setbacks. That's not to marginalize the importance of Johnson, whose high-pitched squeal eased AC/DC in a slightly more metal direction just as metal was about to enter a period of unprecedented popularity.

But no matter his role on AC/DC's biggest record, Johnson was never made to feel 100 percent comfortable in the band.

Malcolm Young, in particular, held on to a modicum of skepticism about his "new" lead singer long after Johnson should've proven himself. Mick Wall's AC/DC biography, *AC/DC: Hell Ain't a Bad Place to Be,* recounts Malcolm's response to the suggestion that Johnson try out for AC/DC way back in 1980, which came from their producer, Robert John "Mutt" Lange. Johnson was known at the time as the singer for Geordie, a nondescript glitter-rock group, and Malcolm wasn't a fan. "He's a fucking big fat cunt," Malcolm supposedly said. "How we gonna have a big fat cunt singing for us?"

Later, when someone brought up the "Bon Scott wrote the lyrics for *Back in Black*" rumors in a 2010 interview, Malcolm didn't exactly throw his arms around Johnson. "I wish we had rehearsed the album with Bon," Malcolm admitted. "You can't compete with Bon's lyrics, he was born with this real talent for that."

I thought about Johnson's "big fat cunt" status in AC/DC when I saw the band perform on 2016's Rock or Bust tour. (By the way, I saw them on Valentine's Day, because the most romantic thing you can do on Valentine's Day is see an AC/DC concert by yourself.) Two things that might otherwise seem unclear about AC/DC become readily apparent once you see them live. One, there's been a long-standing debate among hard-rock fans about whether AC/DC is classic rock or heavy metal. People who know nothing about AC/DC tend to classify them as metal—this likely has something to do with the *Highway to Hell* LP, which is known for the devilish title track and the album-closing jam "Night Prowler," which supposedly inspired the Night Stalker serial killer, Richard Ramirez, to commit his crimes in the eighties. (For the record, "Night Prowler" is about sex, not murder. This is AC/DC we're talking about, not Slayer.) But when you see AC/DC live, it's obvious that this is a classic-rock band. A metal audience resembles the clothing rack at a head shop—it's a sea of black T-shirts emblazoned with band logos. AC/DC, in contrast, drew a strictly khaki-and-golf-shirt crowd. The arena audience looked like a sea of Men's Wearhouse managers.

The second thing that's confirmed about AC/DC when you see them live is that Angus Young is the front man, not Brian Johnson. This is already sort of obvious if you're familiar with AC/DC's album covers, which typically feature a sweaty, duck-walking Angus as a de facto band logo. But in concert, there's no mistaking anyone but Angus as the focal point. Yes, Brian Johnson struts on the platform jutting into the audience, while AC/DC's rhythm section rests in triangle formation at the rear of the stage. But he never struts quite as far as Angus Young. Sure, Brian Johnson squeals with tremendous volume. But Angus Young's Gibson SG is always turned up just a little bit louder. Of course, Johnson has a distinctive look onstage—black shirt, black jeans, black hat, curly brown hair, basically rock 'n' roll *Oliver!* But it's not as distinctive as Angus Young's. When I saw him, Angus's schoolboy outfit was leprechaun green, and it was drenched in sweat almost immediately. By the time Angus was afforded a lengthy guitar solo during "Let There Be Rock," most of the schoolboy suit had been stripped off, as is customary at AC/DC shows. Not only is Angus the leading man; he's also the sex object. Johnson is just the designated c-word.

Three weeks after I saw AC/DC in concert, Brian Johnson an-nounced that he had to quit the road for an indefinite period on the advice of his doctors, who had warned Johnson that he risked total hearing loss if he continued to tour. The band postponed ten concert dates and then, after barely a moment's thought, Angus Young decided to once again replace his lead singer. But he didn't go with an unknown this time. Instead, Young opted for the craziest option imaginable: the one and only W. Axl Rose.

It's impossible to overstate the initial weirdness of Axl joining AC/DC. It would be like walking into that proverbial corner dive bar—the one you love because it never changes—and seeing none other than Axl freaking Rose tending bar. How crazy would that be? Axl's the guy who's going to be pouring your drinks from now on!

Twenty sixteen turned out to be a big year for Axl. Not only did he join AC/DC, he also orchestrated a Guns N' Roses reunion tour with Slash and Duff McKagan. Before the tour, the smart money was on Axl royally fucking it all up. Thirty years of precedent *insisted* that he would fuck it up. When he broke his foot mere weeks before GNR's big unveiling at Coachella—and one month before he was due to join AC/DC's tour—cynics everywhere (including me) chortled. "This is Axl fucking it up! Now he will proceed to derail *two* rock bands."

But you know what? Axl didn't fuck it up. He performed in a leather chair at Coachella and sang like a man wringing every last ounce of spit and venom out of his middle-aged lungs. For the first time since *Appetite for Destruction,* Axl performed like he had something to prove, and he set about proving it. Amazingly, he pretty much pulled it off.

GNR's summer reunion tour garnered positive reviews across the board—*shockingly* positive. Axl sounded good and he was even *punctual.* (I finally saw GNR on the band's 2017 tour, and that dude was still singing his butt off. I couldn't believe what I was seeing.) As for AC/DC, the videos that trickled onto the web as the band commenced its European tour with Axl in tow were improbably persuasive. The first taste was a ninety-second clip of "Shoot to Thrill" from Lisbon, Axl's AC/DC debut. Axl looked a little old and a lot overweight, but he sounded more like Brian Johnson on *Back in Black* than Johnson himself had since around 1995. A video of "Highway to Hell" from Düsseldorf showed Rose equally capable of affecting Bon Scott's snarl over thousands of barking Germans.

As the tour progressed, and video after convincing video accumulated on YouTube, you could see Axl digging in and getting comfortable. He was now doing that stage move where he turns his body forty-five degrees to the left while extending his right arm in a balletic motion, like he's about to throw down in a Wachowski sisters movie. Axl was integrating his own style into the styles of AC/DC's other singers. Axl/DC might've defied all previously known laws of logic, but Axl was using the shit out of this illusion.

Actually, Axl/DC was indicative of late-stage classic rock's new reality, in which aging bands break down and then melt into one another. These are not "supergroups," in which the very best and most famous musicians of an era join together to create an overhyped musical Voltron. These modern melted-together bands—let's call them "shrunkgroups"—are merely composed of whoever is still alive. Whereas supergroups were by-products of a time when classic rock was flush with stars, shrunkgroups have become a necessity as those stars have aged and even died off, making hired guns increasingly important to keep bands (and brands) afloat. It's like the difference between *The A-Team* and *The Dirty Dozen*.

Among the strangest and most successful shrunkgroups is Dead and Company, an offshoot of the Grateful Dead that assembled Bob Weir, Bill Kreutzmann, and Mickey Hart with soft-rock balladeer John Mayer. Like all shrunkgroups, Dead and Company was a marriage of convenience. For the Grateful Dead, this was the latest iteration of the group post–Jerry Garcia. In 2015, the core four—Weir, Kreutzmann, Hart, and Phil Lesh, plus assistance from ringers like Phish's Trey Anastasio and former Dead sideman Bruce Hornsby—staged Fare Thee Well, a series of so-called farewell shows in Santa Clara and Chicago. But after those concerts made $52 million, it seemed unlikely that the Dead was over. Sure enough, Dead and Company was on the road in the fall, and by the following summer they were playing arenas and even stadiums, just like the Grateful Dead in the final years of Garcia's life.

For Mayer, joining Dead and Company was his path into the continuum of classic-rock history. This process began way back in 2010, when Mayer's career was nearly destroyed in the aftermath of a disastrous *Playboy* interview in which Mayer said the following directly into a reporter's tape recorder:

- "My dick is sort of like a white supremacist."
- "I could have fucked a lot more girls in my life if I hadn't been trying so hard to get them to like me."
- "When I'm fucking you, I'm trying to fuck every man who's ever fucked you, but in his ass."
- The N-word.

As if the fallout from that debacle wasn't bad enough, Mayer also faced the more mundane reality of being a white male pop-rock star at a time when rock was being eliminated from the pop world. "The music that was on the radio when I first came up in 2001 would never make it today. It was Norah Jones and Jack Johnson and Coldplay and me. It's just different now," Mayer confessed to *Rolling Stone* in 2013. He had to rebrand himself for the sake of his career, and decided to move on from pop and into perhaps the least fashion-conscious music scene there is—the jam-band world.

This shift officially commenced with his 2013 solo record *Paradise Valley,* which opens with a song called "Wildfire" that blatantly copies the snaky sound of Garcia's guitar. But Mayer truly tips his hand as an ersatz insta-hippie on the album cover—he wears a cowboy hat, poncho, and several jackets and vests. He looks like *Young Guns II* by way of the LP cover for Stevie Ray Vaughan's *In Step.*

On the support tour for *Paradise Valley,* Mayer dipped his toes into jammy waters, inviting the audience to join him on an odyssey of musical exploration between the requisite tunes about quarter-life crises and fathers respecting daughters. But Mayer was never really going to be accepted as a jam rocker without some character references, and who better than the godfathers of the scene, who just happened to need a guitar player?

While Anastasio was respectful of Garcia when he subbed at Fare Thee Well, he couldn't help but sound like himself. Mayer, however, was slavish in his adherence to Garcia's playing. He was eager to sublimate himself to the Dead myth, in the service of making people forget that Jerry was gone and they were actually listening to a man with a racist penis.

By the time Dead and Company reached Bonnaroo, Mayer had more or less perfected his Jerry impression, at least in terms of his guitar tone. These discussions *always* revolve around whether you can replicate Jerry's guitar tone. Mayer didn't have that fluttery quality that Jerry's playing had, where guitar lines flap like butterfly wings. But Mayer also didn't have Jerry's junk addiction. In a band where creativity wasn't a primary requirement, Mayer's consistency was the most desirable attribute.

The role of a shrunkgroup is to maintain the status quo for bands that still have high demand but diminished supply. The Grateful Dead's draw as a concert experience remains strong despite the band itself being significantly eroded. So Mayer was installed like drywall over cracked concrete. And, again, you had to marvel at how well it worked. The illusion dissipates whenever Mayer sings—John's mush-mouthed white-boy blues purr isn't even close to Jerry. But Mayer doesn't sing that much. Besides, this isn't about being the best. It's about being the best that's left.

There will always be purists who argue that these weird new configurations that have been constructed to satisfy the demands of the marketplace are somehow "illegitimate." I'm sympathetic to this point of view, but I feel like the matter has long since been settled. Way back in the late sixties, two of the biggest classic-rock brands ever, the Rolling Stones and Pink Floyd, proved that you could move on from the departure of a founding member (Brian Jones and Syd Barrett, respectively) and actually become more successful. At that point, "legitimacy" was rendered moot in classic rock.

Of course, there are limits. Rock nerds will always point to the bastardized version of the Velvet Underground led by guitarist Doug Yule, who carried on with original members Sterling Morrison and Moe Tucker for a few years after Lou Reed left the band in 1970. Nobody even remembers this incarnation of the

Velvet Underground, because the Velvet Underground without Lou Reed is such an obviously illegitimate proposition. But most of the time, it's not so black and white. For instance, if the Doug Yule situation had been reversed—meaning Lou Reed carried on with the Velvet Underground name after everybody else left— some hard-core fans would've balked but otherwise it would've been more acceptable. Lou was always the most essential part of the Velvet Underground brand.

Going into my AC/DC concert, I felt weird about seeing them without Malcolm Young, who was forced into retirement in 2014 after he was diagnosed with dementia. (Malcolm died in 2017.) If Malcolm Young isn't the greatest rhythm guitarist in rock history, he sits at the table with Reed and Keith Richards. Moreover, Malcolm was half of AC/DC's brain trust. Lead singers come and go but I didn't know if AC/DC would sound like AC/DC without Malcolm Young. Is a monolith that's cracked still a monolith?

(It should also be noted that drummer Phil Rudd wasn't with the band, either—he was forced to exit AC/DC in 2014 after he was arrested and charged with attempting to set up a murder and possession of meth and weed. Rudd still found time to play on *Rock or Bust*, but that album wasn't nearly as AC/DC-like as Rudd's private life.)

As the concert progressed, I felt steadily worse about Malcolm's absence, because AC/DC sounded *good,* and that didn't seem right. Angus Young was the only founding member left onstage, but it didn't matter one bit. Angus Young's nephew, Stevie, held down Malcolm's parts just fine. Frankly, I missed Rudd more—AC/DC's *Razor's Edge*–era drummer, Chris Slade, was filling in, and he was a little too talented and rehearsed to correctly replicate the rudimentary brilliance of Rudd's rhythms. Nevertheless, AC/DC still sounded like AC/DC despite barely being AC/DC.

Maybe I was looking at this the wrong way. Perhaps AC/DC's carrying on without Malcolm Young was the best possible testament to what Malcolm Young built. He created a machine so perfect that it no longer needed him.

"Keep on Loving You"

NOTES ON TRACK 13: Every band did a power ballad. Radio wouldn't play you otherwise. This was ours. Women loved this track. If the guys in the band were in better shape, we could have taken advantage of that, maybe.

Here's a valuable lesson I've learned from working as a music journalist for nearly twenty years: if given the choice between interviewing a hip, up-and-coming musician and interviewing a past-his-prime has-been, take the has-been every single time.

Some of my favorite interviews ever are with artists whose music I don't even like. I'm talking about the time that Poison guitarist C. C. DeVille told me about how he used to drink paint thinner when he ran out of booze. Or when Kip Winger told me he still hates Lars Ulrich for throwing a dart at a Winger poster in Metallica's "Nothing Else Matters" video. Has-beens have nothing to lose, whereas younger, hipper artists must think politically, as being candid can hurt you in the long run. But when you've already been around the block a few times and experienced all the definitive highs and definitive lows in your career, the statute of limitations on your crimes and misdemeanors has long since expired. Now you have the freedom to discuss all the dirt that's actually interesting.

Several years ago, a publicist asked if I wanted to talk to Tommy Shaw of Styx. Growing up in the Midwest in the nineties, I was exposed constantly to Styx's music on classic-rock radio, and I pretty much hated it. "Come Sail Away," "Too Much Time on My Hands," "Babe"—this was rock in its dorkiest, most white-bread form. ("Renegade" is a banger, though.) And yet I jumped at the chance to interview a member of Styx. I had burning questions for Mr. Tommy Shaw, and I had a feeling he would have no problem answering them.

Styx is part of what I call the "underclass" of classic rock that also includes Journey, REO Speedwagon, Kansas, Chicago, Boston, and Supertramp. These bands had their heyday in the seventies, and they either hailed from the Midwest or attracted a Midwesterner-heavy audience. Above all, they prided themselves on a "music first" ethos that superseded the identities of the band members. That's a kinder way of saying that these bands were utterly faceless and largely devoid of personality. Nevertheless, they are inescapable on classic-rock radio to this day.

For every song by Led Zeppelin, Bruce Springsteen, or the Who that WAPL played, I also heard Kansas's "Dust in the Wind," Supertramp's "Take the Long Way Home," Styx's "Renegade," and pretty much every cut from Boston's self-titled 1976 debut. In a way, those songs were invisible to me—they were the foundation upon which the iconic classic-rock bands stood, the stuff you tolerated in order to hear "Baba O'Riley" or "Born to Run." But over time the underclass's pomp-rock synth riffs were cataloged in my brain against my will, and I came to feel involuntary nostalgia for those bygone days when I gritted my teeth through WAPL's workmanlike progressive jams. I came to love how I sort of hated the dregs of classic-rock radio.

Back in the late seventies and early eighties, these underclass bands were dismissed by critics and hipsters of the time as "corporate rock," as they were promoted by major record labels that exploited the corruption of mainstream rock radio to fill the airwaves with power ballads played by out-of-shape white men with poofy hair at the expense of insurgent punk and new-wave acts. Corporate rock bands even adopted the iconography of actual corporations—instead of putting the band members' faces on their album covers, Chicago, Boston, Kansas, and Styx all had distinctive logos that became highly recognized brands.

Self-serious musicians often complain about how rock mythology overshadows the actual music. These are the same people who insist that Christopher Cross—the pudgy soft-rock balladeer who won three Grammys in 1981 for the deathless elevator-music standard "Sailing"—would still be a superstar today if not for the advent of MTV. But the corporate rock bands unintentionally highlighted the shortcomings of the "music first" approach. A band like Styx wasn't just faceless, it was *intentionally* faceless— the guys in the group prided themselves on being blandly anonymous. The most recognizable guy in Styx was campy lead singer Dennis DeYoung, a theatrical cheeseball whose bushy mustache and frizzy mullet made him look like a seventies-era magician. But even DeYoung wasn't a rock star with a well-known persona like Bowie, even if DeYoung's band sold more records than Bowie did in the late seventies. Styx's music might have been more palatable to more people, but it also mattered less to its audience.

However, corporate rock bands were relatively easy to manage, package, and promote. They worked hard, they were generally wholesome, and they didn't ask questions about how their songs got on the radio. Sometimes, they were even willing to get their hands dirty. In Fredric Dannen's 1990 book *Hit Men*, the best-ever exposé of the music business of the seventies and eighties, there's a story about why Epic Records decided to put its resources behind REO Speedwagon's *Hi Infidelity*—the best-selling album of 1981, an otherwise terrible year for the record industry—at the expense of the Clash's adventurous triple album, *Sandinista!* One of the heroes of Dannen's book is Dick

Asher, deputy president of CBS Records, which operated Epic. Asher was a critic of CBS's policy of paying millions of dollars to independent promoters tasked with plugging songs at radio stations.

The system worked like this: Record labels paid these promoters, and the promoters leveraged their relationships with local radio stations to prioritize certain songs for airplay. If labels didn't pay, a song wouldn't get played, even if the song was already insanely popular. For example, Dannen notes that no radio station in Los Angeles was playing Pink Floyd's No. 1 hit "Another Brick in the Wall" the same week that the Floyd was booked to play a series of sold-out concerts at the L.A. Forum, all because Asher refused to pay local promoters to plug that particular song.

CBS was hemorrhaging money at the time, and Asher wanted to cut back on what he correctly surmised was widespread graft. But the corruption at CBS went beyond just independent promoters. People on Asher's own staff were also taking money in exchange for their putting attention on the "right" bands.

In the case of *Hi Infidelity*, Asher wanted to know why Epic's promotion staff was pushing what he believed was a mediocre album, when the label also had a new LP by a critically adored group that had been dubbed "the only band that matters." Asher's suspicions were inflamed when he noticed that Epic's head of promotion—a stout, tanklike man named Frank DiLeo—was wearing an $8,000 gold Rolex, a gift from REO Speedwagon, who also had gifted Rolexes to two other Epic executives.

A little background on DiLeo: He later became famous for managing Michael Jackson for five years in the eighties, and then again near the end of Jackson's life in the aughts. You might also recognize him from *Goodfellas*, in which DiLeo plays Tuddy Cicero, the cigar-chomping mentor of the film's protagonist, Henry Hill (Ray Liotta). DiLeo is the side of beef who says, "You wasted eight fuckin' aprons on that guy!" That was the person who was accepting a gold Rolex in exchange for (allegedly) giving the Clash the shaft.

When I had the chance to interview Shaw, I wanted to talk about Styx's own experience with greasing the wheels of the hopelessly corrupt record business back in the late seventies. While I don't like Styx's music, I am a fan of Styx's *Behind the Music* episode, in which Shaw discusses how he wined and dined radio executives to ensure that the band's breakthrough song, the sci-fi make-out ballad "Come Sail Away," became a hit. When I say "wined and dined," of course I really mean "supplied drugs and microwave ovens as payola."

Fortunately, Shaw was a very nice guy, and he had no problem rehashing all the tawdry acts that he committed to become rich and famous for a spell in the late seventies and early eighties. This is the upside of not having to maintain a persona—you can't disappoint people by telling them how the sausage was made.

"Thank goodness for cocaine," Shaw told me. He added that he was "in an unhappy situation at home" at the time of "Come Sail Away," which gave him extra incentive to get out of the house and party with local promo guys in exchange for future spins of the song.

"We would have a pocket full of, you know, fun-powder, and cash, and we just went around and did everything that we could to get this song on the radio," he said. "We had big plans for that song, so we just went at it like a kamikaze: 'We are going to get this on the radio or we are going to die trying.' We went coast to coast and gave away TV sets and VCRs and promised this and that—plane tickets, anything—and we got the bullet back."

You aren't going to get juicy information like that while talking with the dudes from Twenty One Pilots.

I know these shady back-room dealings should repulse me, and they do—sort of. *Hit Men* suggests that the hegemony of arena rock in the seventies and eighties was propped up by the dishonesty and self-interest of major labels and rock radio, which in turn restricted opportunities for the era's best and most exciting bands to reach a wider audience. This information directly undermines the classic-rock mythos that I hold so dear. It *should* make classic rock appalling to me . . . and yet it doesn't.

I think this has something to do with my mother.

Some of my earliest music-related memories involve my mom singing along very loudly and very off-key to songs off of *Hi Infidelity,* the very REO Speedwagon album that Mr. "You Wasted Eight Fuckin' Aprons on That Guy" pushed when he worked for Epic Records. *Hi Infidelity* was one of two non-Christian music cassette tapes that my mother owned—the other, of course, was the *Dirty Dancing* soundtrack—and it was stored in the same kitchen drawer where we kept the silverware. The kitchen's echoing acoustics made my mom's voice sound even more booming whenever she reached for the high notes on "Take It on the Run."

Heard it from a friend who, heard it from a friend who, heard it from another you been messin' around.

Certainly not an ideal introduction to the Speedwagon. But it stuck.

Now, we can agree that the world would've been better off if Epic had tried to turn *Sandinista!* into a blockbuster, rather than facilitate a path for *Hi Infidelity* to move nine million units. However, I also know that my mother would not have embraced "The Magnificent Seven" with the same vigor with which she accepted "Take It on the Run." The way *Hi Infidelity* entered my mom's life is unquestionably suspect, but once it was there, that album made sense to her. Two things can be true at the same time: Those dorky corporate rock bands got on the radio because the system was rigged in their favor. But they stayed on the radio because millions of normal people heard something in that music that they could relate to.

My mom loved *Hi Infidelity* for many reasons, starting with her age. The average age of an artist with a No. 1 hit in 1980 was 34.2, which means the typical pop star was singing songs reflecting the experiences and attitudes of my mom's generation. On the albums chart, the No. 1 spot for 26 out of 52 weeks in 1981 was held by one of four corporate rock bands with strong followings among Midwesterners like my mom: REO Speedwagon (which was No. 1 for 15 weeks), Styx, Foreigner, and Journey. (Foreigner was actually half-British, which makes them the Mumford and Sons of early-eighties heartland AOR.)

These groups had been around since at least the early seventies (or featured musicians who had played in other prominent bands from that period), and all of them had front men who were at least thirty years old. Styx's Dennis DeYoung turned thirty-four in '81, Journey's Steve Perry turned thirty-two, Foreigner's Lou Gramm turned thirty-one, and Speedwagon's Kevin Cronin turned thirty.

The prototypical hardworking middle-American rock band that packed arenas in Illinois and Michigan and was ignored on the coasts, REO Speedwagon spent the seventies churning out the kind of genial good-time party music that pads classic-rock playlists to this day. Following the seventies arena-rock playbook, the band released a live album, *You Get What You Play For*, in 1977, and was rewarded with its first platinum record. By that time, Speedwagon had already gone through a battery of members, with a revolving door of lead singers. (Cronin originally exited the band after its second album and then returned for its sixth.)

REO Speedwagon had been around the block many times by *Hi Infidelity*, and the album reflected this, in both its "do or die" sense of professionalism and the relatively mature sentiments of the lyrics. This was no wild and crazy collection of drunk and horny rock 'n' roll kids; in *Rolling Stone*, keyboardist Neal Doughty called REO Speedwagon a "family band" and confessed, "We're almost as corny as Donny and Marie." That might be overstating it a bit, but there is something almost refreshingly dorky about the *Hi Infidelity* deep cut "Tough Guys," in which Cronin (who always sounds like he's emphasizing his Midwest twang rather than covering it up) sings about a woman who "doesn't like the rough guys" because "she thinks that they got brains all where they sit." Honestly, REO Speedwagon didn't ask your mom for lyrical input—it just sounds that way.

Hi Infidelity is probably best remembered for helping to usher in the era of the power ballad. The album's big hit was the piano-driven "Keep on Loving You," which was written by Cronin and caused intergroup controversy when he introduced it to the band, apparently because the members of REO Speedwagon had brains all where they sit.

"I walked into rehearsal and sat down at the piano, which I rarely do because I'm a guitar player, and started playing 'Keep on Loving You,'" Kevin Cronin recalled in a 2010 interview with *Louisville Magazine*. "And the guys in the band looked at me like I was from another planet. They were like, 'What are you . . . ?' because we were all bringing in songs for this record we were going to make and they looked at me like I was crazy. And I'm like, 'Dude, this song really means a lot to me.' [And they said,] 'So, dude, that's not an REO Speedwagon song.' And I kind of was like, 'You know what? I'm the main songwriter for REO Speedwagon, so if I write a song, it's an REO Speedwagon song.'"

And, dude, the rest is history.

Heard more than thirty-five years later, "Keep on Loving You" hardly sounds amped up at all; any "rocking" on this song seems to be purely for the band's benefit, in case there was still any lingering embarrassment over having a song so unabashedly romantic in the set list. (Though that discomfort didn't last long, judging from subsequent singles like the even gooier "Can't Fight This Feeling.") In spite of any initial misgivings, the success of "Keep on Loving You" and what it did for REO Speedwagon speaks for itself. After fourteen years in the no-name-rock-band trenches, REO Speedwagon had an instant smash. *Hi Infidelity* went platinum in five weeks as "Keep on Loving You" rose to the No. 1 singles spot in March 1981.

The lyrics of "Keep on Loving You" recall another hugely successful power ballad from that year, Journey's "Open Arms." Both songs concern a troubled relationship, presumably between a husband and wife, or at least a long-term boyfriend and girlfriend. The narrator expresses a desire to remain committed while implicitly acknowledging that it won't be easy. The opening line of "Keep on Loving You"—"You should've seen by the look in my eyes, baby, there was somethin' missin"—recalls the Righteous Brothers' "You've Lost That Lovin' Feelin'," only Cronin (and Steve Perry) still have hope for redemption. Just as Perry in "Open Arms" pledges to "come to you" with "nothing to hide" so "you'll see what your love means to [him]," Cronin wants to leave behind all sins from the past (hinted at in the album title *Hi Infidelity*) "'cause it was us, baby, way before then, and we're still together."

"Keep on Loving You" and "Open Arms" are adult love songs, as opposed to the expressions of overheated infatuation that pass for love in most pop tunes. REO Speedwagon's other peers on the album charts had similar hits in '81: In Styx's "The Best of Times," which went to No. 3 and helped make *Paradise Theater* the band's only No. 1 album, Dennis DeYoung presents a loving relationship as a kind of shelter against tough economic times. Meanwhile on Foreigner's "Waiting for a Girl Like You," from the chart-topping *4*, Lou Gramm tentatively opens his heart to a new woman, worrying that he's "coming on too strong," saying, "This heart of mine has been hurt before."

These power ballads are about damaged people trying to make a go of love despite trying circumstances—and that subject was eminently relatable to millions of recent divorcees like my mom. In 1981, the U.S. divorce rate hit an all-time peak of 5.3 per 1,000 Americans, after rising steadily throughout the sixties and seventies. The National Center for Health Statistics reported that there were 2.4 million marriages that year, and 1.2 million divorces. Those statistics were widely misinterpreted as meaning that 50 percent of nuptials ended in divorce—in reality, it was only 2 percent of the total number of existing marriages—but there were still more people than ever trying to piece their lives together in the wake of shipwrecked partnerships.

Did all of those wayward lonely hearts turn to big, operatic declarations of devotion in the form of corporate rock because it spoke to them, or because the record business ensured that other options were restricted? I suspect it was a little bit of both. But for my mom, it didn't matter. REO Speedwagon, Styx, Journey, Foreigner—it was all divorce rock.

My mom would never describe *Hi Infidelity* in these terms, but I think REO Speedwagon for her represented a more down-to-earth version of the rock mythos. As a kid, I was attracted to larger-than-life rock stars with exaggerated personas rooted in decadent mysticism. I longed to go on a misty mountain hop and venture all the way to the dark side of the moon. But my mother was too experienced to buy into those silly, pie-in-the-sky fantasies. What she longed for was more mundane but in a way no less fanciful—a decent guy who was earnest about love. That's why *Hi Infidelity* made her heart sing. Her notes might've been off-key, but they were true.

While my mom's taste in divorce rock tended toward the bom-bastically sentimental, my dad dealt strictly in emotional vérité. His album of choice was Fleetwood Mac's *Rumours*—it played endlessly in the car whenever he picked me and my brother up for a weekend visit, like a commentary track for our parents' own busted-up marriage.

Because *Rumours* took over FM radio in the late seventies, it was initially lumped into the "corporate rock" underclass. But the tag never suited Fleetwood Mac. For starters, the members of "classic era" Fleetwood Mac emit a powerful erotic charisma. Raffish Mick Fleetwood, rakish John McVie, brooding Lindsey Buckingham, witchy Stevie Nicks, wised-up Christine McVie—these people are the opposite of anonymous or bland. Just try to find an uncompelling photo of Fleetwood Mac taken at any point between 1975 and 1987. I've spent hours scouring Google Images in search of a single Fleetwood Mac band photo to which I am not sexually attracted, and failed every time.

My dad and I didn't talk much—not then, not ever. But maybe that was intentional. While he never sat me down for a traditional "facts of life" chat, he did introduce me to *Rumours,* which was actually preferable. What could he teach me about sex that wasn't better articulated by "Dreams," "Go Your Own Way," or "You Make Loving Fun"? *Led Zeppelin IV* and *The Dark Side of the Moon* were records for adolescent boys who wanted to playact a comic-book version of adulthood. But *Rumours* offered the actual skinny on what it was like to be in way over your head in a grown-up relationship.

I had always assumed that all of your insecurities and neuroses magically disappeared once you exited puberty and became a fully functional adult. But the men and women of Fleetwood Mac seemed to be just as confounded and heartbroken by love as I was. If Stevie Nicks was romantically miserable, what hope did I have as a middle schooler in love with every girl in his class and incapable of dating any of them?

The mythology of *Rumours* is among the most oft-told stories in all of classic-rock lore. But for those who have never seen an episode of *Behind the Music:* Fleetwood Mac originated in London's blues-rock scene of the late sixties, anchored by a powerful rhythm section and led by a mystical guitar virtuoso named Peter Green. But after Green took too much acid and dropped out of the band in Syd Barrett–like fashion, Fleetwood Mac cycled through a series of lineup changes in the early seventies, finally evolving into a highly successful, California-style soft-rock group with the addition of Nicks and Buckingham.

The first LP by this newfangled version of the band, 1975's *Fleetwood Mac,* spent thirty-seven weeks in the Top 10 and sold five million copies, by far the bestselling record that any incarnation of Fleetwood Mac had ever made up to that point. The record put them in the same class as the Eagles at the top of the seventies'

SoCal rock heap. It also marked the beginning of the interpersonal problems that came to define Fleetwood Mac.

During the making of *Rumours,* as Fleetwood Mac toiled for a year under intense pressure to follow up a blockbuster, Nicks and Buckingham's relationship fell apart, as did the marriage between Christine McVie and John McVie. (Fleetwood was also in the midst of divorcing his wife.) Since Nicks, Buckingham, and Christine McVie were all songwriters, the widespread romantic strife became the principal subject of *Rumours,* creating a real-life soap opera that enhanced the album's commercial appeal. *Rumours* went on to sell more than forty million records worldwide.

The most remarked-upon characteristic of *Rumours* is the conversational nature of the songs. This is especially true for the tracks by Nicks (whose "Dreams" is Zen-like and conciliatory) and Buckingham (whose "Go Your Own Way" and "Never Going Back Again" are bitter and borderline nasty). Perhaps because her ex was the bass player who didn't write songs and therefore couldn't respond, Christine McVie struck a balance between the approaches taken by Nicks and Buckingham. In "Don't Stop" and "Songbird," she wishes for a post-divorce friendship. And in "You Make Loving Fun," she sings about having sex with Fleetwood Mac's former lighting director. John McVie, to his credit, supplies the album's funkiest bass line to the latter.

As a rare breakup album offering multiple "he said/she said" perspectives, *Rumours* contained valuable lessons about women, specifically in regard to female desire and agency. Stevie Nicks and Christine McVie wrote about their own wants and ambitions, ultimately defining themselves outside of the men in their lives. Here was something that Led Zeppelin and the Doors never seemed to take into account—that women don't exist simply to pleasure a man.

In "Dreams," Nicks tries to let Buckingham down easy, but she's firm about wanting to live an independent life. In "You Make Loving Fun," McVie sings ecstatically about being with a man who can give her an orgasm. For a teenage boy, this was a real paradigm shifter. Unlike practically every other rock song I had ever heard, "Dreams" and "You Make Loving Fun" didn't put the man first. As dumb as this might sound, I had never even considered that a woman could be as into sex as a dude is. Or that a woman could feel the same hurt and insecurity in the wake of romantic hardship that I did. Stevie Nicks and Christine McVie were among the first women in my life to speak frankly about such things. Teenage boys are already the most solipsistic people on the planet, even without a steady diet of classic-rock sexism, so I needed *Rumours* to set me straight.

Initially, however, I didn't appreciate *Rumours*' feminine side. Like so many young male Fleetwood Mac fans before me, I was all about the Lindsey songs. Lindsey was relatable. Lindsey felt my pain. He didn't get the girl either, and he was angry about it.

When I listen to *Rumours* now, Lindsey kind of seems like a jerk. The line in "Go Your Own Way" in which he essentially calls out Stevie Nicks ("Shacking up is all you want to do") is way over the line. But then I remember that I'm happily married, and that judging Lindsey Buckingham's worldview in "Go Your Own Way" is a luxury if your love life happens to be secure. "Go Your Own Way" is best appreciated as first-person reportage from the front lines of short-term, heartache-induced psychosis.

I wonder what was going through my dad's mind when he listened to *Rumours* on repeat. Did he see himself in the Lindsey songs, as I did in my twenties when I went through the most traumatic breakups of my life? Did he find solace in the sarcasm of "Second Hand News," the defiance of "Never Going Back Again," or the self-pity of "Go Your Own Way"? Was *my* mom *his* Stevie Nicks?

I prefer to believe that my dad loved *Rumours* because he was inspired by the fortitude of Fleetwood Mac—that insane resolve to not break up even as the personal relationships in the band crumbled. As a child of divorce, I learned at a young age that no matter what catastrophe occurs, people find a way to move on. My parents did it, my brother and I did it. And Fleetwood Mac did it, too. In "The Chain," *Rumours'* centerpiece and the only song written by all five members, they pledge to hang on to one another no matter the terrible things they may divulge in the other songs.

When you listen to *Rumours,* you hear deeply sad people refusing to give in to their feelings of defeat and sorrow, and instead pushing ahead to the next catchy chorus. It's a record about making it through to the other side. Isn't anyone who's had their heart broken just trying to do the same?

"You Can't Always Get What You Want"

NOTES ON TRACK 14: Politics. We're in favor of them, and we don't care who knows it. We believe in making the world a better place by telling our audience what to think.

The Rolling Stones recorded "You Can't Always Get What You Want" on November 16 and 17, 1968, at Olympic Studios in London, right before they released *Beggars Banquet*. The song later came out on *Let It Bleed,* released almost exactly one year and one month later, on December 5, 1969. "You Can't Always Get What You Want" was birthed right after Richard Nixon narrowly won the U.S. presidential election, and released the day before the Stones played Altamont, the historic "end of the sixties" moment in rock mythology. Like that, it became the alpha and omega—a beginning for the Stones and an ending for an era, a Significant Anthem That Means Something.

But "You Can't Always Get What You Want" is also just a song. And, like all songs, the meaning is malleable. To Mick Jagger, who wrote it—Keith Richards conceded full credit in *Life*— "You Can't Always Get What You Want" was just "one of those

bedroom songs," a folkie lament that proved surprisingly difficult for Charlie Watts to play along with in the studio. Producer Jimmy Miller tried in vain to demonstrate the song's tricky
rhythm, and eventually Watts threw up his hands and said, "Why
don't you play it then?" So, that's what Miller did. In the end,
only three members of the Rolling Stones—Jagger, Richards, and
Bill Wyman—can be heard on "You Can't Always Get What You
Want," along with Miller, Al Kooper (who played piano, organ,
and French horn), and the London Bach Choir.

Jagger supposedly wrote the song about his then-girlfriend
Marianne Faithfull—at least that's what Marianne Faithfull
thinks. "That's my song," Faithfull told Stones biographer Rich
Cohen in 2016. "Every time I hear it, I'm right back with Mick
in the flat." Two days after "You Can't Always Get What You
Want" was tracked, Faithfull had a miscarriage, which devas-
tated Jagger—at the time his own song must've seemed cruelly
prescient.

The verses aren't just about personal heartache, however.
They're also about the sixties—there are allusions to demonstrations,
drug addiction, and creeping ennui. Clocking in at 7:30, "You
Can't Always Get What You Want" is not just a long song, it's a
big song. A lot of music fans at the time heard "You Can't Always
Get What You Want" as an answer record to the Beatles' "Hey
Jude"—both songs are mini-epics with orchestral flourishes and
sing-along choruses, with a central message that's essentially "Everything's going to be all right." Jagger himself suggested as much
when he expressed admiration for "Hey Jude" before the release
of *Let It Bleed* and hinted in a 1969 interview, "We may do something like that on the next album." But "You Can't Always Get
What You Want" is so much *tougher* than "Hey Jude"—not musically so much, but certainly spiritually. I've always interpreted
that grand choral opening to be at least somewhat satirical, a rasp-
berry blown in the direction of the Beatles' self-importance. Jagger wasn't interested in taking a sad song and making it better. He
was saying that a sad song might be what we *deserve*.

The politics of "You Can't Always Get What You Want" is what most interested rock's early historians. From the beginning, Jagger's bedroom song was viewed as a definitive statement on the failures of his generation to carry forth a revolution. "This era and the collapse of its bright and flimsy liberation are what the Stones leave behind with the last song of *Let It Bleed*," Greil Marcus wrote in *Rolling Stone* when the album was released. "The dreams of having it all are gone, and the album ends with a song about compromises with what you want—learning to take what you can get, because the rules have changed with the death of the '60s."

Years later, long after the Stones had evolved into rock's preeminent stadium-sized Vegas-style extravaganza, there was ample evidence that Jagger could hardly be bothered with "the death of the '60s." For him, the song was popular because, as he said in 1995, "it's got a very sing-along chorus. And people can identify with it: No one gets what they want." Jagger didn't bother to distinguish a specific audience or point out exactly what "they" might want but couldn't have. For him, "You Can't Always Get What You Want" means whatever *they* say it means.

All of this baggage—the alpha, the omega, Marianne Faithfull, the loss of "bright and flimsy liberation"—lingered when "You Can't Always Get What You Want" became a cornerstone of Donald Trump's presidential campaign in 2016. Trump played the song at numerous campaign stops throughout the year, but this song didn't truly reenter public consciousness until it appeared as the outro music for Trump's punishing seventy-five-minute speech at the Republican National Convention in Cleveland that July.

Pundits rapidly pointed out the irony of Trump's utilizing a classic-rock song long associated with the sixties counterculture. But classic rock was already established as the soundtrack for the Republican National Convention—the Rock and Roll Hall of Fame was the favored local attraction that week for attendees, and a guitar was even integrated into the convention's official logo. Weren't these people paying attention to the lyrics to "You Can't

Always Get What You Want"? Did they know nothing about the context from which this Rolling Stones classic sprung?

It's a familiar game with Republican politicians in an election year—a conservative partisan will try to use a classic-rock song at a rally (most likely something by Bruce Springsteen or John Mellencamp), prompting the artist and the media to immediately call out the politician for misappropriation. This happened to Trump repeatedly during his campaign: Queen, Aerosmith, and R.E.M. were among the bands that publicly demanded that Trump stop using their songs to rally Republican voters.

This election-year tradition of rock stars battling Republicans goes back at least as far as 1984, when Ronald Reagan tried to recontextualize Bruce Springsteen's antiwar song "Born in the U.S.A." as simpleminded patriotic sloganeering. What had changed in the thirty-two years between Reagan and Trump was the political purpose of harnessing the power of rock music. In 1984, Bruce Springsteen was a thirty-five-year-old pop star, and Ronald Reagan was a seventy-three-year-old ideologue and enemy to rock 'n' roll going back to his tenure as the hippie-hating governor of California in the sixties. For Reagan, aligning with Springsteen was a naked grab for the youth vote. Trump, meanwhile, was merely representing the preferences of his age group. Here was a seventy-year-old man who had grown up listening to songs sung by Jagger, who turned seventy-three the year "You Can't Always Get What You Want" became Trump's battle cry.

"I like Mick Jagger. I like their songs," Trump said when pressed about Jagger's request that he stop using "You Can't Always Get What You Want" at rallies. It was that simple, and that complicated.

Although "You Can't Always Get What You Want" could be interpreted as an unflattering song *about* Trump supporters, who from the outside resembled an unruly mob of petulant screamers refusing to take responsibility for their own problems, I suspect that Trump's explanation can also be taken at face value: he likes Mick Jagger, and he likes "You Can't Always Get What You

Want." And the people who voted for Trump probably like that song, too. For them, the specific meaning of the words matters less than the way Jagger's voice evokes the past. For anyone who believes that the world has gone to hell, the song is a comforting reminder of how things were when you were younger and more hopeful. Even as seemingly everything else about this country has changed, you can still hear the Stones on classic-rock radio, and there's something comforting about that. "You Can't Always Get What You Want" represents stability—and it's also resolutely white and male, as much of classic-rock radio is, and for some people that's comforting, too.

When you're surrounded only by white people in their sixties and seventies, you can almost imagine that the world you associate with "You Can't Always Get What You Want" is still attainable. For this audience, the song is no longer a salve for those disillusioned by the dawn of Nixon but a taunt to liberals who want to welcome Mexicans into our country and make health insurance accessible to those who can't afford it. No, you really *can't* get what you want, liberal snowflakes. Mick Jagger told us so.

It bothers me how closely these people's myths resemble my own. Because to them and to me, classic rock is a continuum. For them and for me, classic rock feels eternal. They count on classic rock to connect them to their own pasts. Classic rock is *their* great big old tree, too.

The overwhelming whiteness of classic rock is a problem that can't be avoided. There are numerous explanations for why rock evolved from a form of music deeply indebted to black Americans into a genre in which black people are often invisible. Clearly, this is bigger than just classic rock, and you can't break it down without delving into how all art forms seem to inevitably become segregated. Just as there is "black cinema" or "black stand-up comedy," there is "black music," which has long been set apart from white or "mainstream" music. For years, mainstream music was rock,

which marginalized artists of color, who were hardly ever classified as rock by critics, record store clerks, radio, or MTV.

That's how classic rock was first introduced to me on the
radio. The playlist at WAPL was far less diverse than the music
played on the Top 40 station, WIXX, or even the oldies station,
WOGB, which freely mixed fifties and sixties soul and R & B
with early rock 'n' roll.

But on the classic-rock station—with the exception of Jimi
Hendrix and Phil Lynott of Thin Lizzy—there were no black artists. This patently exclusionary narrative was drilled into my consciousness before I was smart enough to question it. It had little
to do with music and almost everything to do with the biases of
gatekeepers. The story of classic rock as told by decades of radio
airplay, magazine profiles, and rock books is a saga about white
guys, because all other kinds of people have typically been re-
routed to other genres, *even when they were making rock music.*
And, yes, the mythology of rock has a lot to do with this. The
lessons I learned about classic albums and historic live shows and
how bands are supposed to look always seemed to have the same
catch—they almost always involved white men.

When I was learning about classic rock as a teenager, I didn't
wonder why I was almost always hearing songs by straight Caucasian males on WAPL, which was staffed almost entirely by
straight Caucasian male DJs, or reading record reviews written
almost entirely by straight Caucasian male critics. It never occurred to me that this might be the result of systemic bias favoring
people who were in my demographic, which supported the white
male musicians making the albums and the white male writers
reviewing them. I just took it at face value that white men were
awesome people who just happened to create all the best stuff. I
was a privileged idiot.

Over the years, I've often wondered to what degree this
white-men narrative drew me into the mythology of classic rock.
In her essential 1991 book *Heavy Metal: A Cultural Sociology,*
DePaul University sociology professor Deena Weinstein observed

that metal fans tend to be white males who are drawn together out of a sense of tribalism that affirms their identity. Outsiders are welcomed so long as they follow the group's "codes of dress, appearance, and behavior, and show devotion to the music," she writes. "Neither sexist, ageist, nor racist on principle, the metal subculture is *exclusivist*, insistent upon upholding the codes of its core membership."

The "exclusivist" heavy-metal subculture of the eighties, Weinstein observed, was an outgrowth of the burgeoning classic-rock tribalism of the late sixties, back when rock was being delineated from rock 'n' roll as a style of music and a way of life. I suspect that Weinstein's astute observations about Iron Maiden fans could also be applied to me when I was a teenage Led Zeppelin obsessive. As a young white kid from Wisconsin who was raised by a single mom, I was confused about what it meant to be a man and looking for something to fill that void. It seems highly unlikely that the preponderance of cool white guys in the classic-rock universe didn't play a significant role in turning me into a fan. I needed role models, and while Jimmy Page was utterly unlike me in every other way, he did sort of look like me, which was enough.

Let's conduct a thought experiment: is it possible to write a history of rock using only black artists? You could start with Ike Turner, whose 1951 song "Rocket 88" is sometimes credited as the first rock song. Then, of course, there's Chuck Berry, ace guitarist and one of rock's most important singer-songwriters. And Little Richard, the model for all future rock 'n' roll screamers, eccentrics, and gender-benders.

All of these artists are already identified as rockers, so let's branch out. Ray Charles, Muddy Waters, Howlin' Wolf, Jackie Wilson, Sam Cooke, and Jimmy Reed played a pivotal role in influencing how rock is sung, performed, and conceptualized. If they were white, they would automatically be classified as rock stars, but because they're black, they are more commonly regarded as blues and soul artists. So, let's annex them into rock history, because they belong there, too.

In the sixties, you have all of the great stars of Motown and Stax, including Marvin Gaye, Otis Redding, Stevie Wonder, the Supremes, and Wilson Pickett, as well as iconoclasts like James Brown, Sly Stone, and the greatest guitarist of all time himself, Jimi Hendrix. Only Hendrix is commonly categorized as rock, but all those artists either influenced rock musicians or sound exactly like the rock bands of their era. So, add them to the historical record as well.

The story continues with the funk and R & B groups of the seventies—George Clinton's Funkadelic self-identified as a rock band and boasted one of the era's top guitarists, Eddie Hazel. The Isley Brothers similarly featured a top-flight axman, Ernie Isley, and recorded their classic 1977 album *Go for Your Guns* at Bearsville Studios in upstate New York, the headquarters for the Band. Al Green's classic albums featured an incredible four-piece band anchored by an all-time great drummer, Al Jackson Jr. The Muscle Shoals Rhythm Section, one of the decade's most acclaimed studio bands, worked out of Muscle Shoals Sound Studio in Sheffield, Alabama—an interracial unit, it played on hits by Aretha Franklin and Bob Seger, though only one of those artists was considered rock.

In the eighties, there were Prince and Michael Jackson, both of whom had hits with straight-up rock songs like "Beat It" and "Let's Go Crazy" that were hardly ever called rock songs. Run-DMC's early hits were guitar-heavy—one of the group's earliest singles is literally called "Rock Box." And then Public Enemy followed up on Run-DMC's cover version of Aerosmith's "Walk This Way" in the nineties by redoing "Bring the Noise" as a surprisingly credible metal anthem with Anthrax, forging the beginnings of rap rock, the most dominant form of rock music in the back half of the nineties.

In the twenty-first century, Outkast, the Roots, Lil Wayne, and Kanye West have made music that draws on rock traditions. And let's not forget rock bands like Living Colour and TV on the

Radio, who were treated as novelties strictly because their membership was predominantly black.

I'm not arguing that the Supremes and Al Green should be thought of as rock rather than soul artists. I'm just suggesting that there's nothing intrinsic about genre. It's a system created by humans who want to make sense of what they're hearing. Ultimately, it's as much about the perception of the listener as it is about the work of the artist.

No artist should be considered strictly one thing or the other. Music should belong to everybody, and if you care to try, you can find a place for yourself inside any great work of art. But just because you've found your own place doesn't mean someone very different from you can't find a place inside the same one. If these differences can't always be reconciled, we should at least recognize that other perspectives can coexist under the same tent.

Amid the Trump-led Republican National Convention came a mini-wave of anniversary coverage about Disco Demolition Night, a Chicago radio promotion gone awry that had instantly become a too-perfect metaphor for pop-music anthropologists thirty-seven summers earlier.

On July 12, 1979, the Chicago White Sox admitted patrons to a home game at Comiskey Park against the Detroit Tigers for just ninety-eight cents if they also brought along a disco record. The promotion was initiated by local rock station WLUP, known among listeners by its number on the dial, 97.9. (Hence the nominal gate price.) Because the White Sox were very bad in '79, they were only drawing an average of about eighteen thousand fans per game, about one-third of Comiskey's capacity of forty-five thousand. But thanks to WLUP's aggressive promotion and the showmanship of star disc jockey Steve Dahl, who conceived the event as "a declaration of independence from the tyranny of sophistication," Disco Demolition attracted seventy thousand very drunken yahoos who wanted to incinerate a metric ton of dance music.

Disco Demolition Night was slated to take place between the games of a doubleheader. During the first game, it was apparent that most attendees didn't care about baseball. They were more interested in throwing bottles and firecrackers on the field, and waving "Disco Sucks" banners.

Twenty-five minutes after the first game ended, Dahl and two associates walked out to center field. The White Sox starting pitcher for game two was warming up on the mound. Dahl, donning army fatigues and a helmet, addressed the audience.

"This is now officially the world's largest antidisco rally!" Dahl declared. "Now listen—we took all the disco records you brought tonight, we got 'em in a giant box, and we're gonna blow 'em up *REAL GOOD*."

You can probably guess what happened next: The drunken yahoos weren't satisfied with just incinerating dance music. After Dahl's explosive routine was over, more than five thousand maniacs stormed the field. Bases were ripped out of the ground and the batting cage was wrecked. A guy even tried to set fire to one of the foul poles. A half hour later, the SWAT team was called in, and thirty-nine people were arrested for disorderly conduct. Comiskey was in such rough shape that the White Sox had to forfeit the second game.

In the aftermath of Disco Demolition Night, two opposing narratives emerged. In the first, the event was viewed as a sign that disco had reached peak saturation, inspiring a backlash. Disco was undeniably the signature sound of pop music in 1979. The number one song the week of Disco Demolition was Donna Summer's "Bad Girls," and the number one album was Donna Summer's *Bad Girls*. Also vying for Song of the Summer status (no pun intended) were Chic's "Good Times," Anita Ward's "Ring My Bell," and the Bee Gees' "Love You Inside Out," all future disco classics.

But by the early eighties, "disco" was a dirty word—though

this was another instance where categorization overshadowed music. Dance music never stopped being popular, it just continued under a different name. Nevertheless, Disco Demolition Night was credited with crystallizing antidisco sentiment right when the genre's pervasive popularity was about to crest.

The second narrative posited that the meaning of Disco Demolition Night was only tangentially related to music, having more to do with the racism and homophobia of the participants. This view was forwarded most prominently by music critic Dave Marsh in *Rolling Stone*, who observed at the end of 1979 that "white males, eighteen to thirty-four, are the most likely to see disco as the product of homosexuals, blacks and [Latinos], and therefore they're most likely to respond to appeals to wipe out such threats to their security."

You can see the parallels to Trump—at both Disco Demolition Night and the Republican National Convention, rock music represented the conservative status quo, a view propagated by an overwhelmingly white majority openly (in some cases violently) opposed to cultural integration.

Marsh's narrative about Disco Demolition Night's reflecting the rock audience's entrenched biases has become the favored view of many pop historians, though the first narrative hasn't been completely set aside. Two accounts of Disco Demolition Night were posted on the Internet on the eve of the Republican National Convention—one was a fifteen-minute documentary produced by the website Red Bull Music Academy, and the other was an oral history produced by *Chicago* magazine. Both accounts followed the same methodology—participants were interviewed, their words were contextualized in the politics of the time, and conclusions were made about what it all meant. However, the conclusions reached by these accounts couldn't be more different.

The Red Bull documentary forwarded the idea that Disco Demolition Night was the product of racism both micro (the neighborhood around Comiskey is depicted as a working-class bastion of white-dude mookery) and macro (it is implied that white rock fans had a general problem with disco's far more racially diverse constituency). Dahl himself denies this, insisting that he was merely making fun of overexposed pop music, but the documentary is clearly pitched to debunk his argument.

The most compelling interviewee is Vince Lawrence, an early pioneer of Chicago house music who worked at Comiskey that night as an usher. As a young black man surrounded by crazed white people intent on burning records by mostly black artists— even records that weren't actually disco—Lawrence could only see Disco Demolition Night as thinly veiled racism. He convincingly connects the riot to a racially motivated beating he once received not far from the stadium. "Steve Dahl from my perspective was the same sort of person resisting the same sort of change," Lawrence concludes.

Lawrence was not interviewed for the *Chicago* magazine story, nor was anybody else associated with Chicago dance music. The treatment of Dahl is much more sympathetic, and his insistence that Disco Demolition Night was an act of rebellion against an overbearing pop trend is supported by other attendees.

"It was like it's OK for a long-haired kid who likes rock 'n' roll to be free and stupid," one attendee says. "For me, Disco Demolition was a license to let your freak flag fly. We took over a ballpark. It was kind of cool. We began to realize we had a tiny bit of power in the world."

"I'm worn out from defending myself [from accusations of being] a racist homophobe for fronting Disco Demolition," Dahl concluded. "This event was not racist, not antigay. It is important to me that this is viewed from the lens of 1979. We were just kids pissing on a musical genre."

I don't know which narrative is correct. I suspect that they're *both* true—people probably hated disco because it inflamed something dark inside of them that they might not have known was there, and they also probably hated disco because disco (like a lot of pop music) was getting pretty fucking ridiculous and played out in 1979.

What's not disputed in either narrative is the suggestion that loving rock 'n' roll derives from a reactionary, conservative impulse—you're either ripping up a ballpark because you hate that rock is being overshadowed by disco, or because you're secretly fearful that white men are being displaced by those whom white men have traditionally subjugated.

I live by one rule: When documentaries are made in forty years about the present day, you don't ever want to be on side of those pushing against history. Rather, you want to be aligned with those who are trying to move the world forward a couple of inches. Therefore, blowing up records for the amusement of musical bigots will never be a tenable position.

When it comes to whether classic rock deserves to be the soundtrack of the reactionary right wing, I defer to musicians, who in 1979 didn't seem to have a problem mixing rock and disco. On one hand, you had Rod Stewart and Blondie, who had No. 1 hits that year respectively with "Da Ya Think I'm Sexy" and "Heart of Glass," which were obvious nods to disco music. On the other hand, you had Donna Summer making overt rock moves on her two big songs from '79, "Hot Stuff" and "Bad Girls," which feature crunchy, pop-metal guitars pumping over disco beats.

Then there's the Rolling Stones, among the first rock bands to dip into disco with their chart-topping song from the previous year, "Miss You."

"In the 70s, of course, there were some fantastic dance records out," Charlie Watts says in 2003's *According to the Rolling Stones,* an oral history of the band. "It was a great period. I remember being in Munich and coming back from a club and Mick was singing one of the Village People songs—'YMCA,' I think it was—and Keith went mad, but it sounded great on the dance floor."

If you can think like the Stones, you'll see there is no beginning and no end to music, only grooves that you can lock into and ride until you find another groove. It's all rock 'n' roll if you want it to be. The point is that the continuum keeps on going regardless of how you process, classify, contextualize, or divide it into myriad subcategories. Instead of trying to bend the groove to your personal whim, it might be better to just plug in and accept wherever it takes you.

Put another way: you can't always get what you want, but if you try sometimes, you might find you get what you need.

But we all know classic-rock history wasn't written that way. Racial lines that should've been blurred were, instead, fortified. Rather than embrace stylistic as well as racial diversity, the parameters of "real" rock 'n' roll were squeezed into a niche that grew narrower and narrower. This narrowing was imposed by the music industry and subsequently codified by the rock press. The audience played a role as well: there's a flawed human instinct to relate most intimately to people who look most like you and slot everybody else in different categories. Again: this is a much bigger problem than just rock music. But rock sadly failed to transcend these boundaries.

The short-term result of all this as it pertains to classic rock is that a lot of great artists were pushed away—they never got the respect or the money they deserved. In the long term, however, the script has been flipped. When the white male rock star, the protagonist of the classic-rock mythos, came to be viewed as passé in mainstream pop by the end of the nineties, there was no alternative to take his place. Women and artists of color have flourished in pop, R & B, and hip-hop, whereas the restrictiveness of rock crippled the genre as demographics shifted. For so long, rock music operated on a "white males or bust" policy. It never dawned on the gatekeepers of rock purity that the public might eventually choose "bust."

"Rock Is Dead"

NOTES ON TRACK 15: Bold statement? Not if you saw how many streams our last album had on Spotify.

A cursory glance at today's pop charts reveals a dearth of anything resembling a traditional rock band. Rock bands barely compete in that arena anymore. Inevitably, this has prompted some onlookers to declare that rock is dead.

In the eighties and nineties, people who were into indie rock were required to hate corporate rock. That was the whole point of being into indie rock—taking a stand against the mainstream version of what was supposed to be outsider music. The significance of a band like Fugazi hinged on playing $5 shows and not selling band merchandise—if you loved Fugazi, these gestures signified a meaningful ethical stance. When viewed through the prism of the era's punk bands, corporate rock appeared bloated and impersonal. Corporate rock could never have the intimacy of music played in clubs or the personal connection of a record sold by hand from artist to fan. So, the unofficial mission of indie bands was to destroy purveyors of bandanas, spandex pants, and power balladry.

In the end, indie rockers got their wish: today, corporate rock as it once existed is no more. But there's a catch: The destruction of corporate rock did not also mean a victory for indie rock. It's just that rock is no longer considered part of pop music. Dave Grohl is a ubiquitous presence at award shows because he's the only musician from the past twenty-five years who can walk onstage and instantly signify "rock stardom" for a mass audience. It might be annoying to see the same guy's mug on TV all the time, but at least Grohl is there to answer the call. Otherwise, rock music as it presently stands would have a serious figurehead vacuum.

But is rock really dead in the twenty-first century?

"Rock is dead" declarations date back to the late sixties. Back then, it was about delineating the difference between the innocence of early *rock 'n' roll* (Chuck Berry, Little Richard, pre-army Elvis) and relatively grown-up rock music (the bearded Beatles, the Altamont-era Rolling Stones, Jimi Hendrix, the Grateful Dead). The Who's manager Kit Lambert, in the introduction to Nik Cohn's 1969 book, *Awopbopaloobop Alopbamboom*, worried that rock might already be part of a "forgotten age." Rock critic Richard Meltzer struck a similarly elegiac posture in 1970's *The Aesthetics of Rock*, which covers rock history from 1956 to 1968, the last year that "the music was unconditionally good," in Meltzer's estimation.

The most famous instance of early rock nostalgia occurred in 1971's "American Pie," in which Don McLean coined the phrase "the day the music died" to signify February 3, 1959, when Buddy Holly, Ritchie Valens, and the Big Bopper were killed in a plane crash. A sprawling eight-and-a-half-minute epic that went on to become a staple of FM radio, "American Pie" was loaded with faux-Dylanesque metaphors describing rock's journey from innocence in the fifties to tragedy at Altamont at the end of the sixties. Intentionally or not, "American Pie" epitomized the very thing that McLean seemed to be against, which was rock's evolution from carefree youth culture to lyrically pretentious and "mature" music for weary adults.

Looking back, it seems strange that McLean would be pining for the past in the midst of one of the great years in classic-rock history—1971 was the year of *What's Going On* and *Sticky Fingers* and *Who's Next* and *Hunky Dory* and *Electric Warrior* and *Every Picture Tells a Story*. Rock was the opposite of dead in '71. Herein lies an important point about "Rock is dead"—it's always more about the perspective of the amateur mortician making the pronouncement than it is about the music. McLean was twenty-six when he wrote "American Pie" and romanticized a tragedy in rock history that occurred when he was around age fourteen. The music you love at fourteen always looms larger in your personal history. When you're young and inexperienced, everything, including music, seems new and exciting. Then you get older and more cynical, and suddenly nothing seems new and exciting, because you can no longer discover what you already loved for the first time. The temptation in this situation is to blame *everything* for turning into *nothing*, rather than yourself for getting older. Hence, "Rock is dead."

When Pete Townshend was young, he wrote enthusiastic anthems about the power of rock. Rock defined his peer group in "My Generation," it was like a drug in "I Can See for Miles," and it pointed the way to enlightenment in "We're Not Gonna Take It" and "Baba O'Riley." But, like McLean, disillusionment was already setting in for Townshend at the still-young age of twenty-six, the year he wrote "Long Live Rock," a sigh of ambivalence posing as a rally cry. (The chorus goes, "Long live rock, be it dead or alive.") The next Who album, 1973's *Quadrophenia,* was a self-referential work of rock criticism, following a protagonist named Jimmy from his teen years as a music-loving mod to a grown man. This coming-of-age process includes a confrontation of Jimmy's favorite rock star. In "The Punk Meets the Godfather," one of the album's bitterest songs, Townshend assumes the voice of the rock star as he confesses that his life's work is, at root, silly and self-destructive:

> *I have to be careful not to preach*
> *I can't pretend that I can teach*
> *And yet I've lived your future out*
> *By pounding stages like a clown*

Townshend was determined to modernize the Who's sound on *Quadrophenia* by integrating state-of-the-art synthesizers into their pummeling attack. This subsequently become a rock cliché: for the next forty years, self-conscious arena bands would "experiment" with technology to deemphasize guitars and embrace "futuristic" music, with mixed results.

So, rock died in the late sixties, and then it died again in the early seventies. But rock still had a lot more dying to do. By the midseventies, rock was dead again because of disco, which threatened to unseat it commercially, and the preponderance of prog-rock bands subjecting audiences to forty-nine-minute keyboard solos, which critics believed undermined rock's artistic validity. In his obituary for John Lennon in 1980, Lester Bangs took time to note that he felt "deeply alienated from rock 'n' roll and what it has meant or could mean," presumably because rock fans preferred the Eagles to Lou Reed. Eight months later, MTV debuted, which signaled another death for rock, as did the wave of razor-haired, pirate-shirt-wearing "New Romantic" bands that the channel favored.

By now, "Rock is dead" was a generational rite of passage—every age group wanted to have its own "Rock is dead" moment, because witnessing the death of a culture is almost as good as witnessing the birth of a culture. The rise of hip-hop, the prevalence of Auto-Tune and drum machines, the multiplatinum success of Hootie & the Blowfish's *Cracked Rear View*—all were used in the nineties as excuses to kick dirt on rock's grave.

In 1993, U2 released *Zooropa,* a self-declared "experimental" record by the era's top stadium band. In interviews, U2's guitarist, the Edge, announced that he was now sick of the guitar, and instead was interested in exploring more synthetic sonic textures. This approach was typified by *Zooropa's* first single, "Numb," in which Edge spoke in monotone over a dense web of keyboard samples overdubbed by producer Brian Eno, the go-to guru for straightforward rock bands who no longer want to rock quite so straightforwardly. The implication was that *Zooropa* represented U2's moving "beyond" rock and toward a new kind of music. (*Zooropa* adhered to the *Quadrophenia* principle, by way of David Bowie's Berlin trilogy. Later, Coldplay would crib from this playbook.) The Edge never said "Rock is dead," but U2 was eager to present itself as something other than a conventional rock band.

A few years later, *Rolling Stone* put an electro-punk band from Essex, England, called the Prodigy on its cover, which was a big deal at the time. Virtually nobody remembers them now, but for about six months in 1997, some very overexcited music critics tried to convince readers that the Prodigy were the Sex Pistols of electronic music. Around the same time, bands that drew on the tradition of classic rock appeared to have been usurped by rap-rock groups such as Korn, Linkin Park, and Limp Bizkit, who proudly professed ignorance of any music recorded before 1987. Korn bassist Fieldy once claimed, in an interview with Chuck Klosterman, that his band's "musical history starts with the Red Hot Chili Peppers and early Faith No More," while bragging about never having heard the Beatles, the Rolling Stones, or Led Zeppelin. When rap-rock became the defining soundtrack of Woodstock 99, an event marred by rioting and dozens of sexual assaults, it appeared the latest wave of aggro bands was literally trampling over classic-rock history.

"Rock is dead" became so fashionable in the late nineties that even artists indebted to classic rock started adopting it. Walking Hard Rock Cafe exhibit Lenny Kravitz put out a single, "Rock and Roll Is Dead," telling ersatz rockers, "You can't even sing or play an instrument / So you scream instead." Three years later, Marilyn Manson released a single called "Rock Is Dead" from 1998's *Mechanical Animals,* his most overt tribute to glam-era David Bowie. "Rock is deader than dead / Shock is all in your head," Manson sings. Manson's audience apparently believed him, as *Mechanical Animals* was his last platinum album, and the era's top shock rocker seemingly disappeared from MTV overnight.

Then something strange (but predictable) happened: *rock music didn't die.* The Edge fell back in love with the guitar, and U2 reestablished itself as a megasuccessful stadium-rock band in the aughts with the single "Beautiful Day." The Prodigy faded away, and *Rolling Stone* went back to putting Paul McCartney and Bruce Springsteen on its cover. Even Lenny Kravitz kept on wearing bell-bottom pants. Rock endured.

Over the years "Rock is dead" has had a symbiotic marketing relationship with an equally tired cliché, "Rock is back!" In the early 2000s, "Rock is back!" took the form of the Strokes and the White Stripes, who made the classic-rock continuum hip again by restoring the Rolling Stones, Led Zeppelin, and the Velvet Underground as contemporary musical touchstones. A few years later, the Killers tried to manufacture a *Born in the U.S.A.*–level phenomenon in the form of their grandiose second album, 2006's *Sam's Town.* Rock critics laughed when Killers singer Brandon Flowers promised that *Sam's Town* would be one of the best albums of the past twenty years (it was not). But when Arcade Fire produced a similarly old-fashioned arena-rock opus with 2010's *The Suburbs,* the Canadian indie band was granted an Album of the Year Grammy.

Rock, indeed, was back. Only not for long. Once again, it seems, rock is dead, and maybe this time it's not coming back. Virtually every conversation I have these days about the "state of rock" is focused on whether rock is dead. And these conversations are typically predicated on the absence of a certain kind of rock band that seemingly hasn't been popular since the turn of the century.

You know the sort of band to which I refer. It resembles a hybrid of Nirvana and Guns N' Roses—punk-tinged hard rock played by troubled young white men who dabble in drugs and tattoos. It's a highly volatile group that emerges from an obscure underground scene to infiltrate and dramatically conquer the culture, forever changing how we hear music in its aftermath. A band that's partly real and partly embellished in our collective memories, in the manner of all rock myths.

A band like that is never going to happen again, because the infrastructure that once made bands like that possible (MTV, commercial rock radio, powerful record labels, influential music retailers, and record stores) has been diminished. The next Nirvana or GNR might sell a hundred thousand units of their "breakthrough" album and perform in the "late afternoon" slot at major music festivals. But that's the ceiling.

Does that equal "Rock is dead"? I'm an optimistic person, so I would say, "No, rock isn't dead, it just doesn't have an easily identifiable cultural identity." Nobody knows how to define rock music anymore.

When the Rock and Roll Hall of Fame was established in 1983, "rock 'n' roll" was understood to be shorthand for the entire spectrum of pop music. In other words, rock was synonymous with "everything"—pop, soul, metal, punk, and rap. But that lack of specificity over time drained rock of its meaning. The influence of rock is so ingrained and widespread now that it's like wallpaper—still everywhere but hardly noticeable. If anything, it's now acceptable for *only* pop stars to explicitly draw on classic rock without risking censure from the coolness police. Most contemporary rock groups would be too embarrassed to directly quote from the Doors or "Hotel California." But Beyoncé and Frank Ocean have both done it without shame, because they're able to remove that music so far from its original context that it suddenly seems cool and postmodern.

If rock has a mainstream identity, it's that faded Nirvana/ GNR "outsider" archetype. But not only is this definition old-fashioned, it keeps out a lot of actual rock bands. If you expect every rock band to be loud, abrasive, and drug-addled, Radiohead is not a rock band. The National is not a rock band. LCD Soundsystem is not a rock band. Maybe rock seems dead because it's easier to say what rock music *isn't* than what it *is*.

This is the crux of rock's identity problem: many bands or artists that could be described as rock—or would've been called rock thirty years ago—are more often than not classified under a different genre. In another time, Taylor Swift would've been classified as a rock star—she's a singer-songwriter who plays confessional songs in basketball arenas, like Bruce Springsteen, Eddie Vedder, or Sheryl Crow. But instead she's called country or pop. The same could be said of Adele—she's part of the diva continuum with Aretha Franklin, Whitney Houston, and Celine Dion, but she also belongs in the history of singer-songwriters with Carole King and Joni Mitchell, who were lumped under the rock umbrella in the seventies. That's two of the biggest pop stars in the world with rock in their DNA, but they are almost never discussed as rock singers.

Let's keep going: If you take the opinions of the band members themselves into account, One Direction is among the most popular rock bands of the 2010s. You can hear it in the music—the title track from 2013's *Midnight Memories* sounds *a lot* like Def Leppard's "Pour Some Sugar on Me." (Harry Styles's 2017 solo debut is even more indebted to classic rock—the record resembles a hybrid of Oasis and the Allman Brothers Band.) But nobody who cares about rock music regards One Direction as a rock band, just as nobody puts the "rock" tag on Maroon 5, even though it's a five-piece group with a conventional guitar-bass-drums formation.

But what if I'm wrong, and the problem is more serious than a simple identity crisis? I might be the only person on Earth who doesn't want his own "Rock is dead" moment. But I have one anyway.

The same week as the Republican National Convention, I ven-tured into the Northwoods of Wisconsin in search of a metaphor for rock's identity crisis. I thought I would find it at Rock Fest, a three-day music festival that bills itself as the "largest rock music and camping event in the U.S." I guess this means that Bonnaroo is technically classified as "a dirty-hippie music and camping event." But only nerds worry about semantics. As Chuck Berry once sang, just let me hear some of that unequivocal, tangible, not-at-all confused, clearly defined rock music.

So, I set my GPS coordinates to "ROCK" and embarked on a two-hour drive through a thunderstorm to Cadott, Wisconsin. I played Black Sabbath inside the car while it looked like Black Sabbath outside the car. The dark vibe made me feel paranoid. All the while I kept my eyes peeled on the horizon for menacing pink swordsmen.

Held annually since 1994, Rock Fest started out as a straight-up Midwestern classic-rock festival—the inaugural lineup included REO Speedwagon, Cheap Trick, BTO, Foghat, and Eddie Money. Subsequent bills were rounded out by groups that might've played arenas had they been touring with their most famous lineups: Fleetwood Mac without Stevie Nicks and Lindsey Buckingham, Electric Light Orchestra without Jeff Lynne, Joe Walsh without the other Eagles.

By the early 2000s, Rock Fest was welcoming nineties pop-rock bands like Counting Crows, Smash Mouth, and the Spin Doctors, all of whom had put out platinum-selling albums just a few years earlier. Eighties hair metal also started to crowd out seventies arena rock—Poison was a reliable draw, but so were also-rans like FireHouse and Jackyl. By the dawn of the 2010s, Rock Fest had devolved into a showcase for "butt rock," a gross but nonetheless appropriate term for lowest-common-denominator hard-rock bands.

A summary of Rock Fest's history echoes the recent history

of modern rock radio, which currently relies on a mix of nineties alt-rock hits and the latest excretions by lifelike Affliction Clothing mannequins such as Five Finger Death Punch, Avenged Sevenfold, and Breaking Benjamin. That is the sum total of what "rock" is now for the people who listen to rock radio and attend festivals like Rock Fest—an inscrutable equation that plugs old-world rock hedonism passed down fourth-hand from Led Zeppelin and Aerosmith into the bludgeoning, sadomasochistic sonic textures of post-grunge and nu metal. It's party music for people who hate their lives.

The key to understanding Rock Fest was *Making a Murderer,* the ten-part Netflix documentary about the questionable conviction of Steven Avery and Brendan Dassey for the 2005 sexual assault and murder of a twenty-five-year-old photographer in rural Wisconsin. When *Making a Murderer* became a cultural phenomenon in 2015, the conversation focused on the particulars of the murder case and the possibility that Avery and Dassey were innocent. But *Making a Murderer* also functioned as a lacerating portrait of an economically depressed Rust Belt community that has been left to rot.

Personal experience caused me to view *Making a Murderer* from this perspective: I grew up about a half hour away from Manitowoc County, where Avery and Dassey lived, and was working for an area newspaper when the story originally broke in 2006. The people standing in the background of every frame of *Making a Murderer*—the townspeople, the news reporters, the befuddled police officers—seemed instantly familiar.

I sensed that these people were fundamentally "good." But I was also aware of how the grind of life in a place like northeastern Wisconsin—marked by punishing winters, slowly decaying industries, a Republican-controlled government intent on reducing public spending, and a hermetically sealed-off culture that embraces outside change like a glacier welcomes an ocean liner—recalibrates the parameters of "good." Life in a small town requires rationalizing the limitations imposed on daily life that are beyond your control. You learn to accept the misery. Eventually, you come to appreciate misery's utilitarianism, and how superfluous comforts don't get in the way of work and sleep. Alcohol helps the process—your inevitable drinking problem enhances the misery, and the misery enhances your drinking problem. Again, *utilitarian*.

The Rock Fest grounds were abundant with utilitarian misery that day. The so-called VIP seating area was just about thirty rows of cold gray concrete benches turned to a cruddy brown by the day's storms, buttressed by a hill offering several acres of muddy pasture to general-admission attendees. Everything looked black and white due to overcast skies choked with cigarette and vaporizer exhaust. Attendees braced themselves against the downpour under rain-soaked hoodies. They were neither friendly nor unfriendly, just hard looking. Everyone seemed to fall into one of two categories: the sweaty sober or the steely drunk. Either way, I knew not to hold anyone's thousand-yard stare.

The headliner that night was the Hollywood Vampires, a shrunkgroup composed of Alice Cooper, Joe Perry of Aerosmith, and Johnny Depp. They had introduced themselves to the world five months earlier at the 2016 Grammys, when they performed Motörhead's "Ace of Spades" in tribute to the late Lemmy Kilmister. If not for Steven Tyler's solo career and Depp's immense supply of disposable income, it's doubtful that the Vampires would even exist. And yet there they were at the Grammys, brandishing flaming torches, smoke machines, spray tans, chains, tattoos, fedoras, and candelabras. The highlight of the performance was a stray audience shot featuring a bemused and purple-suited Bruno Mars, who looked like a guy waiting for Grandpa to stop nattering on at the dinner table about whatever he saw on Fox News that day.

At the Grammys, the Vampires presented themselves to the world as slick professionals who faithfully replicated old rock songs as a tribute to fallen icons, just as they had on the Vampires' largely ignored self-titled 2015 LP. The concept of the album was that each song derived from one of Alice Cooper's old drinking buddies from the early seventies, including Jimi Hendrix, Jim Morrison, John Lennon, Harry Nilsson, and Keith Moon. The other thing these artists had in common, of course, was that they were all dead. The first "meta" shrunkgroup, the Vampires acknowledged rock's decay and celebrated its ongoing decomposition. They were like a walking EKG measuring rock's flatline.

Since their TV debut, the Vampires had fallen upon hard times. Five days before the Rock Fest gig, during a show at Coney Island's Ford Amphitheater, sixty-five-year-old Joe Perry felt faint and braced himself against the drum riser. Eventually, he stumbled backstage and collapsed. Perry's condition was later described as "a combination of dehydration and exhaustion." (Perry returned to the tour two weeks later.) Then there was the matter of Depp's divorce, which had turned messy in light of spousal abuse allegations from estranged wife Amber Heard. Heard alleged that Depp obsessed over her relationship with recent costar Billy Bob Thornton, and in his distress severed part of his own finger with a broken bottle. But none of this had derailed the Vampires as they descended on concert venues that summer in mostly secondary markets like Mount Pleasant, Michigan; Rohnert Park, California; and Cadott, Wisconsin, for Rock Fest.

Before the Vampires arrived, however, there was a set by Marilyn Manson. I had never seen Manson live, but I had interviewed him in 2015 and found the experience both highly entertaining and extremely befuddling. I had wanted to talk to him because I liked the album he was promoting at the time, *The Pale Emperor*, and because he had a reputation for being smarter than you might expect. Really though, Marilyn Manson is smart if you expect him to be kind of dumb, and kind of dumb if you expect him to be smart. Personally, I liked him better as a dumb rock guy than as a supposed sage.

I wanted to talk to Manson about how *The Pale Emperor*'s unexpectedly bluesy sound reminded me of debauched, late-period Doors albums like 1970's *Morrison Hotel* and especially 1971's

L.A. Woman. (Song titles from *The Pale Emperor* include "The Mephistopheles of Los Angeles" and "Third Day of a Seven Day Binge.") Manson brought up the Doors before I did. He called Jim Morrison his "whole inspiration" for becoming a budding poet as a teenager. Later, when he got to jam with Doors members Ray Manzarek and Robby Krieger on some of their tunes in 2012, it seemed to mark the apotheosis of his career.

"They just went with me," Manson marveled. "That's what they did with Jim because he was chaos and they were the tornado, and they just had to go with it. They didn't really have any choice."

I don't know if Manson could tell that I got off on this sort of ridiculousness, but we nonetheless shared an instant kinship over our appreciation of rock mythology. He gamely kept on pumping out hot air. "I'm the third act," he declared. "I'm the person that bends the rules. The hero is just a straight line, but the villain is always the guy who's willing to do things passionately because he wants to do it." I had to stifle my delighted squeals. He went on: "There was a time when, metaphorically, you sold your soul to become a rock star. I think that I stopped paying for a couple years, [or] I didn't pay up as much as I should have. This record was my payment to him, saying, 'Check is through now, motherfucker. This is payment due, plus interest.'"

Onstage, Manson was far less compelling, though it wasn't for lack of trying. Before Manson came out, the Rock Fest grounds throbbed to Rihanna's "Bitch Better Have My Money," and the wobbly bass sounded incredible, the most genuine rock 'n' roll moment of the whole festival. Then Manson entered, slurring his songs like he was wasted, though his inebriation appeared to be affected. When it was time to perform his cover of Eurythmics' "Sweet Dreams (Are Made of This)," Manson came out on twelve-foot stilts. If Manson truly was drunk, his stilt-walking abilities were extraordinary.

After an hour, Manson was done, and then it was another hour's wait in the rain to see the Hollywood Vampires. All there was to do in the meantime was drink. When I'd first arrived at the grounds, I'd bought a Michelob from a curvy blonde wearing a black cowboy hat, a black leather jacket, and spandex pants with rips up the sides. But I soon discovered that you could get whiskey cocktails for the same price. The booze at Rock Fest cost about the same as bottles of water, and it was more essential for surviving the experience.

Upon returning to my concrete slab with another cocktail, I noticed that my seatmates, a beefy dude named Dave and his blond and prodigiously pierced girlfriend, Nona, had departed. They had told me earlier that they weren't so jazzed about that night's lineup; they were more excited to see Slipknot and Five Finger Death Punch later that weekend. The mood before the Vampires was depressingly funereal. The music blaring over the PA was "Down by the River" by Neil Young and Crazy Horse, a song about taking something you love and murdering it.

At eleven P.M., the Vampires came out. At the Grammys, the Vampires had been augmented by GNR's Duff McKagan and Matt Sorum. But Duff had been called up that summer to play stadiums with the reconstituted Guns N' Roses, leaving Sorum to slum it with the Vampires back in the minors.

Cooper might've been the front man, but Depp was both the main attraction and the Vampires' raison d'être. It would have been easy for them to quit after Perry was hospitalized, but Depp's celebrity and ego had kept them going. In a way, you had to admire his commitment. The only glamour in performing for several thousand people in rain-soaked Cadott was that Perry himself had done it two years prior with Aerosmith. Depp was using the disposable income from his movie-star career to pay his dues as a classic-rock musician, and the audience indulged him to bask in the glow of Depp's stardom.

They started off with some Bowie and T. Rex and it was thoroughly not terrible, because even the saddest version of "Jeepster" is still pretty damn invigorating. Throughout the show, Cooper spoke in a fake British accent that underlined the campiness of it all.

"Tonight we'll be doing songs for all of our dead drunk friends," Cooper toasted, and I wondered if he was thinking about poor Joe Perry, who thankfully wasn't dead yet but easily could've been.

After twenty-five minutes, I could no longer stand the rain and left. The problem was entirely mine—the people around me loved what they were seeing and relished the opportunity to get out of their lives for a few hours. I was glad for them. My problem is that I don't like feeling stupid, and the Vampires made me feel like a big fat dunce for caring about classic-rock mythology so much.

I went to Rock Fest because I thought it would help me understand what "rock music" means to the average person. What I discovered instead had less to do with everybody else at Rock Fest than my own lifelong illusions about the music I had grown up with. It's not like I went into Rock Fest expecting greatness. But watching the Hollywood Vampires confirmed some troubling realities. The hot-shit, skinny-ass white guy in leather pants who takes pulls off Jack Daniel's bottles while blasting bloozerock riffs out of his Gibson—that archetype is finished, and it's never coming back. Rock music no longer signifies youth, danger, or rebellion. It is not particularly sexy or especially violent. Even at its best, rock music doesn't command the zeitgeist like it did at Woodstock. At its worst, it can't even personify cultural decay like Altamont. The old myths that once animated rock have essentially evaporated. I could see them dissipate in real time in the Wisconsin Northwoods, where movie-star glamour and rock-god swagger alike withered in the cold, gray rain.

When I was a kid, I became a disciple of classic-rock mythology because I wanted to be part of something bigger and grander than myself; back then, classic rock represented immortality. But at Rock Fest, the music was set on a fixed loop that always seemed to end in death. This is the identity that rock music is saddled with now. In the popular consciousness, rock 'n' roll is a tribute concert played by leathery men hoisting one last toast to dead drinking buddies. It just seems so *small*.

Is rock dead? Not to me, not yet. But it can seem awfully hard to find sometimes. Life-changing bands don't just appear on television or the radio these days. In the twenty-first century, rock mythology has been inverted. Now it's up to listeners to go on a hero's journey to seek out what they're looking for. The music no longer finds you. You must find the music. Straightforward replications of the past always fall flat—the sweet spot is to find a band that can draw on the past just enough that it's able to twist the mythology into something new and surprising.

That's the thing about a hero's journey: you never end up quite where you expect.

"The Hero Discovers the Meaning of Life, Transcending Death, and Finding God . . ."

"You Enjoy Myself"

NOTES ON TRACK 16: We were so high when we recorded this that we're still playing it as we speak.

Starting in the early aughts, the term "guilty pleasure" was phased out of the pop-culture lexicon. This wasn't a matter of jargon associated with a bygone era becoming dated; "guilty pleasure" didn't go the way of "groovy" or "to the max" or "niiice" done in that stupid Borat voice. The change was strictly ideological. Critics and commentators mounted a coordinated strike against "guilty pleasure," arguing that implanting shame onto cultural preferences was at best prudish and at worst prejudicial to various demographic groups. This anti–"guilty pleasure" campaign coincided with the Internet's ascendance as the media's central hub—on the web, you don't have to look hard to find partisans for any cultural artifact, no matter how disreputable. Suddenly, classifying Carly Rae Jepsen or *Gossip Girl* or Mountain Dew as a guilty pleasure seemed not only passé but offensive. It was time for a bold new era in which people were allowed to simply like what they liked without consequences. Now there's even cachet associated with appreciating joyously inane mainstream culture. Which means that if you're a forty-five-year-old man who loves Carly Rae Jepsen, you probably don't ever shut the hell up about it.

However, guilty pleasures haven't *completely* gone away, the definition has just shifted. There are plenty of music opinions that you're not allowed to share publicly without shame, it's just that most of them have little to do with silly, frothy pop. Loving Carly Rae Jepsen is now acceptable, but loving, say, the jam-band stylings of Phish is not. I know this because I love Phish, and I can already feel you judging me about it.

Phish is a four-piece rock group from Vermont that formed in 1983. The group's first album, *Junta,* was released in 1989, and three years later Phish signed with Elektra Records. The band subsequently enjoyed its period of greatest notoriety from 1993 (when it first started selling out arenas) to 1999 (when it played an epic eight-hour concert in front of eighty-five thousand people at an Indian reservation in Florida). The following year, Phish went on hiatus, then re-formed in 2002, then seemingly broke up for good in 2004, and *then* re-formed again in 2009, not long after the band's singer and guitarist, Trey Anastasio, spent fourteen months in a county court drug program for possession of various illegal prescriptions. Since then, Phish has toured every year (though in a limited capacity compared to the nineties) and put out several more albums.

People who care about rock music have almost certainly heard of Phish. But I'd guess at least 90 percent of them aren't aware of even the basic biographical information I just outlined. Phish proves that it's possible to be well-known without being famous; for decades, they have existed in a bubble that has only slightly grazed the mainstream on a small handful of occasions.

The only thing most people know about Phish is that they hate Phish.

When I call Phish a guilty pleasure, I don't mean that I feel bad about enjoying epic guitar solos or goofy lyrics about dogs, antelope, and watchful hosemasters. What I mean is that being a Phish fan *makes me guilty*. When you love Phish, you are instantly alienated from the vast majority of the population. Being into Phish is not merely a musical preference. "Phish fan"—or, ahem, "phan"—is a cultural archetype. And as far as most people are concerned, this archetype is annoying and probably doesn't smell very good.

Let's say you're on a date, and it's going really well. Your date is attractive, funny, kind, and not insane. You are 73 percent sure you want to sleep with this person. Then, over your third round of drinks, your date casually mentions that she is a serious collector of Precious Moments figurines. She has hundreds of them—so many that the figurines have their own room in her apartment.

Would this change your impression of your date? Perhaps not—but it's pretty fucking strange, right? Collecting Precious Moments figurines surely doesn't make a person *more* attractive.

That's what being a Phish fan is like. It's not something you can talk about with most people without its altering the molecular structure of the encounter. Depending on how early *A Live One* comes up in conversation, it might very well be a deal-breaker for a potential friendship or romantic relationship. So, you learn to keep your "What is the best-ever version of 'Tweezer'?" takes to yourself. It's a matter of social graces.

But even if the average music listener didn't instantly recoil at the mere mention of the band's name, Phish would still be a self-contained world. It's that way by design. And as counterintuitive as it might seem, this very isolation is what got me into the band. Learning about them is the closest I've come as an adult to replicating my childhood experience of discovering the gods of classic rock. Because Phish *is* a classic-rock band that just happened to be mistakenly born about twenty years too late.

Led Zeppelin, Pink Floyd, Frank Zappa, Yes, Peter Gabriel-era Genesis, *Quadrophenia*, *Remain in Light*—these are all important touchstones referenced both explicitly and implicitly throughout Phish's career. Classic rock is the music Phish most often covers in concert, and it's the well from which they derive their own material. All of the proggy self-indulgence that the Ramones supposedly destroyed in the late seventies comprises the band's roots. That's the real reason why music critics and cool kids hate Phish so much—they operate as if punk never happened.

Phish interprets classic rock the way Zeppelin and the Stones interpreted the blues. The closer the Brits hewed to tradition, the phonier they sounded. The typical British blues musician was only going to sound gawky and prissy next to Muddy Waters. The only way out for British blues bands was to deconstruct, blow out, and aggressively exaggerate the blues to such a degree that it eventually became something else. This is what Phish does with classic rock: Just as Mick Jagger was a foreigner in the Mississippi Delta, the exceedingly geeky members of Phish were always going to be outsiders in the context of "cool" classic-rock mythology. They turned their geekiness into a positive by acknowledging their distance from the classic-rock gods, reimagining rock history as a fun house for a special breed of rock nerd who is simultaneously reverent and irreverent toward the genre's conventions. In the process, Phish pushed classic-rock mythology into a postmodern realm.

Phish's geeky interpretation of classic rock takes many forms. The band's drummer, Jon Fishman, doesn't play drum solos, but he does execute virtuosic feats on a vacuum cleaner. When Phish covers Lynyrd Skynyrd's "Free Bird" or David Bowie's "Space Oddity," they perform them strictly a cappella. When Phish writes a lighters-hoisting arena-rock ballad, they give it a non sequitur title like "The Squirming Coil."

For this reason, they offer the most authentic classic-rock experience you can get from a band that didn't originate in the classic-rock era, drawing on the mythology without slavishly replicating the past. The uniqueness of this achievement is made clear when you compare Phish to other jam bands. The ones I like— Widespread Panic, Gov't Mule, Chris Robinson Brotherhood— are obvious descendants of the Grateful Dead as well as the

Allman Brothers Band, eternal godfathers of the jam-band scene's Southern wing. (Gov't Mule's Warren Haynes actually made his name playing with the Allmans after their comeback in the late eighties.)

You can't listen to most jam-band records or go to shows without thinking about their predecessors, and this seems intentional. Those bands dress and act like grizzled road dogs straight out of 1973. I'm not knocking it—clearly I'm a person who likes to celebrate classic-rock history—but the backward-looking aspects of those bands are undeniable.

In Phish world, many of the traditional accoutrements of rock mythology—the guitar god, the rock opera, the laser-light show, the drug-fueled hedonistic party, the once-in-a-lifetime "event" rock show—have been turned into opportunities for outcasts to create their own fantasy worlds. At a Phish show, anyone who adores supposedly outmoded rock traditions can come and revel in them in a way that feels organic and unique. It doesn't matter if those traditions don't translate beyond the arena walls. The requirement that a rock band must communicate with the masses in order to be relevant never meant anything to Phish. This band invented its own relevance and left it to the fans (rather than critics and journalists) to write the myths.

The result is a labyrinthian legend that enhances the experience of listening to a band that most people can't stand. Loving Phish will always set you apart, and that's a good thing. For me, it made caring about classic rock feel special again.

Before I loved Phish, I loathed them. And I think my reasoning was common: I despised hippies, and in my mind hippie culture and Phish were synonymous. For a long time this also kept me from appreciating the Grateful Dead. But even after I finally embraced the Dead, I continued to reject Phish because I assumed they were just ripping off what the Dead had created back in the sixties. Besides, the Grateful Dead played Altamont and hung out with the Hells Angels, and their songs were about death and transcendence and riding that train while high on cocaine. The Grateful Dead was sort of cool. Phish was *never* cool.

As my dabbling in Phish went from casual to obsessive, I discovered that pretty much all of my assumptions about Phish were wrong, starting with the belief that Phish was biting the Dead's style. In fact, Phish and the Dead have significantly different reference points. The Grateful Dead was informed by the totality of American music from the first sixty years of the twentieth century: blues, country, folk, jazz, and early rock 'n' roll. Also, the Dead did not exude energy. They were capable of rocking, but only until about 1982. After that, they rolled at decelerating speeds. In their final years in the nineties, they played like a laid-back jazz combo soundtracking Sunday brunch. Their fast songs were slow and their slow songs were like freeze-dried molasses.

Phish, meanwhile, is relatively supercharged. In their nineties prime, Phish would construct jams by storming out of the gate for several minutes. Then the four members would drift into a spacey midsection for several more minutes, and then build to a blazing finish via Anastasio's wildly soloing guitar for an additional several minutes. Phish's musical DNA was also more eclectic and eccentric than the Dead's, indicative of a band that was formed at a time when there were a lot more records to hear. In Phish, you can hear hopped-up bluegrass, jazzy disco, porno-movie funk, Broadway theatricality, and shockingly sincere barbershop harmonies. But it all ultimately stems from classic rock. If the Dead encompasses American music from roughly 1900 to 1967, Phish picks up the story through the AOR era, from '68 to around the time *Stop Making Sense* debuted in theaters in the mideighties.

The only significant links between Phish and the Grateful Dead are (1) a propensity for improvised music, and (2) a friendly attitude toward concert tapers, who preserved Phish's performance history and added significantly to the band's legacy. And yet it's impossible to talk about Phish without also talking about the Grateful Dead, and this is related to our favorite mythologist, Joseph Campbell.

In 1986, Campbell hosted a symposium in San Francisco called "Ritual and Rapture, From Dionysus to the Grateful Dead," inspired by a recent, unexpectedly positive experience at a Dead show. At the time, the Dead seemed consigned to the trash heap of history, an icon of a bygone age marked for obsolescence by the advent of punk, hip-hop, and MTV. As detailed by rock critic Jesse Jarnow in his trenchant book *Heads: A Biography of Psychedelic America*, the Deadhead scene of the early Reagan years was a bastion of marginalized outlaws: Hare Krishnas, bikers, mystics, and drug dealers with ties to the Mexican mafia. There's even a legend about a group of bank robbers that followed the band in '79—they'd hit up a show, knock over a bank, and then speed off to the next tour stop.

By the end of the decade, however, the Dead's fortunes changed dramatically. The band scored its first and only Top 10 single, "Touch of Grey," in 1987, which attracted a sea of wannabes and rubberneckers to Dead shows and transformed the band into one of the world's top touring attractions. In that respect, Campbell was slightly ahead of the curve. While he was no fan of rock music, Campbell was fascinated by the Deadheads' devotion, which he likened to ancient worshippers of Dionysus, the Greek god of wine, fertility, ritual madness, and religious ecstasy. Campbell came away from his first Dead experience a convert, declaring that they were "the antidote to the atomic bomb" because of their power to bring diverse groups of people together.

What Campbell articulated had long been an unspoken understanding among the Deadheads—individuals were drawn to the Grateful Dead because they wanted to be part of something greater than themselves. The Dead became a stadium act in the final years of Jerry Garcia's life because standing amid tens of thousands of sweaty, buzzed, and barefoot people felt meaningful in the classic Woodstock sense. Even as Garcia succumbed to heroin addiction, which hobbled his playing and added years of mileage to his vocals, the Dead's audience continued to grow. By then, the music was beside the point. What neo-hippies shared with the OG hippies was a love for the crowd that matched, maybe even exceeded, their love of the band.

But what if you were born too late for the Grateful Dead? As much as I love collecting Dead concert bootlegs, I'm never going to see Jerry Garcia play live. But I still yearned to join a tribe set off from the mainstream of society, so I chose to make Trey Anastasio my guitar-soloing guru. Phish might not sound like the Dead, but they do provide the listener with a Dead-like experience.

When I watched *Bittersweet Motel,* a documentary filmed during various Phish tours in 1997 and '98 and released in 2000, it was like witnessing an alternate version of the nineties, in which grunge and gangsta rap didn't matter and Phish was the biggest band in the world. *Bittersweet Motel* culminates with the Great Went, a two-day concert held in 1997 at a former air force base in Maine that attracted seventy-five thousand people. The Great Went was an even more successful sequel to the Clifford Ball, Phish's first big-time festival, which was held the previous summer in upstate New York. This was years before festivals like Coachella and Bonnaroo became the norm on the summer concert circuit. It's not a stretch to suggest that Phish—a band that has relied far more on touring and staging massive destination concerts than revenue from albums—was inventing the future of the music business during the pre-Napster era, when most superstar acts were content to reap the benefits of $20 CDs like there was no tomorrow.

The Woodstock overtones of the Clifford Ball were obvious, and media outlets flocked to cover it, including MTV, which made a half-hour documentary starring scores of shirtless dudes and shirtless ladies and their shirtless dogs. But these multiday extravaganzas were ultimately designed for the inhabitants of Phish's self-contained world.

As Anastasio later said of another weekend-long concert, 1998's Lemonwheel, "We had built an alternate reality where the rules of reality didn't apply."

How does one exit regular reality and enter Phish world?

Becoming a fan of Phish is not easy or for the faint of heart. For my journey into the jam-band wilds, I knew I would need a Sherpa, a person who could guide me into unknown territory and point out the important landmarks and dangerous pitfalls. When I was a kid learning about Zeppelin and Pink Floyd, I relied on music magazines and rock books. But there's not a lot of reliable literature about Phish. I read three band biographies, but I still sensed that I wasn't getting the whole picture: The writing about Phish tends to be either reactionary and dismissive, or overly worshipful and inscrutable. You're either on the outside mocking this weird, enigmatic hippie band, or you're an insider speaking in the Esperanto of set-list statistics and "tour" stories. I needed someone who was fluent in Phish but also had enough perspective on the band to offer sound advice to a neophyte.

Fortunately, I was already acquainted with Rob Mitchum, a rock critic who had seen Phish more than fifty times, dating back to his first show in 1996. When I emailed Rob to ask for a primer on the band, he was beyond excited. Two things were immediately apparent: (1) Phish was a topic that he really enjoyed talking about, and (2) very few people ever wanted to talk to him about it. Rob seized this opportunity by writing me a lengthy email.

In retrospect, I could have just as easily consulted Phish.net, a popular resource for set lists and song information. For practically every show they have ever played, there is a post with a comments section in which attendees review the show and recount tall tales about their concert experiences, which often have more to do with the drugs they ingested during the gig than the gig itself. Taken together, these reviews add up to a people's history, doing the work of documenting the band's story that professional critics and journalists have largely avoided.

Before Phish.net there were several editions of *The Pharmer's Almanac,* which collected show information and statistics in hardcopy form, as well as the comprehensive, nearly thousand-page tome *The Phish Companion*. Here you'll find obsessively compiled statistics about all of the hundreds of songs they have played live since the early eighties. You can find "song gap" information on the time that elapsed between particular songs' occurring in a set list. You can see which albums the songs from a particular night's concert were culled from. You can discover how many times they played "Fast Enough for You" in 1993. (Seventeen.) You can learn how many vacuum solos were played in 1997. (Three.) The statistics are needlessly, stupidly, fascinatingly thorough.

No doubt, a lot of hippie dolts enjoy Phish. But the partisans that I've encountered are more akin to nerdy baseball fans who care way too much about Sabermetrics. They're like Mike Hamad, a music writer for the *Hartford Courant* who started diagramming live Phish jams in 2013, drawing a graph of all the shifts in rhythm, tone, and vibe that take place during the long instrumental passages in the songs. Similar to the hundreds of contributors to Phish.net and *The Phish Companion*, Hamad seems to approach them as part science and part religion.

In the early days, the stats were helpful for traders who were looking for concert tapes that featured a rarely performed song or an especially exploratory and exciting jam. Back then, you were forced to be choosy about which tapes you accumulated. By the time I became a fan, however, it was infinitely easier to sample Phish's live work. Right away, Rob emailed me a link to "The Spreadsheet," a massive online treasure trove in which virtually every Phish show is available for download. The Phish On Demand (or PhishOD) app would eventually make all of those shows available in streamable form, along with the official Live-Phish app, which posts pristine recordings of new concerts within minutes of the final encore.

Normally, when you're getting into a new band, you investigate the discography of studio albums. If the band is popular enough, it's easy to figure out what the entry points are. Even when I was a teenager who knew almost nothing about music, I was aware that *Led Zeppelin IV* and *The Dark Side of the Moon* were like a set of double doors leading to that magical palace of classic-rock glory. With Phish, however, it's more complicated. Rob, for one, actively discouraged me from listening to their albums.

"Don't even bother," he told me. "They're all pretty bad."

Now, opinions vary on the quality of their studio work. (I eventually did peruse Phish's albums, and came to love exactly four of them: *A Picture of Nectar, Rift, Billy Breathes,* and *Farmhouse.*) But hardly anybody who likes them defines the band's various eras by the albums. This is the most profound example of Phish deconstructing classic-rock orthodoxy and reassembling it into something entirely different. They invert the recorded music–vs.–live music hierarchy even more than the Dead did—for Phish there is no equivalent to *American Beauty* (the one Dead album even non-Dead-fans know) or "Touch of Grey" (a Top 10 pop hit that became a cultural phenomenon). Instead, they go all in on the transcendent power of the rock show. So, Rob suggested that I focus solely on bootlegs.

Here's how Rob broke down the live eras of Phish's career in his original "primer" email, which more or less squares with the consensus of the band's amateur chroniclers:

Everything up to '93: Jazz-prog nerds

'93–'96: Gradually deeper, busier improv and arena-rock chops

'97–'98: More focused improv, funk evolving to ambient

'99–'00: Harder groove and *spaaaaaace*

'02–'04: The hard drug years (avoid)

'09–present: More crowd pleasing, less improv, occasional flashes of former brilliance

One of the Phish shows that Rob recommended was 3/22/93, an iconic gig played at the Crest Theatre in Sacramento. This show is celebrated for its second set—Phish almost always plays two sets, and Phish fans almost always care more about the second set, which is typically jammier and more experimental. That wasn't the case for 3/22/93, though—the second set was unique because it was one of the rare instances where Phish played its rock opera *The Man Who Stepped into Yesterday*—also known as Gamehendge—in its entirety.

A loopy amalgam of *The Lamb Lies Down on Broadway,* C. S. Lewis, and whatever stoned whimsy is conjured by goofballs trying to kill the boredom of living in Vermont, *The Man Who Stepped into Yesterday* is Phish's very own rock opera, because all classic-rock groups need a rock opera. It's about a retired colonel from Long Island named Forbin who seeks to recover a mythic tome called *The Helping Friendly Book* from the clutches of an evil tyrant named Wilson. Originally Trey Anastasio's senior thesis while a student at Goddard College, *The Man Who Stepped into Yesterday* has never been released as a proper album. But various songs have appeared on Phish LPs, including live staples such as "Wilson," "AC/DC Bag" (named after Wilson's robot henchman), and "The Lizards" (the race of people who inhabit Gamehendge).

As I drifted deeper into Phish, I learned about other obscure but no less essential bits of lore. There was the 3/6/92 gig in Portsmouth, New Hampshire, also known as the "secret language show," in which they initiated no fewer than four signals to generate band-audience interaction in the middle of songs, including "All Fall Down" (a series of four descending notes that cues the audience to fall down), "Aw, Fuck!" (a scraping noise on the guitar that tells the audience to extend a middle finger), "Random Note" (a carnivalesque ten-note sequence signaling fans to sing "Ahhh!"), and "Turn, Turn, Turn" (a quote from the Byrds song that tells the audience to turn around and applaud for an invisible band). I couldn't believe it; Phish literally had its own language!

I studied Phish shows in my thirties like I once studied classic-rock radio in my teens. At first, I couldn't discern the differences between all of the different live versions of "Tweezer," a lightly funky workout from 1992's *A Picture of Nectar* that became one of Phish's most reliable jam vehicles. But my immersion was paying off—my ears had grown stronger and more attentive. I could now absorb thirty-minute excursions into the musical ether without getting lost or bored. At the same time, I'm still not fully confident that I know what "good" Phish is. I am keenly aware that many of my opinions are "wrong" in the eyes of true-blue Phish scholars.

For instance, after I had been listening to Phish for a few years and started going to shows, I felt confident enough to tell Rob that I really liked "Backwards Down the Number Line," a gently melodic midtempo tune from 2009's *Joy*. Rob, with infinite patience, explained to me that "Backwards Down the Number Line" was presently *the most hated song* among Phish fans, because the band always seemed to play it in the second set, where it always interrupted promising jams. (The die-hards referred to this phenomenon as a jam being "lined.") Sure, "Backwards Down the Number Line" was pleasant enough, but it didn't have the elasticity of Phish's most beloved material, Rob insisted. For people like Rob who had hung in for twenty years and scoured every show for magic moments, a nice song with minimum jam potential was basically a nonstarter.

It was all about the jams. He didn't want to hear predictable songs. He didn't want Phish shows to get "too classic-rocky." (Whereas I love it when Phish gets too classic-rocky.) The allure of a band whose body of work grows a little bigger with each concert is that you'll probably never run out of music. For long-time followers like Rob, it wasn't about hearing songs you already liked—it was finding something you didn't know existed.

I don't mind Rob or anybody else telling me that my Phish opinions are wrong. I *like* being wrong about Phish, because it means I have a lot more to learn. I can once again reap the benefits of ignorance, when all that's worth hearing is still unheard, like it was back in my bedroom when I was in middle school. And with Phish, the amount of unheard music grows with every show. I'll probably never reach the end of it.

Is it possible that my interest in Phish stems from a deep-seated midlife crisis that I don't want to acknowledge? Maybe. But at least it's cheaper than a sports car.

"Junior Dad"

NOTES ON TRACK 17: We used to say "Our songs are our children" in interviews. Then critics started calling us dad rock. Pricks.

I am having a debate with myself about Pearl Jam and Wilco.

Here's my dilemma: I love both Pearl Jam and Wilco. Whenever a concert by either band is scheduled in my area, I will see it. However, it turns out that the next Pearl Jam concert in my area will occur on the same day as the next local Wilco concert.

Therefore, I must choose. This won't be easy. But let's break it down.

Overall, I think Wilco has the better discography. I don't know that I've listened to any Wilco album as much as Pearl Jam's *Vs.*, *Vitalogy*, or *No Code*, but I don't like those albums quite as much as *Being There*, *Yankee Hotel Foxtrot*, or *A Ghost Is Born*. Wilco is also more critically acclaimed, though Pearl Jam has sold exponentially more records. Which means that Pearl Jam is more embedded in the times with which it is associated; you can't discuss nineties pop culture without delving into Pearl Jam, whereas

Wilco would only register as a footnote for many rock fans. In that sense, I guess Pearl Jam means more to me, that *Vitalogy* feels like a part of my past in a way that *Being There* doesn't. However, you could also argue that while Pearl Jam's music defines an era, Wilco's music exists outside of time, and is therefore timeless. Who wouldn't rather be timeless?

In a concert setting, I'm slightly more excited to hear Pearl Jam play songs from their best records than I am to hear Wilco play songs from their best records. In fact, I think Pearl Jam is probably the best live band of its generation. Though given the changes to Wilco's lineup over the years, those live versions are often more interesting than Pearl Jam's one millionth rendition of "Rearviewmirror." You can't argue against the stability of Pearl Jam's lineup, though—it feels more like a real band than Wilco does. But isn't Eddie Vedder's place in Pearl Jam roughly analogous to Jeff Tweedy's place in Wilco? If Stone Gossard had been as stubborn about asserting his need for creative control in Pearl Jam as Jay Bennett was about controlling the damn mix for *Yankee Hotel Foxtrot*, I'm sure Vedder would've fired Gossard's ass.

Maybe this conversation is really about Vedder vs. Tweedy.

Let's start over: Vedder is the superior singer, but Tweedy is the superior lyricist. Though Vedder can't quite touch Tweedy's heart-wrenching vocal on "Radio Cure," and Tweedy has never written a first-person narrative as gripping as "Jeremy" or "Elderly Woman Behind the Counter in a Small Town." What if we pitted Vedder and Tweedy against each other in a mythical arm-wrestling contest, *Over the Top*–style? Vedder seems to be in better shape than Tweedy, but Tweedy likely has the psychological edge, given his years of mind games with Jay Farrar back in Uncle Tupelo. I suspect it would be a draw.

One thing is clear: this is the most dad-rock moment of my life.

Given that you are holding a book in which topics such as *Frampton Comes Alive!* **and "Turn the Page" and David Bowie's**

cocaine habits in the seventies are discussed at length, I'm going to assume that you've heard the term "dad rock." I'm also going to assume that you *like* dad rock. This is good, because I (obviously) also like dad rock. A lot.

But let's say you have no clue what dad rock is. In the parlance of our times, "dad rock" is used to describe three kinds of bands.

1. A dad-rock band is a band that your dad liked when he was young.

The most straightforward definition. Initially, dad rock was meant to describe popular if also unfashionable groups from the sixties and seventies—Steely Dan is probably the most emblematic dad-rock band of all time, though dadness is also strong with the Eagles, Jimmy Buffett, Paul Simon, and Crosby, Stills, Nash and Young. However, dads have gotten younger over time, so now it also applies to bands from the nineties, including Pearl Jam and Wilco. (The current generation of dads might very well be the last for whom rock is popular enough for "dad rock" to work as a recognizable signifier.)

2. A dad-rock band is a band that is consciously and unapologetically influenced by bands from the sixties and seventies.

This version of dad rock was born in the eighties with groups like U2 and R.E.M., who came up during the first decade in which rock music was divided into distinct halves by the advent of punk and the rise of classic-rock radio. These twin events severed modern rock from its past, even as rock's past survived and weirdly carried on a parallel life *in competition* with modern rock. To some, the act of plugging in a guitar was now automatically construed as "retro" or "nostalgic" (i.e., the judgmental form of "retro"). It was now possible to sound like a rock band and act like a rock band

and perform rock-band-like tasks in a contemporary setting and be viewed as *not* contemporary.

This gap between rock's "classic" and post-"classic" periods created a battle of conflicting impulses—burying the past vs. building upon the roots—that every subsequent important rock band has had to reconcile. For dad rockers, many of whom came to the music as it started its cultural decline, rock 'n' roll was like folk music, a tradition handed down as a box of tools that could be used to build and fortify a subculture outside of the pop mainstream. Chris Robinson of the Black Crowes—one of the defining dad-rock bands of the nineties—once referred to this continuum in a *Behind the Music* episode as "the song," an ongoing collaboration between an unborn future and the mythical past to create something that feels a little realer and more permanent than the latest trends.

3. A dad-rock band is a band composed of dudes who are old enough to be dads.

This one is tricky, because a band can start out in stark opposition to dad rock in one decade and then age into dad rock in another decade. Sonic Youth was not a dad-rock band in the eighties but became a dad-rock band in the aughts. Yo La Tengo also became a dad-rock band at that time. So did Pavement. Sleater-Kinney became a dad-rock band in spite of being made up of women. This is all just a function of the space-time continuum.

No matter which of the three definitions apply, classifying a band or artist as dad rock is generally understood to be a put-down. For starters, the word "dad" has a terrible connotation in rock history. Jim Morrison wanted to kill his dad. Harry Chapin suggested that karma eventually screws your dad over, because (of course) he's a jerk. Paul Westerberg and Kurt Cobain both distinguished dads (bad) from fathers (less bad) in "Androgynous" and "Serve the Servants," respectively, agreeing on the overall failure of their respective patriarchs as male role models.

In terms of dad rock, the modifier "dad" is meant to weaken the word "rock," divorcing it from any sense of power, danger, or sexual excitement. This matters if you care about classic rock, because the implicitly negative epithet "dad rock" has overshadowed the implicitly positive "classic rock" as the favored term for how rock 'n' roll is now discussed.

It's hard to pin down who exactly coined "dad rock." It seems to have derived, as so many memorable insults have, from the British music press of the 1990s. According to legend, a nameless English scribe came up with the term as a snarky dismissal of a photo featuring Oasis's Noel Gallagher, the Jam's Paul Weller, and Paul McCartney hanging out at a recording session in 1995 for a charity album benefiting Bosnian refugees. (This sounds like a setup to a joke but I swear it's not.)

While searching for dad rock's rhetorical roots, I reached out to Simon Reynolds, the best and probably most famous British rock critic of the last twenty-five years. (He's certainly the best and most famous British rock critic for whom I had an email address.) I fired off a terse, half-baked, five-sentence email asking if he remembered hearing fellow writers use "dad rock" back in the nineties. Forty minutes later, Reynolds replied with a pithy four-hundred-word response that could've appeared with minimal editing in a special dad-rock issue of *Uncut*. This man produced insightful music commentary with the improvisational flair that Duane Allman once applied to ten-minute guitar solos.

"It was an insult term by people who didn't like this sort of traditional, backward-looking band and were vaguely disturbed by the erasure of the generation gap," Reynolds told me. The biggest British band of the era, Oasis, epitomized the "sort of traditional, backward-looking band" that dad-rock critics despised, Reynolds wrote.

Dad-rock bands view rock history as a tapestry that connects present-day bands to the icons of the past—it's an argument in favor of young people *empathizing* with their parents, which is always going to be a hard sell for some people. For Gen X critics systematically dismantling the boomer-rock canon and replacing it with post-punk and hip-hop records, it was pretty much impossible.

Now, we wouldn't be talking about dad rock today if the term had only been used to admonish young Tony Blair voters for liking the Verve instead of Roni fucking Size. It only matters because "dad rock" eventually migrated to America and became a commonly used cliché for stateside music writers, due in large part to one review of Wilco's languorous sixth album, 2007's *Sky Blue Sky,* by the popular indie-music site Pitchfork.

When Pitchfork was founded in 1996, its mission was to cover all the bands that never got mentioned in *Rolling Stone.* The site represented a stand by Gen Xers against the boomers, but also a strike against mainstream rock by the underground, foreshadowing the impending end of the classic-rock era. In the Pitchfork universe, Neutral Milk Hotel and the Smiths mattered more than the Foo Fighters and U2, and the site's polarizing ten-point scoring system clearly delineated the "haves" (who scored 8.0 or higher) from the "have-nots" (6.0 or lower) in a new, emerging caste system now defined by elite tastemakers rather than the unwashed masses.

Pearl Jam was way too popular to ever have a chance with Pitchfork, but Wilco was one of the site's pet bands in the late nineties and early aughts, peaking with a perfect 10.0 review for *Yankee Hotel Foxtrot.* But then the members of Wilco got a little older and a lot mellower, and their records suddenly featured a lot more guitar solos. This was something Pitchfork would not stand for.

Sky Blue Sky proved to be Pitchfork's departure point. The review accused *Sky Blue Sky* of "nakedly expos[ing] the dad-rock gene Wilco has always carried but courageously attempted to disguise." For Pitchfork, dadness didn't just denote nostalgia—it was posited as a disorder, like epilepsy or pedophilia, that had to be concealed at the risk of a band being exposed as "passive," "soft," or "lackluster," the most damning adjectives used to describe *Sky*

Blue Sky. (By the way, the author of the Pitchfork review is none other than Rob Mitchum, my friend and Phish Sherpa. We still argue about it whenever we see each other.)

It should come as no surprise that I love *Sky Blue Sky.* The album contains some of Jeff Tweedy's most trenchant songs about marriage, including the ways in which husbands suck up to their pissed-off wives by offering to do the laundry. *Sky Blue Sky* came out the year before I got married, and Tweedy's meditations on domesticity (and the quiet storms that linger beneath the surface of long-term relationships) struck a chord. I welcomed *Sky Blue Sky* as a kind of guidebook for how to survive the next phase of my life, which is probably the best compliment you can give any work of art. Even the most polarizing aspect of *Sky Blue Sky*— Nels Cline's wonky, meandering guitar solos—sounded awesome to me. Cline channels Glenn Branca and Dickey Betts simultaneously; his playing is equal parts cerebral and badass.

But I get where Pitchfork is coming from: *Sky Blue Sky* is reminiscent of a classic-rock record released before the late-seventies punk revolution—a hyper-proficient, well-pedigreed soft-rock LP. It's music about dads made by dads that would appeal most to other dads. In the view of the contemporary music press, that made *Sky Blue Sky* automatically suspect.

"It's music for squares," *Billboard* **declared of dad rock in 2014.** "The younger, more multicultural world views it as not just passive, but patriarchal, because its values exclude almost all people of color, anyone who uses a turntable or a sampler and a wide range of female artists, from Taylor Swift to Azealia Banks. A vote against dad rock is a vote for inclusiveness."

Right now, I'd like to give a brief lesson in how culture critics can rig the discourse. As a professional culture critic, I've been sworn to protect these trade secrets. However, circumstances have compelled me to be the Edward Snowden of pop criticism. At the risk of imprisonment in music-critic jail, I must be a whistleblower and leak this highly effective and oft-used three-point plan.

1. Invent a genre that only critics care about or even know how to define. (This applies to dad rock, but also chillwave, seapunk, backpack rap, hipster metal, alt-country, or anything attached to the suffix "-core.")
2. Construct the criteria for the made-up genre in such a way that it applies to artists you personally cannot stand.
3. Turn that made-up genre against the artists and blame them for not being "inclusive," even though critics were the ones who decided which artists belong in said genre.

Critics don't have to make words up to rig the discourse. They also do it by selectively applying certain language to certain artists, and *not* applying it to other artists. I saw this a lot in the run-up to the 2016 Grammy Awards. In the Album of the Year category, the one rock record—*Sound & Color* by the very good Southern band Alabama Shakes, led by black singer-songwriter Brittany Howard—was the nominee invariably described as "nostalgic." Anybody who has ever read a record review knows that "nostalgic" is the worst thing an album can be, next to "problematic" and "by the Dave Matthews Band." "Nostalgic" is code for "out-of-touch and conservative," the very charge that inspired that anonymous snarky bloke in the British press to invent the term "dad rock" in the first place.

Meanwhile, the other nominees that year included a country LP reminiscent of the "outlaw" music of Willie Nelson and Waylon Jennings (Chris Stapleton's *Traveller*), an R & B album anchored by highly successful Michael Jackson sound-alikes (the Weeknd's *Beauty Behind the Madness*), and a hip-hop record informed by soul and jazz classics from the seventies (Kendrick Lamar's *To Pimp a Butterfly*). The winner was Taylor Swift's *1989*, a record that explicitly referenced the past in its album title. But none of those other albums were called nostalgic.

This is not to say that the Alabama Shakes record isn't steeped in the past—*Sound & Color* has an easily discernible connection to Led Zeppelin and early Outkast LPs like 1998's *Aquemini*. But *Sound & Color* doesn't exactly sound like any of those references. You would never mistake Brittany Howard for Robert Plant or Andre 3000, as the record's swampy, soul-infused sound evokes the essence of blues rock and hip-hop without ever quite settling into either genre. You can pick out the component parts of *Sound & Color*, but they've never been put together in that specific way before. The point is that *all* music derives from what came before, not just rock. Inside every genre lurks a whole lot of dads.

The irony of rock critics inventing dad rock in order to criticize neo-classic-rock bands for eliminating the generation gap is that the generation gap was a by-product of classic-rock mythology *invented by baby boomers.* Don't trust anyone over thirty, the man can't bust our music, your sons and your daughters are beyond your command—this is the stuff of one million documentaries about the sixties, the ones that always include the same grainy stock footage of hippie yahoos dancing in circles. (Grown-ups in the sixties apparently hated it when young people danced in circles.) Pop historians credit the rise of Elvis Presley with establishing teenagers as a marketing demographic distinct from adults, leading to the dawn of a new era in which pop music was viewed as a progressive force initiating social change driven by youth culture. Before then, "youth culture" didn't exist as a concept. Modern pop subsequently became the story of forward-thinking young people embracing music performed by marginalized people—early on, it was blues and R & B played by African Americans and country and folk music associated with impoverished rural whites. Later, it was dance music derived from gay and Latin communities, and hip-hop from the poorest and blackest sections of the Bronx. All of these styles were eventually absorbed into the stew that was broadly defined as rock 'n' roll.

The mythology of Elvis Presley was that he "invented" a new style of music by synthesizing many styles that were largely unfamiliar to white fifties teenagers. But the contradiction of the myth is plain to see—it's not really "new" if you are combining elements of music that already exists. Actually, I would argue that it *is* new, because if you don't accept that synthesis plays a part in pretty much every great rock record ever made, then *nothing* is ever truly original.

Our ability to easily deconstruct anything "new" has made everything seem like a retread. If Presley existed today, he would be dismissed as derivative, because the sources of inspiration for superstars are more readily available. When Presley sang "Hound Dog," it sounded like a revolution only if you hadn't already heard Big Mama Thornton's original version. That many people hadn't heard Big Mama Thornton in 1956 is what enabled the Presley myth to persist and flourish. But it's not just Presley who would seem unoriginal, it's every artist who has ever mattered as a paradigm shifter. The Beatles and Rolling Stones loaded their first several records with covers of songs by Chuck Berry, Buddy Holly, and Little Richard. Bob Dylan did a straight-up Woody Guthrie impression during the first three years of his career. Jimi Hendrix's early stage show ripped off the Who. When David Bowie invented Ziggy Stardust, he was jacking Marc Bolan's act and Lou Reed's songwriting style. The first Ramones record sounded like the Beach Boys if the Beach Boys were from Queens and sniffed glue. Bruce Springsteen stole from Dylan and Phil Spector, U2 stole from Springsteen, and Arcade Fire stole from U2 (and Springsteen).

Of course, Big Mama Thornton deserved to be heard as much as Elvis, and it's also true that throughout rock history, white male artists have hogged the credit for "inventing" music that had already been made by African Americans for decades. (There's also a credible counterargument that Elvis's massive celebrity raised the profile of Big Mama Thornton, along with countless other artists who entered Presley's orbit, playing a pivotal role in integrating pop culture.) The problem is that we're looking at music history incorrectly. The truth is that all music has elements of borrowing and invention. Elvis Presley became a legend because he combined different kinds of music and culture in new and exciting ways. But Elvis was also clearly indebted to many artists who came before him. He was a revolutionary, and a dad rocker.

I wound up choosing Pearl Jam over Wilco.

When you must choose between two of your favorite bands, it feels as though you're betraying a friend. I felt guilt and remorse over what I did to Wilco. I wouldn't be surprised if Jeff Tweedy never spoke to me again—I mean that theoretically, in a fantastical scenario in which I have Jeff Tweedy's contact information, and we phone or text regularly, and he's now so infuriated over this Pearl Jam situation that he blocks my number.

Anyway, my reason for choosing Pearl Jam wasn't purely musical. Pearl Jam was playing at Wrigley Field, and I had loved seeing PJ play the Friendly Confines a few years earlier. It was one of my favorite concerts ever, in part because there was a three-hour rain delay that divided the concert into two parts. Admittedly, this is an odd, contrarian view of the gig. Many Pearl Jam fans hated this Wrigley show, because it didn't wrap until after two A.M. and the band was forced to cut many of the songs that it had promised to play that night. But for me it was awesome because I spent that delay drinking between three and fifty Old Style beers and talking about high school girlfriends with my lifelong friend Mark.

Pearl Jam is a band that Mark and I listened to when we were teenagers, and Pearl Jam is one of the only things still bonding us together, now that we are both married with kids and living in different states. Our conversation during the rain delay—the text of which has been expunged and will forever remain top secret, to prevent prosecution from our respective wives—remains one of my happiest (and drunkest) memories from the last ten years.

It was as though my Pearl Jam show experience had magically been transformed into an emotionally uplifting Pearl Jam song.

This Pearl Jam memory highlights something important about my relationship with the rock bands from the nineties that I love, which is different from my relationship with the classic-rock bands from the sixties and seventies that I love, even though I was listening to all of those bands at the same time when I was growing up. The difference is that I grew up *with* the nineties bands— when I was young, they were also young. This has affected how my brain processes nineties bands as I've aged.

When I listen to Zeppelin, I feel basically the same way as I did when I was a kid. In my mind, Zeppelin will always equal "Zeppelin circa 1971 or '72." It's like a stationary monument that lies along the path of my life. Listening to Pearl Jam, however, makes me feel older than listening to Zeppelin does. That's because that band is traveling down the path with me. Led Zeppelin will always exist outside of time, whereas Pearl Jam will always exist in *my* time.

This is true for all of the nineties bands that meant something to me as a teenager. For a generation of millennial rock fans, Weezer is classified as classic rock, and they appreciate Weezer in the same way that I appreciate Zeppelin and Pink Floyd. For them, 1994's *Weezer* (also known as *The Blue Album*) and 1996's *Pinkerton* are as mythic as *Led Zeppelin IV* or *The Dark Side of the Moon*. Weezer to them will always equal "Weezer circa around the time I was born." And they tend to be more forgiving of bad Weezer albums, like 2008's *Weezer* (also known as *The Red Album*), which includes the single worst tune Rivers Cuomo ever wrote, "Heart Songs." (Sample lyric: "Eddie Rabbit sang about how much he loved a rainy night / Abba, Devo, Benatar were there the day John Lennon died." *Ugh.*) For them, *The Red Album* is Cuomo's version of *McCartney II*, a work of batshit genius that can only be appreciated by subsequent generations.

I can't see Weezer that way, because I've lived with them from pretty much the beginning. I love *Pinkerton*, but that album will never seem mythic to me, because I remember buying it the week it came out during my freshman year of college and being the only person I knew who liked it. *Pinkerton* didn't become an iconic record among rock fans until many years later, long after I had already forged my own relationship with it. When I hear *Pinkerton* now, I don't think about the mythology of that record, I recall what it was actually like to hear it in the fall of 1996. As for bad Weezer albums, well, I have my own connections with those, too. I heard an advance copy of *The Red Album* before writing a review for the AV Club, so I had the opportunity to hate that record before most people even heard it. I was part of the initial consensus opinion on *The Red Album* that future listeners could decide to rebel against.

When people say, "Rock is dead," they're really making a statement about themselves—they're saying, "This thing that once mattered *to me* is now dead *to me*." The flip side is that every year there is a new group of teenagers for whom the world is being created just as they're discovering it for the first time. Anything that existed before them might as well have been around forever. When I was a teenager, classic-rock bands signified forever. For teenagers now, forever is represented by the dad-rock bands that I loved back when the dudes in those bands were unattached and getting drunk every night, just as I was back then.

With Pearl Jam, it has always seemed like Eddie Vedder has not-so-secretly wished to be a classic rocker. In the nineties, Vedder disdained ephemeral celebrity, but he revered historical icons. When he was the biggest young rock star in the world, Vedder chose to hang out with grizzled veterans like Neil Young, Pete Townshend, and Mike Watt. Right as Pearl Jam was peaking as a phenomenon on MTV, the band retreated to making anticommercial albums like *Vitalogy* and *No Code* that were designed to be appreciated decades later rather than adored in the moment. When Pearl Jam was invited to the Grammys in 1996, Eddie Vedder griped about the awards being meaningless. But he always made himself available to induct personal heroes like Young, the

Ramones, and R.E.M. into the Rock and Roll Hall of Fame. Given his level of exposure at the peak of his fame, Vedder could've been a major pop star. But he instead acted like a man who really wanted to be a fifty-year-old journeyman.

I think that's why, when you see Pearl Jam now, Eddie Vedder seems so much happier and more relaxed than he was in the nineties. He's finally achieved his lifelong goal: he's a middle-aged guy in a rock band that's been around for more than a quarter century. He's now as old as Mick Jagger was when I saw the Stones for the first time back in the nineties.

It's the same but different. Mick Jagger is Mick Jagger, and he'll always be Mick Jagger to me. But Eddie Vedder was once young, and now he's a dad.

"Pressing On"

NOTES ON TRACK 18: This is where we found religion. Not our most popular period, but some things are more important than record sales. Besides, the only thing more universal than God is death, and we already have enough tunes about that topic.

L et me tell you a story about a park known for the face it attracts.

Exactly six months and one week after Prince died, I drove to the Minneapolis suburb of Chanhassen in search of Minnesota's answer to Graceland—Paisley Park. Prince's iconic recording studio and occasional residence had just opened its doors to tourists, and I wanted to feel the spirit of the artist formerly known as the world's sexiest MF-er.

According to the song "Paisley Park," which was released three years before Prince finished construction on the actual building in 1988, this mythical palace was once the exclusive party premises of "colorful people whose hair on one side is swept back." Now, for those willing to pay $38.50 (for a standard tour) or $100 (for the VIP experience), a physical manifestation of Prince's legacy was accessible to the hoi polloi, no matter their hair persuasion.

The man was gone, but you could stare at the vast infrastructure he left behind.

The first thing you notice when you walk into Paisley Park is that you are being watched—by purple-shirted tour guides, by black-suited security people, and finally by a large pair of eyes planted on a wall facing the lobby entrance. The eyes, like the facility, belong to Paisley Park's purple-suited proprietor. "Prince sees everything," said Niccole, my tour guide, who shepherded me and eight other VIP Prince fans from Los Angeles, Seattle, and Fargo through the sixty-five-thousand-square foot complex.

Prince envisioned Paisley Park as a business headquarters, a home base, a creative playground, and, finally, a shrine to all things Prince. During our tour, Niccole promised, we would see his private study; his pet doves, Divinity and Majesty; the kitchen where he ate pancakes and watched Minnesota Timberwolves basketball games; and the remains of Prince himself, now resting inside a small purple box encased in a model of the Paisley Park building situated in the atrium.

What we wouldn't see was any of the rooms on the second floor, the private areas where he presumably lived, slept, and got freaky. And we definitely wouldn't gain entrance to the elevator in which he was found slumped over without a pulse on that fateful morning of April 21, 2016. A display for 2004's *Musicology* tour now blocked the elevator door. It's not known exactly how often he lived at Paisley Park—he owned more than a dozen properties in the neighborhood, and also was known to have houses in L.A. and Toronto. What's clear is that he worked there, hosted concerts, threw parties, and then died in this place.

This was the first day that tours had resumed after community concerns over traffic and safety issues put a temporary hold on the building's business permit earlier in the month. Chanhassen is one of Minneapolis's tony suburbs, the kind of place where even the neighborhood Goodwill store is housed inside "classy" red brick, in the manner of all well-off Midwestern communities. This isn't the kind of town that seeks to establish a tourist attraction.

The whole point of moving to a place like Chanhassen is to get away from other people.

When I arrived, I felt a twinge of cynicism. I had read about Paisley Park's drab, all-white, oppressively rigid exterior—*Forbes* aptly described it as having the charm of "an Amazon warehouse"—but it was still strange to ponder that Prince conjured wondrous musical universes imbued with the magical powers of sex and God just down the road from a mundane swath of Target and OfficeMax stores. Prince was an extraordinary figure—and yet he chose, like Superman, to live in the most ordinary of environs. Inside Paisley Park, it was much funkier. While the outside walls are strictly Chanhassen-friendly norm-core, the inside walls resemble the sky-blue cover of *Around the World in a Day*—they're covered with symbols, gold and platinum records, and dozens of photos of Prince in all his different guises.

In his final years, Prince routinely hosted impromptu concerts in Paisley Park's hangarlike performance space. But the rest of Paisley Park for years remained a mystery to outsiders. "It's a strange place, even to visit," *GQ*'s Chris Heath wrote in 1991. "It's not anything physical . . . It's something more intangible, and you see it in the faces of the people who work there. They're like students taking a long, perplexing exam, trying to work out what the question means before they can start writing. And the question is this: What does Prince want?"

"What does Prince want?" seemed to still be the central question for those now running Paisley Park, as well as those who visited. Inside every room, people asked, "Is this how it was . . . you know . . . *before*?" That Paisley Park had swiftly been transformed into a museum with the requisite overpriced gift shop might've struck some as unseemly, but the whole enterprise was predicated on *being the way that Prince would have wanted it*. Prince had warmed in his final years to semiregularly admitting outsiders into Paisley Park, and his confidants claimed that he always intended to turn the facility into a kind of Prince Hall of Fame. In a way, opening Paisley Park was the only way to keep

Prince alive—it was the one place where he still seemed to be in control, even from beyond the grave. In death, as in life, Prince demanded unquestioning obedience from his staff. That power was still detectable as soon as you walked in the door.

Early on, our tour entered a dimly lit editing room to watch brief clips of unreleased concert footage. Posters for Fritz Lang's *Metropolis* and Clint Eastwood's Charlie Parker biopic *Bird* hung on the walls. Behind the editing console sat Sean Johnson, whose father, Kirk Johnson, was a key member of Prince's inner circle tasked with various duties, including the management of Paisley Park. Kirk was with Prince when his private plane made an emergency landing en route from two concerts in Atlanta, the final shows Prince ever performed, just a few weeks before he passed. Johnson was also the one who informed the media that Prince had suffered from "bad hydration" on that plane, though it's believed that Prince actually overdosed on opioids.

Sean was on hand to answer questions, though he seemed reluctant to divulge even vague platitudes about his former boss. A dark purple couch stood between us, the tourists, and Sean, Prince's erstwhile employee. (Niccole informed us that we were not allowed to sit on the couch.) When I asked Sean what it was like to work for Prince, he paused, as if figuring out what to say. Someone volunteered that Prince was "difficult." "No," Sean said. "Exacting. Who isn't difficult? Everybody is difficult."

Some aspects of Paisley Park had to be altered before it could open to the public. The albums on the walls were put behind Plexiglas and the candles flickering in nearly every room were replaced with LEDs. A large room devoted to *Purple Rain*—outfitted with Prince's purple motorcycle, stage clothes, and Oscar for best original score—was conceived and at least partly installed by Prince, but not finalized until after his death. (There were also much smaller adjoining rooms commemorating Prince's other films, *Under the Cherry Moon* and *Graffiti Bridge*.)

Other rooms appeared to have been rearranged to suit Paisley

Park's newfound status as a museum. In cavernous Studio A, where Prince recorded albums like 1988's *Lovesexy* and 1991's *Diamonds and Pearls,* you could peer past the control room glass at Prince's Linn LM-1 drum machine, a vital contributor to the sound of so many of Prince's eighties hits. Otherwise, the same multicolored tapestries that Prince picked out to hang on the studio walls remained where he'd left them, only now they were freighted with significance.

"What do the tapestries *mean*?" a fellow tourist asked Niccole.

"Perhaps they help with the sound?" Niccole guessed. Niccole confessed that there were many things about Prince that she did not know. She read her Prince factoids off well-worn index cards, though she wasn't all that confident about their veracity. Earlier, she'd explained that the significance of the name Paisley Park, "*we think,* is that a paisley takes many forms," the inflection in her voice suggesting a question mark at the end of that statement.

Prince, a notoriously private man who carefully curated his public image, is a person about whom much is still unknown, even among his close associates. (I wonder how many fascinating facts about Prince will never end up on an index card.) Nevertheless, care was taken to preserve Paisley Park the way it was on April 20, 2016, the day before Prince died. In Prince's office, adjacent to the atrium, there was a stack of books near a conference table devoted to religion and ancient Egypt: *The New Oxford Annotated Bible, The Secret Teachings of All Ages, Pharaohs of the Sun.* While a pile of LPs topped with *Cookin' with the Miles Davis Quintet* seemed staged, the CD tower behind Prince's desk did not. I can buy that Prince—notoriously averse to streaming music—was a fifty-seven-year-old guy who preferred CDs for his workday jams.

Prince's distaste for twenty-first-century technology also informed Paisley Park's no-cell-phone policy. In Prince's time, restricting access to screens no doubt made Paisley Park its own island. (You also won't find any clocks there—it's like a casino.) Now that it's a museum, I suspect that taking away your cell phone also provides added incentive for visitors to pony up another $10 for a "unique and exclusive photo opportunity" in Studio B reserved for VIP guests. (No photos or videos are allowed otherwise.) This gambit worked on me, anyway. I lined up to have my picture taken next to a twelve-foot photo of Prince while the other guests played Ping-Pong on Prince's table.

The end of the tour wrapped with a swing through the enormous 12,500-square-foot performance area, outfitted with five stages memorializing five different Prince tours. Guests were then led into the NPG Music Club, a nightclub that doesn't serve liquor in accordance with Prince's faith as a Jehovah's Witness. It was there that Prince had entertained Madonna while she was on tour not long before he died, Niccole informed us.

As my eyes traced over a nearby wall, I suddenly froze—staring back at me was none other than Prince, peeking out from behind a curtain. Years ago, Prince had himself painted onto the wall so guests would know he was always watching, even now.

What compels people from all over the world to visit the out-skirts of Minneapolis just to look at Prince's books and assless pants? Surely the man's undeniable genius attracted an intensely loyal fan base. But at the time of Prince's death, it had been many years since he made music that anyone besides die-hards cared about. Prince's last Top 10 single, "The Most Beautiful Girl in the World," came out in 1994. He continued to release multiple singles per year through 2015, but his last song to chart in the U.S., "Black Sweat," petered out at No. 60 in 2006.

The final album that Prince released during his lifetime, 2015's *Hit n Run Phase Two*, sold just two thousand copies in its first week. *Pitchfork* gave the album a measly 4.7, calling it "underwhelming" and "predictable." The review's most damning assertion—that Prince was trying in vain to re-create past glories—is the most common criticism of late-period work by classic-rock artists. Nobody would come out and say directly that Prince was washed up, but there wasn't much excitement about his work in the twenty-first century. Not until Prince died, anyway.

After he died it was a different story. Twenty Prince albums reentered the album charts, including five in the Top 10. People who wanted to listen to Prince while mourning him *had* to buy Prince's records, because in the immediate aftermath of his death, they weren't available on any streaming services. Suddenly, fans who couldn't be bothered to keep up with his recent work—and likely hadn't listened to his old albums in years unless they had held on to their CD collections—rushed to social media to talk about the important role his music played in their lives. Prince went from being a respected but marginal figure to an incredibly vital linchpin in popular culture, just like that.

I don't mean to suggest that this post-death conversion was insincere, or that it was unique to Prince. As the classic-rock generation ages and falls away, I suspect that this rapid revisionist history will become more and more common. The generational provincialism that has long shaped the narrative of popular music has softened. Even those who normally bristle at the overbearing influence of so-called boomer culture have been moved by the loss of iconic artists who have loomed more like architecture than human beings. The tension between valorizing the superstars of the sixties, seventies, and eighties and smarmily delegitimizing them seems to have given way to melancholic acceptance that all things must pass.

The visitors to Paisley Park wanted to walk around inside the one place where Prince still felt like a living presence. But it was also a place to say goodbye—not just to Prince, but to a part of themselves. Grumpy cultural critics who question the validity of public displays of grief for rock stars don't understand that rock stars function as flesh-and-blood metaphors for the human experience. Rock stars live, they love, they falter, they come back—we pay attention because the exaggerated arc of rock stardom creates a framework for understanding our own lives. Now classic rock is also helping us to understand, and accept, the inevitability of death. When a rock star dies, what people are mourning is their own mortality.

Is it a surprise that the classic rocker who is most sensitive about this grieving process is Bruce Springsteen? In 2016, Springsteen published his memoir, *Born to Run,* an instant classic that swiftly entered the A-list of rock autobiographies with Keith Richards's *Life,* Bob Dylan's *Chronicles,* and Patti Smith's *Just Kids. Born to Run* covers a lot of ground: It details Springsteen's rise to fame, dispenses historical trivia about New Jersey's rock club culture in the sixties and early seventies, dishes a little dirt on the E Street Band, pulls back the veil to reveal aspects of his private life (especially his battles with mental illness), and functions as a kind of coping manual for new fathers and longtime disappointed sons. (I wish this book existed before my first child was born.) But the primary subject of *Born to Run* is the passage of time, and how it turns the young into the old, the child into the parent, and the innocent into the weary.

Many reviewers noted Springsteen's funny, rollicking, ALL CAPS jocularity, which distinguishes the first two-thirds of the book, because this conforms to Springsteen's public image. But the parts that stuck most with me are when Springsteen turns somber, and the capitalization becomes more restrained, in the closing chapters of *Born to Run.*

One of the most valuable insights that *Born to Run* provides is just how desperately Springsteen needs to perform. While pharmacology contributed to his mental health in his later years, playing live remains his most effective treatment. During a low point in the early 2010s, Springsteen writes, he desperately reached out to manager Jon Landau to set up a tour as a tonic for chronic depression. "I called Jon and said, 'Mr. Landau, book me anywhere, please.' I then of course broke down in tears."

By the end of *Born to Run,* Springsteen seems to be in a better place, in part because he's made peace with his own humanity. In the process, he ponders the unthinkable: a world without himself, without Bruce Springsteen, without the Boss. Favoring a

River-like metaphor that also alludes to Joseph Campbell, Springsteen writes of an old tree near his boyhood home that was recently felled. At first, the tree's absence fills him with dread. But then he looks to the sky and is reassured that what is gone will live on in those who are left behind.

"We remain in the air, the empty space, in the dusty roots and deep earth, in the echo and stories, the songs of the time and place we inhabited," Springsteen writes. "My clan, my blood, my people."

In the final film that he completed, 1974's quasidocumentary *F for Fake*, Orson Welles profiled Elmyr de Hory, known in his time as the world's most famous art forger, and Elmyr's biographer Clifford Irving, who was later implicated for fabricating an exposé of Howard Hughes. *F for Fake* is a movie about a fake being profiled by a fake. But it's really an excuse for Welles to riff on the legitimacy of authorship, the slippery nature of artistic authenticity, and the impermanence of artistic achievement. It's cinema's greatest auteur scoffing at the idea that auteurs truly matter in the grand scheme of things.

The centerpiece of *F for Fake* is a monologue in which Welles pontificates on the French cathedral Chartres, which was built somewhere between 1194 and 1220. At least five other iterations of Chartres Cathedral have stood on the same ground since the fourth century. The current version has remained remarkably well preserved—no renovations have been required to keep it intact for visitors in the past seven centuries.

"The premier work of man perhaps in the whole Western world, and it's without a signature," Welles says of Chartres. The irony is plain given Welles's narrative in *F for Fake*—Elmyr's forgeries of classic paintings were so convincing that they hung undetected in many of the world's finest galleries. Elmyr was eventually caught, but before he was due to be extradited to France from his home in Spain to stand trial on fraud charges, he committed suicide. In the end, how much is a signature worth anyway?

"Ours, the scientists keep telling us, is a universe which is disposable," Welles says. "Our works in stone, in paint, in print, are spared, some of them for a few decades or a millennium or two, but everything must finally fall in war or wear away into the ultimate and universal ash. The triumphs and the frauds, the treasures and the fakes. A fact of life. We're going to die."

If that's what Welles saw when he gazed upon Chartres, what thoughts are worthy of the Nobel Prize, which was awarded with great controversy to Bob Dylan in 2016? Awards are denials of the "ultimate and universal ash" that Welles talked about, a self-inflicted con about how a legacy can be set down and made to stand for eternity, the paramount myth. Dylan was seemingly alone in understanding this. When the award was announced, it took Dylan two weeks to publicly acknowledge the honor. When British newspaper the *Telegraph* finally tracked him down for a comment, Dylan's response was gracious but cryptic: "Isn't that something?" he mused, adding that he wouldn't be there to accept the award, due to vague "pre-existing commitments."

Dylan's apparent disregard for the Nobel Prize provoked a series of backlashes and counter-backlashes. After one Nobel committee member called him "impolite and arrogant," Dylan defenders rushed to point out that *of course* Dylan would act this way, because Dylan *always* acts this way when somebody tries to turn him into a figurehead. What did these Swedes expect anyway?

Around the time that Dylan was awarded his Nobel, I became obsessed with his "gospel" period, which includes the albums *Slow Train Coming* and *Saved,* and about half of *Shot of Love.* These albums are Dylan's version of Welles's Chartres monologue—he gives up on the ephemeral in order to directly address the divine. Some Dylanologists (including Clinton Heylin, as sharp and as cantankerous as a man devoted to studying Dylan minutiae should be) have claimed that this God-obsessed period never ended—it's just that Dylan, after a brief flirtation with forthright evangelism, returned to obscuring his spiritual beliefs behind an enigmatic veil. (That recent Dylan albums such as 2012's *Tempest* contain enough bloody retribution to rival the Old Testament supports this thesis.)

Still, there was a time when Bob Dylan was moved to write directly and explicitly about his love for Jesus and his belief that the world would soon be over. And then he went on the road and for many months refused to play any of his old songs, fearing that they were "anti-God." And then, after the relatively restrained *Slow Train Coming* sold well and produced a Top 40 hit, "Gotta Serve Somebody," Dylan doubled down yet again with the album cover for the overtly born-again *Saved,* in which God reaches down with an oversized paw to touch the outstretched hands of true believers. Dylan conceived the cover himself, and later told *Rolling Stone*'s Kurt Loder that he wished he could have had the image "posted up on Sunset Boulevard—[this] big bloody hand reaching down."

It's fair to assume that the Nobel people weren't thinking of Dylan's gospel albums when they honored him for "having created new poetic expressions within the great American song tradition." When Dylan became a Christian, it temporarily silenced his poetic side. For years, people had asked Dylan to explain himself and plainly articulate his vision of the world. On his Christian albums, Dylan finally codified his lyrics into a clear message that left little wiggle room for interpretation. If you were sick of Dylan playing games, well, this was as close as he would ever come to unequivocal. Rock's most famous enigma finally embraced literalism.

"I follow God," Dylan told a Tucson radio station in 1979. "So, if my followers are following me, indirectly they're gonna be following God too, because I don't sing any song which hasn't been given to me by the Lord to sing." It doesn't get any clearer than that. But because this is Bob Dylan we're talking about, the most straightforward version of himself somehow wound up being the most confounding.

Even among Dylan fanatics, Dylan's spiritual material is often derided—these albums are widely regarded, at best, as good "bad" albums, though many people just think they're plain bad. *Slow Train Coming* has a decent reputation—due mostly to the production by Jerry Wexler and Barry Beckett, who helped the studio-averse Dylan sound professional in accordance with high-tech late-seventies standards. But *Saved* and *Shot of Love* are defended only by the staunchest of hard-core Dylan heads. When I was going to as many Dylan concerts as I could in the early aughts, the percentage of people who loved *Saved* would go up the closer I pushed to the stage. Many of these people resembled fans profiled in David Kinney's excellent 2014 book *The Dylan-ologists,* particularly the woman who keeps a shrine in her home that comingles photos of Jesus and Dylan with excerpts from the Bible and Dylan's gospel-era concert rants. I met a lot of people like that, and they always weirded me out. The strange intensity of Dylan's spiritual albums, coupled with the strange intensity of Dylan's spiritual-minded fans, kept me away from that music for a long time.

What finally opened Dylan's gospel songs up for me was delving into the concert bootlegs from Dylan's gospel tours, including a show in Toronto from 1980 that was originally recorded for a live album that Dylan's label, Columbia, declined to release. (This concert was officially released in 2017 as part of a boxed set devoted to Dylan's gospel period.) In a live setting, backed by one of his finest bands ever, Dylan's gospel songs swayed and rocked with newfound force and passion. It was a big, warm, bouncing ball of sound. On the breathtaking version of "When He Returns" from the Toronto tape, Dylan sings about as well as he ever has, opening his heart and making himself vulnerable onstage in ways that he rarely does now. On the albums, Dylan can come off as preachy and judgmental; *Slow Train Coming* and *Saved* are unique Dylan LPs in that the lyrics must often be completely ignored to be enjoyed, at least for nonbelievers. In concert, however, Dylan let the music carry him toward a more ecstatic and heavenly place. Even if you don't believe in God, you feel the spirit. You want to go where Dylan is going.

Dylan has always been an artist who has looked past this life and to a world that is hidden but omnipresent if you've trained yourself to see it. "I'm pressing on," he sings in "Pressing On," one of his best gospel-era tracks, "to the higher calling of my Lord." If you love Dylan, this constant pushing against all that's temporary and fleeting is what makes his work so powerful. When that's your mission, who has time for something as inconsequential, and reactionary, as the Nobel Prize? You have to keep pressing on—to the next song, to the next record, to the next show in the next town. It's like Welles said: everything that gets set down eventually fades. But what if you don't set anything down? Maybe you can't outrun death simply by touring forever. But you *definitely* can't evade the big dark empty by sitting still and worrying about your legacy. Forward motion is restorative. Higher ground is redemptive. "Our songs will all be silenced," Welles concludes in *F for Fake*. "But what of it? Go on singing."

Nothing lasts, so let's appreciate what we have while we can. Press on, Bob.

"Death Don't Have No Mercy"

NOTES ON TRACK 19: Our long-term career plan is to die because that *always* helps your record sales and also you have no choice.

Way back in 1977, the year I was born, the Clash imagined a world without classic rock. Over a whirlwind of power chords and Topper Headon's frantic drum fills, Joe Strummer screamed in the song "1977" about "no Elvis, Beatles, or the Rolling Stones." On one hand, this was wishful thinking—a core tenet of punk ideology was the destruction of rock's dinosaurs. (Keep in mind that "1977" was recorded six months *before* Elvis Presley actually died.) On the other hand, "1977" has a decidedly apocalyptic, opposite-of-wishful-thinking vibe. Strummer can't get a job, so he's fired up to engage in some class warfare. "The papers say it's better," he snarls, "I don't care, 'cause I'm not all there." For the Clash, the demolition of classic rock was simply part of a widespread cultural evisceration.

More than forty years later, modern society is still more or less intact, and so is classic rock. But the Clash weren't wrong about the impending end of this culture, even if they did become just another band from the seventies that gets played on classic-rock radio. The world without classic rock that's posited in "1977" is now upon us.

In the next ten to fifteen years, most if not all of the major rock stars from the sixties and seventies will be gone. The two surviving Beatles, Paul McCartney and Ringo Starr, will either be pushing ninety or . . . well, you know. At some point very soon, the Rolling Stones will play their final concert, whether by choice or by . . . well, you know. Keith Richards endured Altamont, heroin, Anita Pallenberg, more heroin, Mick Jagger's solo career, and that one time he fell out of a coconut tree in the midaughts. But he's still a human being, believe it or not, so he won't actually *survive* this world. Even Bruce Springsteen, who has restored his body time and again like a classic Cadillac, will eventually break down and be unable to run.

What happens then? When the twilight of the gods finally turns to darkness, what will the world look like the next morning?

Here's my best guess: the resulting void will inalterably change how the music is perceived. Once all of the rock gods are dead, they will cease to be people and become *only* myths. Which means it will be up to those of us who still care about vinyl and rock shows and tall tales about medium-sized British guitar players to keep those myths alive. When you can't actually view Mick Jagger or Ozzy Osbourne or Neil Young in the flesh, loving classic rock will require a process of animation not unlike a religious ritual. (Also: holograms. Hologram tours in which dead musicians are brought back to digital life are going to become commonplace in the 2020s and beyond.) Rock shows won't be *like* church—a metaphor for the divine for overexcited fans—they will *be* church. Faith in that which is no longer tangible will become the basis for a small but committed community of true believers. I'm not saying that all rock fans in fifty years will be wearing tiny guitars around their necks and studying Lester Bangs's *Psychotic Reactions and Carburetor Dung* like it's the Bible. But *some* might.

The groundwork for a world without classic rock is already under way. And I'm doing my part. For instance, I just paid $9.99 to watch a concert by a Grateful Dead tribute band on Pay-Per-View.

Actually, the members of Joe Russo's Almost Dead would probably object to being classified as a tribute act. And I don't think the "tribute" tag suits them, either. The goal of a typical tribute band is to create the illusion that the genuine article is performing onstage. So long as you close your eyes and pound enough beers, you can imagine that you're actually witnessing David Lee Roth at the Starwood in 1978, and not a part-time hairdresser named Harold and his Van Halen cover band Atomic Punk vamping it up at a sports bar. But that's not the intent of Joe Russo's Almost Dead (or JRAD). What JRAD does is reconfigure the Dead's catalog like British bands in the sixties reconsidered the blues—it's a three-pronged approach that utilizes the Dead as a songbook, a sonic blueprint, and a set of tools. At a JRAD show, classic tunes by the Dead provide starting points for long, improvised jams that salute the spirit of the Dead without explicitly re-creating any specific era of the band's history. The idea is not to pretend that JRAD is actually the Grateful Dead, no more than the Stones pretended to be Robert Johnson when they put "Love in Vain" on *Let It Bleed*. It's to evoke the spirit of what has been lost out of thin air.

How does that happen? In the show that at this very moment is being beamed live to my computer from a bowling alley in Brooklyn—JRAD still performs at Brooklyn Bowl periodically ever since playing its first show there on a lark in 2013—the band treats the Dead's music like a turntablist remixing classic funk cuts. A jam that starts with "Hell in a Bucket" takes an unexpected turn into Led Zeppelin's "Moby Dick." (The members of JRAD also play in a band called Bustle in Your Hedgerow that specializes in instrumental versions of Zeppelin songs. Bustle in Your Hedgerow, by the way, is also awesome.) After a few minutes of communing with the spirit of John Bonham, JRAD slips into the chorus of the Dead's cheesy half-hearted disco experiment "The Music Never Stopped," before eventually winding back to "Hell in a Bucket."

Along the way, there are plenty of interstellar excursions in the form of improvised jamming. The star of JRAD in that regard is Marco Benevento, a keyboard wizard who has straddled the jam, jazz, and experimental rock worlds since the late nineties, in his own groups and as a sideman for musicians such as A. C. Newman and Rich Robinson of the Black Crowes. In the Grateful Dead, Garcia was invariably the lead instrumentalist, and whoever was playing keys usually receded into the background. But while JRAD provides ample space for guitar solos, Benevento also adds keyboard textures far more creative than anything supplied by the succession of bearded gentlemen who played in the original Dead. (The Grateful Dead had four keyboardists die on them, which is really taking the Spinal Tap joke about dead drummers too far.)

Is this really "new" music, or is it just a clever repackaging of what's already familiar and comforting? I've asked myself this question many times since I started collecting JRAD concert recordings. My interest in this band feels a little weird to me—has my classic-rock obsession come to *this*, loving a band that covers an older band that I love? Why would I listen to a band interpret the Dead when I can still hear actual members of the Dead play these songs?

More than any other classic-rock band, the Grateful Dead have been directly involved in mentoring those who might replace them one day. Along with Russo, the other members of JRAD have done time in Dead side projects such as Phil and Friends (with Phil Lesh) and Billy and the Kids (with Bill Kreutzmann). When Russo played with Bob Weir and Lesh in Furthur, the lead guitarist was John Kadlecik, the "Jerry" from a popular Dead cover band called Dark Star Orchestra. The Dead established alternative methods of distributing music outside of the corporate record industry decades before that industry imploded, so the cultivation of their replacement talent could be chalked up as another instance of prescient thinking. The market for classic-rock bands won't instantly evaporate the moment that all the original classic-rock musicians are dead. In 2016, artists over the age of fifty accounted for 50 percent of the $4.5 billion grossed by the year's top-earning tours—among the cash cows were Springsteen, the Rolling Stones, Paul McCartney, and Guns N' Roses. In the future, so long as there are still paying audiences, it will be up to repertory bands to play classic-rock music, like orchestras performing the great works of classical composers from centuries past. What the members of the Dead have done is take a lead role in handpicking the people who will carry their music forward once they are gone.

When all the classic-rockers are gone, there will still be the dad-rockers. The void left by the Stones will be filled by the Foo Fighters—I'm sure Dave Grohl has been studying for this gig ever since he left Nirvana. Over time, "Start Me Up" will be gently phased out as interstitial music at sporting events in favor of "My Hero." Even people who are neutral on the Foo Fighters' music will pay to see their concerts, in the same way casual listeners pay to see the Stones now, because it will be considered a rite of passage, like visiting the Grand Canyon. But dad-rockers aren't getting any younger, either. Once they fade away, bands capable of filling arenas and stadiums will suddenly become very scarce.

This makes me sad, though maybe it shouldn't. What am I mourning when I lament the death of stadium rock? I've always loved the idea of larger-than-life rock music more than the actual practice of seeing a band play on a football field or inside of a hockey shed. I adore the mythology of stadium rock, but the reality of it kind of sucks. Only a fool would romanticize overpriced parking, bad sight lines, piss-poor sound, and the emotionally disconnected performances that are endemic to the stadium-rock experience. I much prefer bands that ape the aesthetics of arena rock—enormous choruses, thundering guitars, booming drums, hyperactive stage antics that can wow the people all the way back in the last row—while performing in clubs and theaters. Outsized energy packed into a relatively small space is always a winning formula. Stadium rock belongs in a bar.

One of my favorite bands of the 2010s is Japandroids, a guitar-and-drums duo that hails from Vancouver. Japandroids are the ultimate "stadium rock crammed into a rock club" band. (If Jack White had studied Kiss as closely as he pored over Son House, the White Stripes would've sounded like Japandroids.) In 2012, Japandroids put out their second LP, *Celebration Rock*, which was essentially a modern version of an AC/DC album in the best possible way. All the songs are about either drinking too much or driving too fast on the highway, and every chorus is accented with a crazy drum roll, guitar squeals, and about a dozen "whoa!"s. It's not a complicated formula, but it's deceptively difficult to nail down perfectly. For the two dudes in Japandroids, guitarist Brian King and drummer David Prowse, it all stems from an unabashed love of classic-rock mythology. For instance, every Japandroids album has exactly eight tracks, because many of the classic-rock albums that King and Prowse love have eight songs: *Led Zeppelin IV*, Black Sabbath's *Paranoid*, Bruce Springsteen's *Born to Run*, Patti Smith's *Horses*, Metallica's *Master of Puppets*. For them, classic rock is a religion that relies heavily upon numerology.

In 2017, Japandroids followed up *Celebration Rock* with a relatively grown-up sequel, *Near to the Wild Heart of Life*. Now, instead of emulating *Highway to Hell*, Japandroids aspired to the stateliness of *Who's Next*. The album's best song is "Arc of Bar," a seven-minute story song about drinking and gambling (but mainly drinking) that's reminiscent musically of "Baba O'Riley" and lyrically of Bob Dylan's "Lily, Rosemary and the Jack of Hearts." It's the perfect melding of stadium-rock aesthetics and classic-rock mythology, and you'll never have to stand farther than fifty feet away to experience it.

"I love stadium rock bands. That type of music that's made to be performed and enjoyed in a massive place like that is just part of my DNA in a way," King told me a few weeks after *Near to the Wild Heart of Life* was released. "I like to think in a way that we've always kind of been a stadium rock band. It's not like Dave and I ever had a conversation when we started the band like, 'We want to be stadium rock and we want to play a stadium someday.' I mean, that's obviously ridiculous."

A few hours after I interviewed King, I saw Japandroids play an incredible two-hour show at the Minneapolis club First Avenue, a 1,500-person-capacity venue. The local 18,000-seat basketball arena was across the street. The distance between where Japandroids were playing and where a band like Japandroids might've played in a different era was literally only about 100 feet. Metaphorically, however, those 100 feet seemed insurmountable.

"But we've just always been a stadium rock band," King insisted. "We've been writing and performing in a way as if it was a stadium full of people even though a lot of the times there were only five people there."

Playing for five people like it's an audience of fifty thousand people is an ethos that harkens back to Springsteen: Bring your songs home, play every show like it's your last, *prove it all night*. For Bruce, that work ethic paid off in rock superstardom. Is it a betrayal to Springsteen acolytes like Brian King if the path forged by the Boss no longer seems viable? Maybe. But as a fan, shrinking the size of rock 'n' roll hasn't reduced my enjoyment of the music. Stadium rock played in actual stadiums isn't all it's cracked up to be. Stadium rock without the stadium part actually seems like an evolutionary improvement.

Perhaps the question shouldn't be, "Why can't a band like Japandroids play stadiums?" but rather, "How great would it be if Springsteen still played clubs?"

What's important is that rock 'n' roll continues to matter. And I don't think that hinges on whether rock bands in the future play stadiums or sell millions of albums. Rock started out as a subculture before it became a monoculture, and it can still matter as a subculture. I just keep going back to how classic rock made me feel when I first discovered it—I want to believe that this music can still connect me to something important and immortal. The mythology matters. But the mythology must also change.

After classic rock, rock music will matter by losing the exclusionary aspects of the culture that imposed unnecessary limitations on musicians and the audience. The old classic-rock myth about the white-male superman who pursues truth via decadence and virtuosic displays of musicianship has run its course. The time has come for new legends about different kinds of heroes.

In the 2010s, rock music is more diverse than ever—more female, more black and brown, and infinitely more open to LGBTQ musicians. When I was growing up, I fetishized the rock show as a den of iniquity, a place where danger reigned. It was easy for me as a privileged white guy to romanticize danger because I was hardly ever *in* danger. But now when I go to see young up-and-coming bands, I see the rock show being reclaimed as a safe space for a diverse population to express themselves without fear of judgment, persecution, or violence. This is what progress looks like.

As I write this, the best writer of rock songs on the planet is a funny and keenly observant Australian named Courtney Barnett. In many ways, she looks like an old-school rock star: she plays left-handed guitar like Jimi Hendrix, and her hair is identical to the perfectly unkempt coif that Keith Richards sports in *Gimme Shelter*. But unlike those guys, Barnett is a twentysomething lesbian who writes hilarious songs about being stuck inside your own head even as the world goes crazy around you.

One of my favorite Courtney Barnett songs is called "An Illustration of Loneliness (Sleepless in New York)," which is a play-by-play account of the night after Barnett's first show in America. "An Illustration of Loneliness" is Barnett's entry in the venerated "life on the road" song genre, only instead of saxophone wails and hard-bitten tales of drunk customers and no-good groupies, Barnett describes her hotel room in darkly comic detail—she likens the cracking plaster on the walls to the skin on her palms, and wonders whether those jagged lines can predict the future.

I lose a breath, my love line seems entwined with death
I'm thinking of you too

If Barnett is the best young writer of rock songs on the planet, then Will Toledo of Car Seat Headrest is in the top five. Toledo is certainly among the most prolific—before he signed a deal with Matador Records in 2015, he released eleven albums under the name Car Seat Headrest in just four years. The best of these early albums is 2011's *Twin Fantasy,* a concept album about a young man locked in a toxic relationship with a much older man. But like Barnett, Toledo's sexuality is neither the focal point of his persona nor a deep dark secret that he's reluctant to divulge. It is a reference point in his songs, but so are allusions to Beatles trivia.

This is in keeping with shifting attitudes that have occurred gradually in the greater culture. But in terms of rock history, it's a sea change. "Gay rock" was practically its own subgenre in the seventies. Back then, it was a big deal when Elton John (factually) and David Bowie (opportunistically) spoke about being homosexual. The climate of intolerance was severe enough to keep Freddie Mercury—a man who lived with the utmost flamboyance in every other area of his life—in the closet right up until he died of AIDS in 1991. Even a relatively modern rock star like Michael Stipe didn't officially come out until 2001 in a *Time* magazine interview.

The latest advance in rock-related progressivism pertains to transgender and non-gender-binary musicians. In 2014, I traveled to northern Michigan to attend an Against Me! show in Grand Rapids. Before the gig, I interviewed the band's front woman, Laura Jane Grace, who had announced two years prior that she was transgender in a *Rolling Stone* story. Back in the aughts, Grace was known as Tom Gabel, and Against Me! was signed to Sire and garnered public support from Bruce Springsteen, a primary influence on Against Me!'s populist, meat-and-potatoes punk rock.

In the wake of Grace's announcement, it was unclear whether Against Me!'s fans would stick with the band. The group's album *Transgender Dysphoria Blues* directly addressed the fear, anger, sorrow, and sense of liberation that Grace felt in the immediate aftermath of coming out. But as uncompromising as Grace was in her lyrics, the music on *Transgender Dysphoria Blues* was as rousing and catchy as anything Against Me! had ever recorded. It sounded like the most subversive Green Day LP ever made.

That night, I wondered how these Midwestern Against Me! fans would respond. This was the first time that they'd be seeing Grace as herself, and not as "Tom Gabel." The tension was palpable when Grace and her bandmates came onstage. But then something incredible happened: Grace strummed the furious punk-rock guitar riff to *Transgender Dysphoria Blues'* title track, and the dudes in the audience started slamming into one another. In that moment, all that mattered was the music, and it fucking rocked.

I studied Grace closely, making note of every important detail—the tangles of dark hair clinging cinematically to her cheeks, the way her voice turned hoarse after she hollered for over ninety minutes, the sea of flannelled arms waving in unison as Grace transformed her intensely personal confessionals into raging rock anthems. I remembered it all so I could pass the legend along to subsequent generations.

How long does classic rock have? As long as the old guys and gals are still on the road, I'm going to keep on seeing them. Classic rock will always be my country—it's where I come from, and the place that still feels like home in spite of the countless ways my life has changed since middle school. That doesn't mean I can't see or criticize the flaws—the suppression of women and people of color, the glorification of alcohol and drug abuse, the reactionary conservatism, the endless Woodstock retrospectives, the phony Satanism, the drum solos, the stubborn sleaziness of Gene Simmons. My love for classic rock is complicated but remains undying.

Some shows will be better than others, I'm sure. For every unexpectedly transcendent night, when the legends recover their lost powers and reaffirm their greatness, there will likely be many more nights when the gap between what was and what is will seem disconcertingly wide.

Nevertheless, I will keep going. If the Who takes *Quadrophenia* back on the road, I will pay to see it. If Black Sabbath decides that its farewell tour wasn't the end, I will send my regards to Satan and buy tickets. If Bob Dylan wants to keep on weirdly covering American standards popularized by Bing Crosby and Nat King Cole, I will keep on trying to understand why. If Neil Young wants to perform with actual cows onstage, I will hold my nose and demand an encore.

What can I say? I still believe. When I was a kid, classic rock was a fantasyland populated by the impossibly cool and occasionally wise, where revelatory feats of daring and moxie were perpetuated in smoky concert halls and expensive recording studios by damaged geniuses and noble fools. Inside every album lay mystery, danger, sex, laughs, and maybe a good tip or two on how to live. It was a seductive place that I never wanted to leave, even after I grew up. And, I guess, I never did.

No matter how many depressing classic-rock shows I must sit through, that handful of transcendent nights will always make it all seem worthwhile. Because at some point, these people won't be on the road, and I won't have the option of even being disappointed by my heroes. They'll just be gone, forever. But for now, they're here. And to me, they'll always be larger than life.

ACKNOWLEDGMENTS

A special shout-out is in order for Kevin Doughten and Paul Shirley, who encouraged me to see the Who in 2012 and write about it. That piece was the catalyst for the book you're holding right now.

This book wouldn't exist without Matthew Daddona, who bought the pitch, and Anthony Mattero, who helped me sell it. Thank you for allowing me to go on this journey and making the writing of this book such a rewarding experience.

I'm indebted to the work of the following writers, authors, journalists, critics, and thinkers: Stephen Davis, Mick Wall, Greil Marcus, Nik Cohn, Richard Meltzer, David Fricke, Joseph Campbell, Charlie Gillett, Bill Simmons, Chuck Klosterman, Lester Bangs, Anthony DeCurtis, Kim Neely, Jancee Dunn, Kurt Loder, Gary Lachman, Levon Helm, Peter Ames Carlin, Paul Trynka, Cameron Crowe, Zach Everson, Rich

Cohen, Dave Marsh, Pamela Des Barres, Clinton Heylin, Jann Wenner, Dave Hoekstra, Jesse Jarnow, Chris Heath, David Kinney, Simon Reynolds, Donald Fagen, Danny Sugerman, Jerry Hopkins, and Keith Richards.

These friends and colleagues provided invaluable support during the creation of *Twilight of the Gods:* Steve Gorman, Rob Sheffield, Rob Mitchum, Bob Mehr, Shea Serrano, Lizzy Goodman, Ian Cohen, Dave Hartley, Michael Azerrad, Derek Madden, Josh Modell, Jarret Myer, Brett Michael Dykes, Keith Phipps, and Caitlin White.

Apologies to the following classic-rock gods about whom I regret not writing more in this book: Queen, the Beach Boys, Rod Stewart and the Faces, Rush, Genesis, Elton John, John Mellencamp, Joni Mitchell, the Kinks, ELO, Cheap Trick, the Guess Who, Billy Joel, and Warren Zevon.

Thank you to Josh Tillman, whose first three albums as Father John Misty soundtracked the writing of this book, particularly the song "Only Son of the Ladiesman."

Most of all, eternal thanks and eternal love to Henry and Rosemary. I'm sorry we never got to see Tom Petty together. Let's go see Wilco in a few years. And, finally, I dedicate every hyperbolically romantic classic-rock power ballad to Valerie—the love of my life, my best friend, my cinnamon girl, my long cool woman in a black dress, my stairway to heaven.

INDEX

ABOUT THE AUTHOR

Steven Hyden is the author of *Your Favorite Band Is Killing Me*. His writing has appeared in the *New York Times Magazine, Washington Post, Billboard,* Pitchfork, *Rolling Stone,* Grantland, The A.V. Club, Slate, and Salon. He is currently the cultural critic at Uproxx, and the host of the *Celebration Rock* podcast. He lives in Minnesota with his wife and two children.